# Practical Product Management for Product Owners

# The Professional Scrum Series by Scrum.org

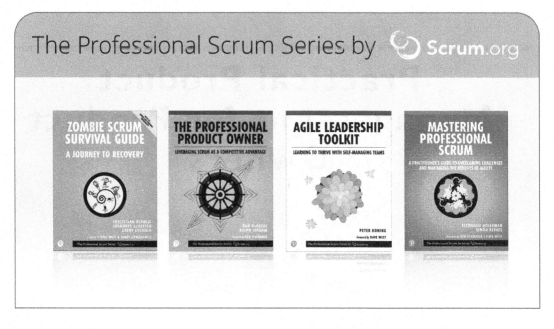

Visit **informit.com/scrumorg** for a complete list of available publications.

---

The **Professional Scrum Series** from Pearson Addison-Wesley and Scrum.org consists of a series of books that focus on helping individuals and organizations apply Scrum and agile leadership to improve the outcomes of customers and organizations. Approaching the challenge from different perspectives, each book provides deep insights into overcoming the obstacles that both teams and organizations face as they seek to reap the benefits of agility.

All Scrum.org proceeds from the series go to Year Up, an organization whose mission is to close the Opportunity Divide by providing urban young adults with the skills, experience, and support to empower them to reach their potential through professional careers and education.

 Pearson
Addison-Wesley

twitter.com/informIT

**informIT.com**
the trusted technology learning source

# Practical Product Management for Product Owners

## CREATING WINNING PRODUCTS WITH THE PROFESSIONAL PRODUCT OWNER STANCES

Chris Lukassen
Robbin Schuurman

**♦♦Addison-Wesley**

Boston • Columbus • New York • San Francisco • Amsterdam • Cape Town • Dubai
London • Madrid • Milan • Munich • Paris • Montreal • Toronto • Delhi • Mexico City
São Paulo • Sydney • Hong Kong • Seoul • Singapore • Taipei • Tokyo

Library of Congress Control Number: 2023930521

ISBN-13: 978-0-13-794700-3
ISBN-10: 0-13-794700-3

1 2023

## Pearson's Commitment to Diversity, Equity, and Inclusion

Pearson is dedicated to creating bias-free content that reflects the diversity of all learners. We embrace the many dimensions of diversity, including but not limited to race, ethnicity, gender, socioeconomic status, ability, age, sexual orientation, and religious or political beliefs.

Education is a powerful force for equity and change in our world. It has the potential to deliver opportunities that improve lives and enable economic mobility. As we work with authors to create content for every product and service, we acknowledge our responsibility to demonstrate inclusivity and incorporate diverse scholarship so that everyone can achieve their potential through learning. As the world's leading learning company, we have a duty to help drive change and live up to our purpose to help more people create a better life for themselves and to create a better world.

Our ambition is to purposefully contribute to a world where:

- Everyone has an equitable and lifelong opportunity to succeed through learning.
- Our educational products and services are inclusive and represent the rich diversity of learners.
- Our educational content accurately reflects the histories and experiences of the learners we serve.
- Our educational content prompts deeper discussions with learners and motivates them to expand their own learning (and worldview).

While we work hard to present unbiased content, we want to hear from you about any concerns or needs with this Pearson product so that we can investigate and address them.

- Please contact us with concerns about any potential bias at https://www.pearson.com/report-bias.html.

**Definition of stance**

/stɑːns, stans/

noun

The way in which someone stands, especially when deliberately adopted (as in jujutsu, golf, and other sports), a person's posture.

"She altered her stance, resting all her weight on one leg"

—Oxford Languages

# CONTENTS

*The Product Owner is one person, not a committee. The Product Owner may represent the needs of many stakeholders in the Product Backlog. Those wanting to change the Product Backlog can do so by trying to convince the Product Owner.*

—Scrum Guide 2020[1]

For many organizations, the accountabilities of Product Ownership are a challenge. When discussing the subject, people working in those organizations ask questions like, "Is a Product Owner a Business Analyst?" or "Is the Product Owner a Product Manager from the business?" The reality is that when organizations adopt Scrum, there is a mindset change that might make it hard to fit into an existing organizational structure. Ultimately, these organizations are wrestling with the idea that someone will be accountable for ensuring that the work on the product will be the most valuable. Single accountability in most organizations does not fit. They want groups of people, hierarchies, processes, controls, and governance to ensure that the right thing will be done. Or, if there is a mistake, everyone, which means no one, is accountable for that mistake. The Product Owner was introduced to Scrum to enable teams to deliver stuff and to remove the impediment of traditional organizational decision making. The purpose is clear, but the details are vague. How does the Product Owner decide what is most valuable? What does the Product Owner do every day? How do they interact with stakeholders and the team? How many teams do they support?

Those questions are tough to answer because the application of Scrum is so varied, and context matters. For example, a Product Owner at a genetic research organization will need a very different set of skills from one at a bank or retail organization. Also, how Scrum is being used in each organization will be different. For some organizations, Scrum teams are connected directly to customers and have the autonomy to deliver value directly. For others, Scrum teams are part of an elaborate and complex release process comprising tens of teams working toward connected, dependent goals. Each situation will encourage a different focus and approach to ordering value and working with the team.

---

1. https://scrumguides.org/scrum-guide.html#product-owner

But there is a set of skills from which all Product Owners need to draw. And more importantly, those skills can be grouped into stances that provide context and boundaries. Stances are a fun way to describe the approach the Product Owner takes. I was first introduced to the preferred and misunderstood stances of the Product Owner by Chris and Robbin when we developed the Professional Scrum Product Owner-Advanced course for Scrum.org. These stances became a great way to teach the ideas of Product Ownership and form a bridge to Product Management. They also can enable Product Owners in challenging situations to clarify what is essential.

For example, in a complex, multi-team environment where the Product Owner is more of an order taker than an order maker, the stance of the Visionary can add some clarity to how the Product Owner supports the backlog helping the team to at least understand the context of the Product Backlog items. Using the Visionary stance will not change the situation for the Product Owner, but it will encourage the use of additional skills that might help the team see more context in the Product Backlog items they receive. By applying the stances, a Product Owner will slowly expand their reach.

Each stance includes connections to product management, Lean UX, Lean Startup, Coaching, Facilitation, and other bodies of work. This illustrates the breadth of skills a good Product Owner can draw on to drive value effectively. It is also ironic that the description in the Scrum Guide, four paragraphs and one bulleted list, can introduce so much. But that is the power of Scrum as described by the often-used phrase "easy to learn, hard to master."

In this book, Chris and Robbin present a comprehensive list of the stances and skills a Product Owner can use. They present great examples that illustrate both the challenge of Product Owners and the value that can come from excellent Product Ownership. As the Product Owner of Scrum.org, I have applied many practical examples and ideas from the book. Reading the book also made me refresh my focus, which often gets sidetracked by detail and distractions. Value is my destination, but other things often confuse and obscure my route. In this book, Chris and Robbin have presented a flashlight, or six flashlights, that can help me find my way to delivering more value for my organization.

The accountabilities of the Product Owner are not easy to master, and maybe you will never master them. From personal experience, I still wrestle with balance, focus, and communication, and I have been on this path for many years. But with every excellent increment, delivered Sprint Goal, and every Product Goal realized, you are changing the world! Good luck, and enjoy the book.

*Dave West*
*CEO & Product Owner, Scrum.org*
*December 2022*

# INTRODUCTION

*Practical Product Management for Product Owners* helps Product Owners understand and avoid common pitfalls that inexperienced Product Owners face. It provides them with better alternatives; more effective behaviors; and useful tools, concepts, and techniques to become great Product Owners, delivering products and services that delight their customers. It uses a case study approach to illustrate these problems and describe alternative solutions. The case study, while fictitious, is based on the authors' experiences working with, and in various cases as, real Product Owners.

Everyone has experienced poorly conceived products or services, despite the vast amounts of time and vast sums of money that organizations spend building these products and creating the services. We believe this is because Product Owners (Agile product managers) often lack the fundamental accountabilities, experience, and skills they need to deliver great products and services. Because of their inexperience, they fall into bad habits such as trying to please stakeholders by agreeing to build what stakeholders want, even when those stakeholder ideas may not be best for customers.

Inexperienced Product Owners lack the skills, and often the empowerment, to chart their own course based on feedback from real customers. They frequently don't even understand what customers are trying to achieve with the product or service; they make decisions based on anecdotal and subjective secondhand information that doesn't reflect real customer needs. In short, they are largely shooting in the dark, hoping to hit something.

## BOOK STRUCTURE

The book helps Product Owners and Product Managers to replace ineffective and destructive Product Owner behaviors that lead to bad products with effective behaviors that lead to great products. It starts with an introduction to the misunderstood and preferred stances.

The Customer Representative stance is then discussed. Readers learn how advanced Product Owners empathize with customers, how they identify value for customers, and how they connect customers, value, and features in a coherent story.

The Visionary stance covers how to tell better stories, set clear Product Goals, create effective product roadmaps, and work company value and product pricing.

Readers then learn about the Experimenter stance, discovering how to do business model innovation, design and run experiments, and scale products effectively.

Great Product Owners are great Decision Makers. Making decisions, deciding how to make decisions, deciding whom to involve, and effectively evaluating decisions are the main topics of the Decision Maker stance.

Of course, collaboration with other people is done continuously, but there are some patterns around Agile governance, Agile budgeting, and Agile contracting that will help readers to become great Collaborators.

Finally, readers learn about the Influencer stance. Great Product Owners are masters at influencing their customers, users, stakeholders, and teams. Mastering the Influencer stance is critical for success.

## TARGET AUDIENCE

The primary target audience for this book includes Product Owners, product managers, and product leads who wish to advance their careers and/or increase their personal impact on the product. After having attended a Professional Scrum Product Owner I (PSPO-I), Certified Scrum Product Owner (CSPO) training, or having read *The Professional Product Owner*,[2] people will understand the basic principles of their role within the Scrum framework. However, turning understanding into effective behaviors and turning effective behavior into actual value maximization of a product is a whole different matter. The audience typically has a few years of working experience as a Product Owner/Manager.

A secondary target audience includes Agile Coaches/Consultants and Scrum Coaches/Masters. The practitioners struggle to effectively coach, train, and mentor their Product Owners, managers, and leads. Many of them struggle to coach product people and company management on effective product management practices and skills, resulting in misunderstood stances of the Product Owner. This book will help Agile Coaches and Scrum Masters to learn about the Product Owner stances, tools, and techniques needed for success so that they can help their Product Owners to become better visionaries, customer representatives, collaborators, decision makers, experimenters, and influencers.

Finally, many product and company leaders, managers, and executives struggle with advancing the profession of product ownership/management in their organizations. This book will help them to coach and guide their product

---

2. Don McGreal and Ralph Jocham, *The Professional Product Owner: Leveraging Scrum as a Competitive Advantage*, Addison-Wesley, 2018.

people and teams on a journey of personal growth and growth of the product team and product.

Register your copy of *Practical Product Management for Product Owners* on the InformIT site for convenient access to updates and/or corrections as they become available. To start the registration process, go to informit.com/register and log in or create an account. Enter the product ISBN (9780137947003) and click Submit. Look on the Registered Products tab for an Access Bonus Content link next to this product, and follow that link to access any available bonus materials. If you would like to be notified of exclusive offers on new editions and updates, please check the box to receive email from us.

# ACKNOWLEDGMENTS

Chris and Robbin want to thank their families for all their support with this book and for providing us with the time and space to get the job done. In addition, Scrum.org especially has been instrumental in providing an environment of inspection and adaption, envisioning, and knowledge sharing about Professional Scrum product ownership.

Another big thank you to everyone who took the time to review our book and provide invaluable feedback, especially Kurt Bittner, Gillian Lee, Tommy Norman, and Kent J. McDonald.

Finally, we want to thank all our friends, peers, and students. We thank all the people who joined our training courses, asked tough questions, and motivated us to put our story on paper. We also thank all the great product folks from the Value Maximizers community who joined our talks and workshops and shared their experiences and stories.

# ABOUT THE AUTHORS

 **Chris Lukassen** has been active in product management for more than 20 years and has worked in both start-up and established enterprises. His products have led to awards and, in other cases, to failures. His mission is to teach people to create products in such a way that they can never go back to the old method.

Chris's inspiration is the world of martial arts, in particular jujutsu, where he continuously sees analogies with the world of product management. His first book, *The Product Samurai,* earned him his nickname and continues to be an inspiration for talks at conferences around the globe.

In his spare time, Chris plays anything with anything that has strings, repairs or sails his sailboat, or just has fun with his four children and loving wife.

With Robbin, he cofounded the Value Maximizers and was co-creator (and course steward) of the Professional Scrum Product Owner-Advanced course at Scrum.org. Being an active Professional Scrum Trainer, Chris trains many product managers in Scrum, Leadership, User Experience, and Metrics.

Currently he is the Chief Product Officer (CPO) at Expandlor, bridging the worlds of product management and data by creating new products in newer ways.

Chris appreciates feedback, and the best way to provide it is through his LinkedIn page: https://www.linkedin.com/in/chrislukassen/.

**Robbin Schuurman** works as a product leader, trainer, and consultant. He leads the Product Management Academy within Xebia Academy and is co-founder of the Value Maximizers. He also supports and advises organizations in Digital, Agile, and Product transformations. Through coaching, training, and consultancy, Robbin helps Product Owners, Product Managers, and Product Leaders to improve their impact on customers, improve the agility of the organization, and improve their time-to-learn.

Robbin is also a Professional Scrum Trainer at Scrum.org, the official training and certification body for the Scrum framework. He is co-creator and course steward of the Professional Scrum Product Owner-Advanced course at Scrum.org. Robbin offers various Scrum.org certified courses, including the Professional Scrum Product Owner courses, Professional Scrum Master courses, and the Professional Agile Leadership Essentials course.

Robbin has over a decade of experience in Agile, Scrum, Project Management, Product Management, and (Product) Portfolio Management. In recent years, Robbin has fulfilled various roles in organizations, including being a Project Manager, Product Owner, Agile Coach-Consultant, Transformation Lead, Software Development Manager, and Head of Product.

You can contact Robbin via his LinkedIn page: https://www.linkedin.com/in/robbinschuurman/.

# THE STANCES OF THE PRODUCT OWNER

I

*Your stance against the world is more important than the stance of the world against you!*

— Mehmet Murat Ildan

## QUICK QUIZ

To connect to Part I, answer each of the following statements by checking the Agree or Disagree column. The answers are shared in the Part I Summary.

| Statement | Agree | Disagree |
| --- | --- | --- |
| Product Owners and product managers require the same knowledge, skills, and competencies to be successful. | | |
| A Product Owner should be concerned only with product development and is only a tactical and development-execution role. | | |
| A Product Owner is essentially an Agile project manager with subject matter expertise or product development skills. | | |
| The Product Owner accountability is implemented in the same, consistent way across organizations. | | |

| Statement | Agree | Disagree |
|---|---|---|
| Being an effective Product Owner requires versatility. You can't be a great Product Owner unless you take different stances in different situations. | | |
| If you are not responsible for contracts, governance, pricing, budgeting, or marketing, then you do not need to learn about and demonstrate ownership for these topics. | | |
| A Product Owner is a product manager. A product manager can be a Product Owner. | | |

# AGILE PRODUCT MANAGEMENT

## IS IT PRODUCT OWNER OR PRODUCT MANAGER?

One of the biggest problems that Product Owners face is that the accountabilities and authorities they *should* have are not connected to only a single person in the organization. Their accountabilities are commonly distributed among multiple people and positions. For example, defining and communicating the product vision is (traditionally) done by folks other than those who order the work to be done. The difficulty may come from the fact that the words "Product Owner" originate from and are used mostly in the context of the Scrum framework. Since not all teams and organizations have adopted Scrum, organizations struggle to connect all the Product Owner accountabilities to a single person in the organization.

Ken Schwaber and Jeff Sutherland[1] managed to grab everybody's attention when communicating that things are different when applying Scrum. With the creation of the Scrum framework and Product Owner accountability, Schwaber and Sutherland revealed an important question: Who *owns* the product? What we found and experienced is that this is a difficult question to answer in many organizations, as they often have a product management team but also business teams, IT teams, design teams, and software

---

1. Jeff Sutherland and Ken Schwaber are the creators of the Scrum framework.

development teams. In most organizations, people from each department claim to know what is best for their customers and their product(s). We often find that there is a need for a clear owner of a product.

Before we dive into the nuts and bolts, let's go back in time to the point where the concept of Product Management was first introduced.

## WHAT IS PRODUCT MANAGEMENT?

The year was 1931, and Neil McElroy was working for Procter & Gamble, where he noticed that much of the competition he faced came from people within the company. There seemed to be little alignment and focus on the different aspects of making a product successful. Ownership and management of products were divided over many people in the company. Based on his observations, McElroy wrote a memo in which he introduced the concept of brand men—individuals within the company who would be accountable for a brand, including its sales, marketing, product management, development, supply chain management, and so on. Procter & Gamble implemented McElroy's idea and became one of the first brand-centric organizations. With this introduction of brand men, the profession of product management was born.

A couple of years later, McElroy worked with two young entrepreneurs, Bill Hewlett and David Packard, the founders of HP. These gentlemen interpreted the brand men concept as *"putting decision making as close as possible to the customer."* With this implementation, HP became one of the first companies to implement product management as a job. It changed the way they worked as they started organizing themselves by products, and thus the concept of a product-led company was born.

In the late 1970s, product management got more systematic with the help of Michael Porter, who wrote about the five forces that impact products and the classic marketing mix that product managers need to focus on to fulfill the needs of the customers. However, as the world became increasingly complex, the role of product manager, rather than being expanded to handle the added challenges, was split over multiple people and domains. The idea of splitting roles was that various departments could focus almost exclusively on specific aspects or complexities of a product. Consequently, we saw a move away from the original brand men concept, which recreated some of the problems it was meant to solve.

This approach led to a split between marketing, engineering, and strategy in many organizations. Unfortunately, many organizations today still separate these domains. As a result, all departments feel that they "own" the product, that they know what is best for customers, and that they best understand the marketplace.

Since the 1970s, marketing has evolved to be more about owning the brand and about customer acquisition. Engineering owns the development (process) of the product. The product organization owns the products, services, and/or value proposition, but this part of the organization doesn't formally exist in all organizations.

The alignment of the different aspects that contributed to product success led to attempts to clarify the interfaces. And so, marketing created requirements, production did the same, and both passed the requirements on to engineering. When the product failed, people doubled down on documenting and clarifying specifications rather than increasing the collaboration between the departments. This whole approach slowed down product development, and it became increasingly difficult to respond to changes in the market, adopt new technologies, or incorporate new insights.

In the 1990s, a rise of agile development frameworks, practices, and ways of working emerged. The common denominator is that they focused on speeding up the feedback cycle by simplifying the process and, ironically, getting back to the idea of brand men. A single person manages the product and the value it generates for customers, users, society, and the organization itself.

This approach led to a new problem in the industry. For the last 60 years, the accountabilities of managing a product had been implemented in a way that was not in line with the concept of a single "owner" of the product. Initially, industry innovators talked about the "agile product manager," but the concept led to more confusion than real change. So, somewhere between 1995 and 2001, the title was changed to Product Owner to signal the importance of mapping accountabilities to a single person.

In the end, the job title does not matter. Whether you call the person who owns the product a Product Owner or a product manager is up to you and your company. What matters is that your organization is product led.

## WORKING IN A PRODUCT-LED, SALES-LED, OR MARKETING-LED ORGANIZATION

Being a product-led company means that an organization is fully focused on product and product experience. Everyone in such an organization is relentlessly focused on creating value and great experiences for customers, users, society, and the organization itself. The core belief in such an organization is that if they all focus on solving real customer problems, satisfying their pains and gains, and building the right product or service to solve their problems, the positive business results will follow naturally.

An organization, however, can also be marketing led or sales led (which many organizations still are). Being a sales-led organization means that the company is focused primarily on driving sales with a sales team. Many of its decisions and actions are driven by opportunities to sell to (big) clients rather than by delivering the best product (experiences). A sales-led company is less focused on building an awesome product than on selling the product. Marketing-led organizations are focused mainly on improving revenues from a (content) marketing perspective. They invest in and focus on marketing strategies such as creating whitepapers; eBooks; webinars; infographics; radio, television, and print ads; social media conversations; and other forms of content  to attract potential buyers to the organization.

Especially in the early stages of an organization, being sales led or marketing led might be helpful to drive growth. In general, most modern companies move toward a product-led strategy. Such an organization is usually where a Product Owner or product manager can have the biggest impact on the product and make a real difference.

# WHAT IS A PRODUCT OWNER?

Before moving on to the more advanced product management topics of this book, let's establish a shared understanding of what a Product Owner in the context of Scrum really is. The Scrum Guide states, "A Product Owner is accountable for maximizing the value of the product resulting from the work of the Scrum Team. How this is done may vary widely across organizations, Scrum Teams, and individuals."[2]

The Scrum Guide does not list all the accountabilities, responsibilities, or work that a Product Owner does. It is purposefully incomplete, not a detailed instruction manual. It describes only core Scrum concepts and acknowledges that many patterns, processes, insights, practices, and responsibilities can be added to Scrum. Additional practices and concepts used by an organization are highly context dependent and therefore are not defined in the Scrum Guide.

Product discovery, customer research, market research, and product marketing, to list only a few, are various product management activities that are not listed in the Scrum Guide. They are all, however, core to the product management function. They are also core to the Product Owner function, even though not explicitly mentioned in the Scrum Guide.

It's much like the various implementations of the product manager position. Some product managers are focused on product development (technical PM), some are more focused on business (growth PM) or on data and artificial intelligence (data PM), and others are more generalists (generalist PM).

The activities a Product Owner performs is context dependent. A Product Owner may delegate the execution of various activities to other people while remaining accountable for overall product success and value maximization. The Scrum Guide states:

---

2. https://scrumguides.org/scrum-guide.html#product-owner.

The Product Owner is accountable for effective Product Backlog management, which includes:

- Developing and explicitly communicating the Product Goal.
- Creating and clearly communicating Product Backlog items.
- Ordering Product Backlog items; and,
- Ensuring that the Product Backlog is transparent, visible, and understood.[3]

The Scrum Guide does not elaborate on all of the product management work that Product Owners perform; however, product management activities are vital. Product Owners may do some of that work themselves or may delegate the responsibility to others. Regardless, Product Owners remain accountable. For Product Owners to succeed, it is important that the entire organization respects their decisions. Product Owners should be the final decision makers when it comes to product-related decisions. It is also important to note that the Product Owner is one person, not a committee. Again, this doesn't mean that Product Owners will do everything themselves, but they are accountable and should have decision-making authority. Product Owners may represent the needs of various stakeholders, such as customers, users, and internal stakeholders. People who want a change in the product can try to convince the Product Owner of their idea's potential value.

The essence of this message in the Scrum Guide is that within the Scrum framework, there is one accountable person who *owns* the product (the Product Owner). This Product Owner has accountabilities that are defined within the Scrum framework but potentially has many additional responsibilities and accountabilities as well. This is exactly what Figure 1.1 illustrates. The Product Owner has certain accountabilities that are core to product ownership in the context of Scrum along with many additional responsibilities that are part of the wider product management profession.

Examples of product management responsibilities may include (but are not limited to) work such as product visioning, product strategy, strategic product

---

3. https://scrumguides.org/scrum-guide.html#product-owner.

planning, product roadmaps management, product marketing, customer analysis, competitor analysis, product launch, product retirement, and product operations. This is *not* a complete list. Many additional responsibilities and work may be done by Product Owners, and that work is context dependent. As stated earlier, Product Owners may do such activities themselves or delegate them to someone else (while remaining accountable).

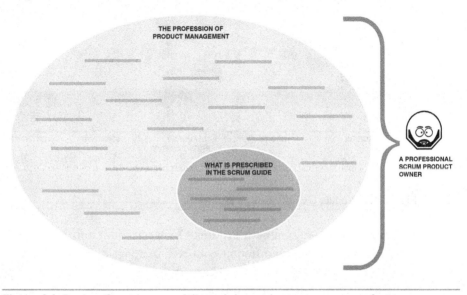

**Figure 1.1** Product Owner accountability and the product management profession

## DIFFERENT TYPES OF PRODUCT OWNERS

In this section, you explore various types of Product Owners, as illustrated in Figure 1.2. Although these types are all considered Product Owners, their effectiveness, impact, and core focus are quite different. The different types have emerged over the past 20-plus years as the Scrum framework gained popularity and as people modified Scrum practices to make the framework fit their organizations' unique contexts.

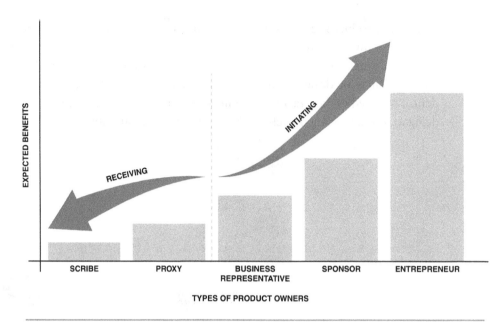

**Figure 1.2** Product Owner types by expected benefits

Although Scrum—along with Product Owner accountability—is applied in many ways and in many different contexts, in adapting Scrum to their needs, people and organizations sometimes borrow terms, ideas, and concepts from Scrum but fail to apply *Professional* Scrum. Following are signs that Professional Scrum is not being practiced:

- The team does not do a Daily Scrum every day.
- The Sprint Review is a demo.
- The Scrum Master role rotates between the Developers.
- The Product Owner is unempowered and needs permission from stakeholders (e.g., a steering committee) for many decisions.

When an adaptation of Scrum, rather than Professional Scrum, is implemented, teams often struggle and face limitations imposed by company governance and/or by misunderstandings about Scrum. Consequently, the benefits of Scrum are reduced, and the company experiences slower time-to-market and reduced value delivery. The limitations also strongly affect the implementation and effectiveness of the Product Owner accountability.

Practicing Professional Scrum means applying Scrum in accordance with the Scrum Guide and doing more than just following the mechanics and fundamentals of the framework. Professional Scrum requires mindset techniques for ways of working and thinking and an environment that supports it, including trust. It requires embodying the Scrum Values and being outcome oriented. It requires people to have a growth mindset and to behave professionally and ethically, for example, when it comes to decision making and product quality.

A way to identify whether your organization is experiencing a suboptimal implementation, and therefore reduced benefits, of Scrum is to recognize the various types of Product Owners. Let's explore them.

## THE SCRIBE

Scribe Product Owners are most often seen in organizations that have recently adopted Scrum or that have not yet really embraced the Agile Product Management Mindset. These organizations see the Product Owner mainly as someone who manages "a list of work" (i.e., the Product Backlog) for the Scrum Team(s). Scribes gather the stakeholders' wishes and translate them into work for the Developers. They often have little if any authority. They make sure that the stakeholders' wishes and demands are described in a way that makes sense for the Developers. To grow as a Product Owner and become more effective at their job, you the Product Owner could explore the person asking for the requirements and what that person's goals are.

## THE PROXY

Like Scribes, Proxy Product Owners are often seen in organizations that are not very mature in their Agile and/or Scrum adoption. Proxies have a bit more authority than Scribes have. For instance, a Proxy gets the authority to make (limited) decisions regarding the order of the Product Backlog. However, the vision, goals, desired results, and scope are still decided by other parties, such as a steering committee or product manager. Proxies are sometimes referred to as "Adidas Product Owners." They tend to run up and down the organization, gathering requirements, clarifying requirements with the business stakeholders, and taking those requirements to the Developers. Although Proxies understand the requirements from a business perspective, they still do not provide the most effective form of product ownership.

## THE BUSINESS REPRESENTATIVE

Close collaboration with business stakeholders, marketing, commerce, and customer care provides Product Owners with knowledge about the market, customers, product, and organization. Having this knowledge allows Product Owners to represent customers and the product more effectively, which raises the Product Owners to the Business Representative level. Business Representatives do more than merely receive requirements and demands from people. They also generate ideas. They take initiative. A Product Owner who does not understand the business well is unlikely to be very effective in this role.

## THE SPONSOR

Sponsor Product Owners operate much like Business Representative Product Owners, but they are also given budget responsibilities. They may struggle to decide on and receive proper funding for their product, often because they are unfamiliar with the lingo and practices. They sometimes feel that an invisible wall stands between "executing" the product and "owning" the product. On the other side of the wall, people are speaking a different language that revolves around return on investment, operating expenses, capital expenditures, cash flow, inventory, and so on.

*When in France, speak French.*

— Robbin

The way to move forward and to become a Sponsor type Product Owner is to learn to speak the language of people from finance, risk, and legal, for example, and of course, the executives. Sponsors often decide how the budget is spent, that is how much budget is allocated to the team, infrastructure, marketing, sales, support, and so on. Ultimately, the budget drives the product forward. The easiest way to get into this world is to make friends, pair with them, learn, create transparency about budget (and time and resource) spending, and slowly but steadily, you'll increase your ownership.

## THE ENTREPRENEUR

The final type of Product Owner is the Entrepreneur. Some people also refer to a Product Owner as the "mini-CEO," which is unfortunately rarely the case. Entrepreneurs are the type of Product Owner envisioned in Professional Scrum and found in some of the early discoveries/implementations of Scrum. Entrepreneur is not a theoretical concept, it's just rare to find this type of Product Owner (especially in large enterprises). In startups, it is easy to point at the Product Owners, as they have typically invested directly in the company, and they carry the risk and success of the product. In larger organizations, this is not always possible, but Entrepreneurs can exhibit the same mindset, the same hunger for value, the same joy of success, and the same tears for failure.

The Entrepreneur Product Owner can make the biggest impact for customers, users, and the organization. This person takes full accountability for the product and has complete decision-making license around the product. The Entrepreneur is someone with a strong vision of the market and the product. It is someone with a passion for the product and strong leadership and communication skills. Entrepreneurs are ultimately accountable for the product's success or failure, including its financial success (profit and loss).

*If you don't have a plan, you become part of somebody else's plan.*
—Terence McKenna

## Introduction to the Case Study: World News

*Beep, beep, beep.* Noa opened one eye as she smashed the snooze button on her alarm clock. She would not let the alarm ring again, because today was going to be a great day. She was excited and ready to get started at her new job as Product Owner–Digital at World News.

As Noa cycled through the early morning fog, she imagined some of the first conversations she was about to have at her new company. Company onboarding would kick off with a meeting with Dave, the CEO of World News.[4] Although Noa realized that she would be able to get only a couple of questions answered given Dave's packed agenda, a million questions burned in the back of her mind: What would be the best place to start? What are your key expectations? What's your biggest challenge right now? Do you have any specific things you'd like to see me do in this role? What's your view of what makes a Product Owner successful at this company?

Noa caught her breath as she waited for a red light. Her new job title would be Product Owner–Digital. Despite having a few years of experience as a Product Owner, she wondered what her new job would really include. Noa knew what the job should entail in theory. However, in her previous Product Owner role, Noa found that the role wasn't exactly implemented in an optimal and effective way. In fact, the role was so far off from professional Product Ownership that she decided to quit her previous employment, and she was not looking to repeat her previous experience.

"Okay," she said to herself as the traffic light turned green. "I need to get a clear understanding of the definition of my product first. It all boils down to what Dave considers to be part of the product and whatnot." This would make a great question to ask. She stepped on the pedal and accelerated toward World News.

"Welcome to World News!" said Dave. "I'm Dave, the CEO. I'm happy that you have decided to join our company as our Product Owner–Digital. There is a lot of work to be done. I trust my onboarding package was helpful to make a good start?"

---

4. World News is a fictional company in the context of this book. It is inspired by real-life events, cases, and situations that we and/or other Product Owners have experienced, but the company itself does not exist.

Noa had indeed received a detailed information package as part of her onboarding. The financial details of the company, how it had been doing for the last few years, a couple of customer personas, the mission and vision of World News, an organizational chart, and most interestingly, a market analysis that had been performed in the months before her arrival. She had about a million questions but quickly learned that Dave was more of a talker than a listener.

"World News was founded as a news company in 1989 by our three founders, who are now retired shareholders. We design, print, and distribute our newspapers daily and have all the services in-house to do so." Dave gazed at a photo on the wall of what Noa presumed were the founders.

"The company grew quickly in 1989 and had 110 employees at the end of the year," Dave continued. "In the nineteen nineties, the company grew very fast, acquiring multiple printing businesses, publishers, and media companies. In 2005, World News had about 700 employees and a revenue of 100 million dollars. The following years were rough for World News. We acquired more companies to keep some of the market share, but in 2010, we had to go through some major reorganizations, letting go of 250 employees."

Noa could see that Dave had been affected by that experience and asked what the current state of the business was. "It feels like we have been in survival mode for more than 10 years, trying to remain profitable," Dave replied. "As in many other news companies, many good people from the printing business have left, and we now have 400 employees and 52 million dollars in revenue."

Dave looked straight at her. "I acknowledge that we've been stuck in our printing business for too long. Although we have made some digital efforts, we are way behind our competitors regarding digital media. This is where you come in."

*Sure, no pressure,* thought Noa. None of her previous questions made any sense now, and she was unsure what was the right question to ask. At least Dave had not completely misunderstood the Product Owner role. This would be an interesting journey!

# Introducing the Product Owner Stances

## The Misunderstood Stances of a Product Owner

The accountabilities of a Product Owner are often misunderstood, leading to interesting implementations of Scrum, and of Product Ownership in particular. The misunderstanding occurs in part because organizations try to map the Scrum framework and Product Owner accountabilities to existing processes, roles, artifacts, and events. Such implementations of Product Owner accountability often result in attitudes and behaviors that are not very productive in practice. These ineffective behaviors and attitudes are referred to as the *misunderstood stances* of the Product Owner.

What are *stances?* You can think of them as patterns. They are attitudes and behaviors that Product Owners display *at times*. Because most people do not display these stances continuously and consistently over time, but rather only in moments, *stances* is a more fitting term than *patterns*. Let's explore the six most frequently displayed misunderstood stances and how you can recognize them.

## THE CLERK

*The Clerk is also referred to as the admin, secretary, waiter, yes man, or order taker.*

Clerks are the waiters who gather the wishes and needs of stakeholders and serve them up in the form of user stories to the Developers. They aren't focused on achieving the product vision or on crafting clear goals and objectives. Clerks never say no to stakeholders but instead try to please everyone by delivering on their wishes and needs. There's nothing wrong with servant-leading customers and stakeholders, but Product Owners whose main purpose each day is to get new "orders" from stakeholders are missing the point of being a great Product Owner.

The following patterns are associated with the misunderstood stance of the Clerk:

- Clerks tend to have an endless (or at least extensive) Product Backlog, primarily because they rarely if ever say no to the stakeholders. When a stakeholder poses an idea, requests a new feature, or tells them what to do, Clerks typically respond, "Sure, let me add that to the Backlog."
- Clerks typically have an internal focus. Internal stakeholders tell them what to do and what to build. Clerks don't (often) interact with external stakeholders, rarely with external users, and (almost) never with real, paying customers who buy the product. They seldom talk (or allowed to talk) to

external influencers or governance stakeholders, such as legal authorities and/or regulators.

- Clerks act as a go-between (carrier pigeon) between the Developers and the stakeholders. They need to put people on hold frequently to get more information from others. They can't make any decisions because they need approvals and permission before acting. This reactive, permission-seeking stance often demotivates everyone. Clerk Product Owners struggle to say no because they try to please everybody. They tend to micromanage, distributing tasks among team members, managing via spreadsheets, utilizing people, reducing effort estimates by the Developers, maximizing output, and being a team coordinator.

## THE STORY WRITER

*The Story Writer is also referred to as the analyst, technical writer, legacy system copycat, scribe, and note taker.*

It's often in the language that you can detect a Story Writer. Many conversations they have are about the details in the Product Backlog items. The Developers in the Scrum Teams push back when work is not compliant with the Definition of Ready (DoR). They push the Product Owner to make items ready for Sprint in accordance with the DoR. A DoR is a practice (not required in Scrum) that Story Writers and Scrum Teams sometimes use.

Although helpful to some teams, a DoR can also result in counterproductive behavior if it starts to feel more like a contract in the hands of a Story Writer than a simple, handy checklist.

The point, however, is not really about the DoR. The point is that a Story Writer is focused on all the details, such as requirements descriptions, acceptance criteria, nonfunctional requirements, and other details in tickets. When a product increment does not produce the value or outcomes the Scrum Team hoped to achieve, the Developers often point to a lack of clarity and specifications. This often reinforces the Story Writer stance, and the Product Owner focuses even more on documenting all the details, keeping this misunderstood pattern intact.

The following patterns are associated with the misunderstood stance of the Story Writer:

- Story Writers typically have a very well-organized Product Backlog. The Product Backlog items (usually user stories) on the top are small, specified, designed, detailed, estimated, and refined to be clear. They focus on specifying the work to a great level of detail, making sure that the Developers have no further questions because all the details are in the tickets.
- Story Writers have a keen eye for details, and they love to dig into all the nitty-gritty stuff. They are great at specifying user stories. They tend to write user stories, acceptance criteria, and functional descriptions all day long.
- Other associated behaviors are acting as a business analyst, acting as a technical writer, copycatting legacy systems, scribing, and note taking.

## THE PROJECT MANAGER

*The Project Manager is also referred to as the velocity maximizer, resource utilization maximizer, wish list administrator, sidekick to management, and progress reporter.*

Project Managers are typically concerned with the day-to-day progress of the Developers. They rarely if ever miss a Daily Scrum, even if only to ask individual team members what they've done, what they're going to do, and whether anything is blocking them. They measure the success of the team in the form of increased velocity and tend to "report" on story points, burndown charts, and velocity to the stakeholders during the Sprint Review. All in all, many of these Project Manager stance takers are focused on progress, resource utilization, dependency management, and the basic application of the Scrum framework (e.g., doing the Events and ensuring clear roles and accountabilities). All of these activities are useful; however, they should not be of primary concern to Product Owners. Also, they distract Product Owners from their core accountability: maximizing the value of the product.

The following patterns are associated with the misunderstood stance of the Project Manager:

• Project Managers are used to managing projects, not managing products. Projects have a clear start and end, are temporary, and are executed by a temporary team/organization. The project manager role is designed to deliver output, which is then delivered to the line organization for further implementation and the actual realization of the expected outcomes. However, being a Product Owner is not a temporary endeavor! Product Owners are in it for the long run (not just for delivering some outputs) and are (or should be) accountable for the total cost of ownership and profit and loss of the product.

- Project Managers are typically concerned with the day-to-day progress of the Developers. Now just to be clear, it is not necessarily bad to know what is going on with the Developers. However, a Product Owner's job is not to manage the progress that the Developers are making. Your job is to maximize the value delivered by the Developers by making sure the (potentially) most valuable (or most risky) work is done first.

- When a Sprint produces more story points than were delivered in a previous Sprint, Project Managers usually get excited.

- Project Managers are often used to reporting on (traditional) measures of progress, such as scope, time, and budget, as well as on deliverables, progress percentages, risks, milestones, and deviations from the original plan. Although it is not a bad practice for Product Owners to keep an eye on the budget and potential risks, the way to deal with them in Scrum framework is quite different.

- Project Managers are used to getting projects/assignments with a clear scope, timeline, and budget. They are also accustomed to asking a steering committee for permission or approval to guide their actions and decisions. Product Owners do not answer to a steering committee. They don't go out to get new projects and assignments. They create a product vision and strategy and start maximizing value. Product Owners are accountable and responsible for the outcomes.

- Other associated behaviors of Project Managers are micromanaging, managing the metrics, setting deadlines, distributing tasks among team members, managing via spreadsheets, utilizing people, reducing effort estimates by the Developers, maximizing output, and being a team coordinator.

## THE SUBJECT MATTER EXPERT

*The Subject Matter Expert (SME) is also referred to as the senior user, key user, process manager, domain expert, or business expert.*

SMEs are expert at explaining how things work. Product Owners who favor this stance are a blessing and a curse. When they bring relevant domain knowledge to the Scrum Team, the team can make more informed decisions and create a better plan to achieve Sprint Goals and other goals. The SME stance can also lead to a single point of knowledge, and rather than forgoing discussion, as in the Story Writer stance, its stance manifests as micromanagement and spoon-feeding the Developers. Another manifestation is that the domain expertise can lead to biased judgments because SMEs often assume that they know what is right for the customer, even when direct feedback from customers indicates otherwise.

Many organizations seem to expect Product Owners also to be SMEs with detailed knowledge about business processes. Although there's nothing wrong with understanding the business processes well, Product Owners don't have to be the experts.

The following patterns are associated with the misunderstood stance of the SME:

- SMEs can specify work up to a great level of detail. They are, as the term says, experts in their business, domain, or technical field, and some don't hesitate to share their knowledge with everyone else. Consequently, one of the traps of having SME Product Owners is that they can talk about their area of expertise for hours. It's not uncommon that meetings take much longer than expected and that, despite the SME's lengthy discourse, nobody understands the goals that they're working toward.

- Other SMEs, by contrast, frequently make comments such as "You don't need to know that" or "I'll let you know about the next steps when we get there." The information they have may be valuable, yet they guard it closely—sometimes by design, sometimes unconsciously. Knowledge is power, and some SMEs perceive their knowledge as job security. Some SMEs, therefore, aren't necessarily in favor of knowledge sharing; they instead spoon-feed the Developers tiny pieces of the total picture, keeping themselves constantly involved throughout the development effort.

- Another risky behavior that SMEs frequently display is to be both Product Owners and Developers. For example, a SME Product Owner might simultaneously serve as a software/enterprise architect, a business developer, or maybe a customer journey expert There is a risk in having multiple jobs and roles in the team. Being the senior or expert on the team often reveals the pitfall of stepping in and doing it yourself. It is not unheard of that the senior Developer or architect rearranged the codebase overnight or that a Marketing Product Owner redesigned the whole marketing campaign plan over the weekend.

- Other associated behaviors are being the architect, being the technical (development) expert, being the test manager, being the senior (technical) person on the team who decides on all the details, being the UX designer, being a micromanager, distributing tasks among team members, and reducing effort estimates by the Developers.

## THE GATEKEEPER

*The Gatekeeper is also referred to as the protector, guard, shield, gateway, or single point of contact.*

Gatekeepers are the single point of contact between the Scrum Team and the outside world. They tend to block all connections between the Developers and its stakeholders; all communication goes through the Gatekeeper. Product Owners with a Gatekeeper stance must answer all of the Developers' questions, but they do not have much time for the team. Also, Gatekeepers typically want to sign off on all requirements.

There's nothing wrong with "protecting" the Developers from the outside world. There is also nothing wrong with explaining to stakeholders that they should not approach individual team members directly because they work as a team, not as individuals. Product Owners can help the Developers to stay focused by collaborating with the Scrum Master in coaching stakeholders about how the Developers do teamwork. However, Product Owners who make themselves the single point of contact between the Developers and the outside world are missing the point of being a great Product Owner. Also, being overprotective of the Developers—shielding them from stakeholders and preventing them from getting direct customer, user, and stakeholder feedback—often results in missed opportunities for maximizing value.

The following patterns are associated with the misunderstood stance of the Gatekeeper:

- The Gatekeeper is great at keeping stakeholders away from the Developers and blocking all communications. The agreement made between the Gatekeeper and the Developers is that all questions are asked and answered through the Gatekeeper, who will consult with stakeholders if necessary. The Developers do not pose questions directly to users or stakeholders, let alone customers.

- Another typical Gatekeeper pattern is that all the ideas, wishes, demands, and work should be communicated directly to the Product Owner. In this way, Gatekeepers ensure that not even the smallest stakeholder request reaches the Developers without the Gatekeeper's knowledge.

- Gatekeepers also block feedback from the stakeholders to the Developers. They tend to see 2- to 4-hour Sprint Reviews as a waste of the Developers' time—time that could be better spent writing code. They therefore host the Sprint Reviews alone; gather feedback from the stakeholders, users, and customers; then share that feedback with the Developers.

- Gatekeepers insist on signing off on all the requirements and deliverables that the Developers produce.

## THE MANAGER

*The Manager is also referred to as the team boss, team lead, technical lead, Product Owner & Scrum Master, and HR-responsible person.*

The Manager is concerned with the well-being of the Scrum Team. The Manager loves to see happy, engaged, and motivated people. They love it when people are developing themselves, learning new skills, obtaining new knowledge, and making mistakes. The Manager is a real people person, focused on people's growth. Another goal of the Manager is to evaluate individual team member performance.

Product Owners as Managers typically are responsible for performance management and evaluating the team. They have many one-on-one conversations with individual team members to learn more about their personal goals and performance. There's nothing wrong with caring for the Developers or with stimulating the Developers to try, learn, experiment, and fail. However, Product Owners who make performance management a big part of their job are missing the point of being a great Product Owner.

The misunderstood stances of the Product Owner are typically driven by confusion about what product ownership is (really) about. Fortunately, there are many things you can do to correct these misunderstandings of the Product Ownership accountabilities. By exhibiting the preferred stances, attitudes, and behaviors, for example, and by explaining why the system is misinterpreting Product Ownership, you can help to change the system. If you are not a Product Owner yourself, you can help your Product Owner by influencing the system toward a positive outcome.

*Don't change the people, change the system and the people will follow.*
—Serge Beaumont

## THE PREFERRED STANCES OF A PRODUCT OWNER

The misunderstood or nonpreferred stances of a Product Owner should be countered with preferred stances. Based on coaching and training thousands of Product Owners and product managers for more than a decade, we've learned about various stances that can help Product Owners to be more successful. The preferred stances are related to the constructive, positive, and valuable stances that we have seen many successful Product Owners display. The preferred stances are the Visionary, the Collaborator, the Customer

Representative, the Decision Maker, the Experimenter, and the Influencer. Let's dive into the preferred stances of the Product Owner!

## THE VISIONARY

*The Visionary is also referred to as the inspirator, challenger of the status quo, the dreamer, or the imaginative Product Owner.*

Visionary Product Owners have a clear vision (or dream) for the future, they actively challenge the status quo, and are generally seen as inspiring leaders to follow. They have a relentless focus on what can be instead of on what is. It is their mission, vision, passion, and inspiration that is appealing for many people to follow.

Not everyone has the ability to envision a faraway and very different future, and that's okay. A vision doesn't always have to be a "10 years from today, put a man on Mars" kind of vision. Some visions are big, others are small—and not every vision necessarily succeeds. The main quality of a Visionary is the ability to share their vision in a way that motivates their team to work toward that goal. So, be inspired by Visionaries; consider what you might learn from them, what makes them effective, and what they might improve; and then improve your own Visionary stance as a Product Owner.

## THE COLLABORATOR

*The Collaborator is also referred to as the team player and team worker.*

Product management is a team sport. To represent customer needs effectively, and to translate those needs into a valuable product, Product Owners need to collaborate with a wide range of stakeholders, teams, and departments. A Collaborator Product Owner tends to support people in their own discovery process, whether it's about defining goals, clarifying Product Backlog items, or analyzing customer needs.

Collaborators are team players who place the well-being of the team ahead of the well-being of themselves. A team with members who act cooperatively and seek to achieve the common goal functions better than a team with members who focus only on their own individual goals. Collaborators are open and transparent. They proactively share information, insights, and knowledge. They listen to understand, not to respond. They allow others to do what they are good at, and they do whatever they can to help the team succeed.

## THE CUSTOMER REPRESENTATIVE

*The Customer Representative is also referred to as the customer advocate, voice of the customer, user representative, user advocate, or voice of the user.*

Customer Representative Product Owners are the go-to people for those in the organization who want to gain an understanding of what customers (and/or users) are looking for in the product or service for which the Product Owner is responsible.

Product Owners who take the stance of the Customer Representative tend to focus on helping other people (Developers or others) to understand what customers need, what their challenges are, what pains and gains they have. When taking the Customer Representative stance, the Product Owner tends to explain how the team's work affects customers, users, and business processes.

## THE DECISION MAKER

*Decision Makers help the stakeholders and team to keep time-to-market short by keeping decision-making time short. All sorts of decisions must be made daily. Some can be delegated to the Scrum Team or stakeholders; others must be made by the Product Owner.*

The term *decision* ("act of deciding") was coined in the mid-fifteenth century from the Latin *decisionem*:

> *Decisionem (nominative decisio), "to decide, determine"; literally "to cut off."*[1]

Making decisions is about "cutting off" choices—cutting off some other course of action. It may sound limiting, but it's not. It's liberating. Creating products presents us with endless options and possibilities, but at some point, we need to make some decisions and commit to next steps.

What do great Decision Makers do? Well, they listen! Great Decision Makers make sure the other party feels heard and understood. Next time someone voices concerns over a decision, try to note whether you (a) negate their concern: "That's not happening"; (b) minimize it: "That's not a problem"; (c) top it: "Compared to what I had to do, . . ."; or (d) interrupt them in the middle of their sente——.

## THE EXPERIMENTER

*Sir Isaac Newton, Louis Pasteur, Marie Curie, Albert Einstein, and Nikola Tesla; these are some of the greatest scientists of all time. If not for people like Nikola Tesla, then maybe you wouldn't have been able to read this book and maybe we wouldn't have written it in the first place. These and other scientists, innovators, and Experimenters are the driving force of innovation.*

---

1. Etymonline.com, s.v. decision (n.), accessed October 2019, https://www.etymonline.com/search?q=decision&ref=searchbar_searchhint.

When taking the stance of an Experimenter, Product Owners explain what we know AND what we don't know. They state hypotheses and assumptions instead of user stories and requirements. They see the work that the team does as experiments to discover new and hidden value rather than executing and delivering set-in-stone work packages. Experimenters understand that there is more unknown than known and therefore feel the need to try new things: explore, innovate, and experiment.

## THE INFLUENCER

*The Influencer is also referred to as the politician.*

Some of the most famous and influential leaders of all time include people like Mohandas K. Gandhi, Nelson Mandela, Martin Luther King Jr., and Abraham Lincoln. These gentlemen are in all the top-ten lists of the best politicians, Influencers, world changers, and so on. Indeed, these leaders have all had a big impact on their people, countries, and/or the world. Most of these people eventually were elected to positions of power, which offered them even more opportunities to change the world. However, they all started with no authority, but they were visionary, inspirational people and, above all, great Influencers.

Product Owners who are great Influencers get things done without exercising formal authority over a person or team. Great Influencers act and speak in ways that may hardly be noticed when present but are dearly missed when they are gone.

Influencers help the stakeholders to align around the product vision, strategy, goals, and objectives. Influencing the stakeholders and Scrum Team is a hard but very important job. Influencers uses effective communication, negotiation, and persuasion to get people to join the cause. Influencers are aware of their environment, both the official and unofficial reporting structures, and they know who influences whom.

> *Tact is the ability to tell someone to go to hell in such a way that they look forward to the trip.*
>
> —Winston Churchill

# THE STANCES OF THE PRODUCT OWNER

# SUMMARY

## KEY LEARNINGS AND INSIGHTS

This concludes Part I, in which you were introduced to the misunderstood and preferred Product Owner stances. You learned that Product Owners must be versatile in their ability to take the right stance depending on the situation. You also explored the fundamentals to product ownership and product management.

## QUICK QUIZ REVIEW

If you took the Quick Quiz at the beginning of Part I, compare your answers to those in the following table. Now that you have read about Product Owner stances, would you change any of your answers? Do you agree with the following answers?

| Statement | Agree | Disagree |
|---|---|---|
| Product Owners and product managers require the same knowledge, skills, and competencies to be successful. | ✓ | |
| A Product Owner should be concerned only with product development and is only a tactical and development-execution role. | | ✓ |

| Statement | Agree | Disagree |
|---|---|---|
| A Product Owner is essentially an Agile project manager with subject matter expertise or product development skills. | | ✓ |
| The Product Owner accountability is implemented in the same, consistent way across organizations. | | ✓ |
| Being an effective Product Owner requires versatility. You can't be a great Product Owner unless you take different stances in different situations. | ✓ | |
| If you are not responsible for contracts, governance, pricing, budgeting, or marketing, then you do not need to learn about and display ownership for these topics. | | ✓ |
| A Product Owner is a product manager. A product manager can be a Product Owner. | ✓ | |

## WANT TO LEARN MORE?

Are you ready to learn more about Product Ownership, the profession of product management, and the preferred stances of the Product Owner? That's great! You can continue to read this book from cover to cover or dive right into one of the stances that you want to learn more about. Each of the chapters to follow takes a deep dive into a stance. The first one coming up is the Customer Representative stance.

# THE CUSTOMER REPRESENTATIVE

*Solve real problems. People don't argue the cost of a fire hose when their house is on fire.*

— Steve Johnson

# QUICK QUIZ

To connect to Part II, answer each of the following statements by checking the Agree or Disagree column. The answers are shared in the Part II Summary.

| Statement | Agree | Disagree |
| --- | --- | --- |
| People buy, hire, or absorb products to solve their problems, not for the features that products have. | | |
| If you ask customers what product they need, the only answer you get is "faster horses." | | |
| There is always a product, a customer, and a producer, but they are not always easy to define. | | |
| The best people to talk with to learn more about customers are sales, customer support, UX, and marketing people. They know best what customers really want. | | |
| The best way to express value for customers is in how much revenue they bring in for the company. | | |
| Visualizing user information (e.g., with personas or empathy maps) provides a better understanding of customer and user problems and needs. | | |
| Company goals, company impacts, personas, value for customers, and the features to be built are all interconnected in nonlinear ways. | | |

# How to Identify and Define Product

## Introducing the Customer Representative

Some positive outcomes and benefits are observed when Product Owners take the Customer Representative stance. For example, the Developers have a greater understanding of their customers and users. With this increased understanding of customers and users, including their needs, pains, fears, and objectives, the Developers can build the product or service that best fits their customers' needs. The bottom line is, the better you understand your customers, the higher your chances of building the right product.

Besides building a better product, the Developers become more self-managing, as they can relate to and empathize with customers and users. This increased self-organization allows the Product Owner to spend less time explaining all the details to the team members.

An increased focus on long-term visions, goals, and objectives starts to grow (while, of course, the team delivers in a steady and frequent cadence) because the team's focus is shifted from delivering features and user stories to delivering what truly matters to customers and users. And although there may be other benefits as well, focusing more on the customer hopefully leads to an increased customer satisfaction or net promoter score.

What it is that great Customer Representatives do?

- **Name the customer and user:** Customer Representative Product Owners can list and name customers and users. They have a clear understanding of the customer and user personas and know them by heart. Product Owners with a Customer Representative stance can talk about, say, "Dave" and know that Dave is a CEO who's married, has two kids, and loves baseball and cycling. They also know Dave's biggest challenges: What is the next Big Thing his company must do to keep growing? How will his company stay relevant in the future? Product Owners tend to use anecdotal evidence to support broader trends. This is a pitfall, however, and not what great Experimenter Product Owners do. They go and visit some large customer who says they want some capability in the product, which they generalize to all customers. This leads to the classic Innovator's Dilemma described by Clayton Christensen.[1]

  The high-performing Product Owner must be able to put these conversations in context and understand when personal preferences of specific customers are truly representative of a broader base of customers. Doing so means deeply understanding the problem that customers face, not just the symptoms and imagined solutions they express. I liken this to the way a doctor interviews a patient to understand root causes. The patient may come in asking for a more potent pain medication, but the doctor is irresponsible if they simply give the patient what they ask for. Doctors have a responsibility to treat their patients' ailment, and Product Owners must do the same for their customers.

- **Value listening over talking:** Customer Representatives understand that listening to customers is much more important than talking to them. Customer Representative Product Owners have regular meetings with real customers and users just to listen to their pains, gains, needs, and wants. They're not selling them the product or trying to solve their current prob-

---

1. *The Innovator's Dilemma: When New Technologies Cause Great Firms to Fail*, Harvard Business Review Press, 1997.

lems. These Product Owners are just there to listen, observe, and maybe try to spot hidden opportunities.

• **Identify customer and user needs:** Identifying customer needs is not the same as asking, "What do you want? What do you need?" Product Owners who have mastered the stance of the Customer Representative can listen, observe, and ask powerful questions to get a better understanding of customers and users. Creating a great product that customers love isn't done by asking simple questions. It's achieved through truly understanding customers and users.

> *When I worked with an electric vehicle–charging company, a new Product Owner came on board. After meeting the Developers and going through the company boot camp, he wanted to understand customers and users. He first talked to a lot of people in the company, to get their ideas. But what was great was that he rented an electric vehicle for two weeks, ordered a whole bunch of charging cards from different companies, downloaded several mobile apps to support them, and then he just experienced E-mobility for himself. This is a great example of a Product Owner who tries to understand what customers experience by walking in their shoes.*
>
> — Robbin

• **Understanding the why of the customer:** Though the previous points may have made this clear already, remember that we should not talk too much about what. We should talk mostly about why, and this is what Customer Representatives do. They focus on the goals and objectives of customers. They focus on the pains and gains. They focus on what people want to achieve, instead of what people want to do.

• **Identifying customer value:** Another core element of being a Customer Representative is to clearly understand and be able to express what customers value and how to qualify and quantify value.

To help you become a more effective Customer Representative, we discuss the following concepts, tools, and practices in this part:

- **Understanding your product well:** What is a product? What makes a product successful?

- **Understanding your customers:** How can you talk to customers (and users) effectively? What do you talk about? And how can you capture your findings through personas?

- **Finding value:** How to find or identify value for customers and users (by using the Elements of Value)?

- **Connecting customer needs to goals:** How do you connect company goals to customer personas, customer needs, and features to build?

### What Is the Product?

As Noa walked through the already familiar hallways of World News, she noticed the distinct smell of ink from the printing press. Decades of continuous printing had infused the walls, ceiling, and furniture with the smell of printing ink. It was not unpleasant, but as a newcomer, it served as a constant reminder of the organization's DNA.

Noa paused in front of Shanice's office. Shanice ran the circulation department and oversaw "getting newspapers on doormats," as she called it. The more Noa tried to understand what "news" meant, the more questions popped up in the back of her mind. How did digital news relate to printed news? How did the mobile app relate to the website? Somehow, the digital and analog realms within World News felt worlds apart.

Noa's thoughts were interrupted by Kemal's cheerful voice, "Ah, the new face!" he said as he walked up to her. "Shanice isn't in today, but do you want to have a cup of coffee? I have some ideas I want to run by you." Kemal ran marketing and advertising and still had control over the World News App team. Noa felt that the App team should be part of her responsibility as the Product Owner–Digital, and she was keen on finding an opportunity to take control of the app. However, she wasn't sure how to achieve it.

An hour later, she had managed to become Product Owner for the mobile app as well, but she had discovered that many people within the World News company considered themselves "owner" of "products." Artifacts such as photos, articles, advertisements, marketing campaigns, videos, and feedback tools were considered products. *But are those products?* she wondered. At the same time, she was pretty sure that if everybody owns everything, nobody owns anything. Perhaps she could start with the customers, see what they buy from World News, and then trace back to learn how everything was connected. . . .

## WHAT IS A PRODUCT?

A common misconception when implementing Scrum is that every team must have a product and/or Product Owner. Perhaps it is because when the framework is explained, people try to simplify it by framing it in a way that suggests a single team can deliver the whole product.

This is often not the case, and in response, we see a traditional divide-and-conquer tactic. The product is broken up into subproducts, and each team starts to own a part of the product. Often these teams have individual Product Owners, and before you know it, everybody owns bits and pieces that do not directly create (customer) value. As a result, it becomes difficult to align teams, goals, and initiatives.

For example, Figure 3.1 illustrates how World News's product(s) can be split into many components or "internal products." But how can you ensure that they deliver value? What is the value proposition? Take the photo component as an example. The photos themselves are not that valuable unless they are combined with other content and delivered to a newsreader. For a newsreader, the combination of photos, an article, relevance, and a medium to read it makes it a product that can generate value.

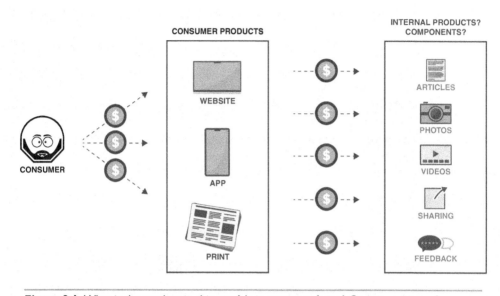

**Figure 3.1** What is the product in this case? Is it consumer-facing? Or is it an internal component?

This doesn't mean that the component photos don't have any value! For example, if you were a freelance photographer who sold photos to World News, your product would be a photo or set of photos. In such cases, where people or components are so good that other people or companies want to buy them, they have value in themselves for other parties. Think of how Amazon created a product out of its AWS services, which in turn are just a component of the Amazon store. Al Jazeera did something similar with its news and photos, but those cases are not common.

When you examine World News's products from a customer point of view, you can see three touchpoints where they can consume the products: the printed paper, the website, and the native mobile app. Perhaps the printed newspaper fulfills a different need for customers than the app or the website fulfills. A printed newspaper might be read on Saturday as part of a deep dive, or perhaps it appeals to a particular customer segment. The website might be used by people who are diving into the details, whereas the app might be used to skim the headlines.

> *Any organization that designs a system (defined broadly) will produce a design whose structure is a copy of the organization's communication structure.*
>
> —Melvin E. Conway

Organizing people and teams around the "real" product is important since people tend to optimize their work for their organizational structure. This was first discovered by Conway, and though it is typically used to explain why some architectures have come to life, you can use it proactively to create the desired conditions for your product by designing the structure.

So, depending on whom you ask, you may get different answers to the question, "What is your product?" Figure 3.2 illustrates how different people and/or functions may have different answers to this question.

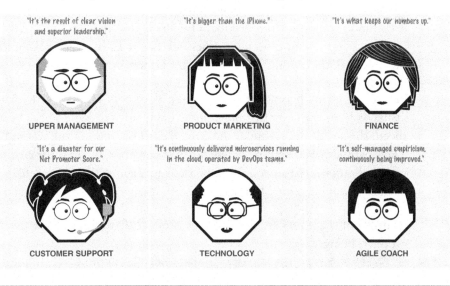

**Figure 3.2** What people consider to be the 'product' is a matter of perspective.

So, what is a product? And why is it important? These questions reveal an organization's key drivers. The answers will reveal the organization's primary focus. Does it focus on customers? Are there multiple parties to be satisfied? What is the organization optimized for doing? Often, the answers are incoherent. You'll likely get ten different answers when asking ten different people.

Even many product leaders in organizations think in terms of optimizing internal processes and systems or think about internal products, without being able to translate the value that the products create into outside-in value.

> *A product is a vehicle to deliver value. It has a clear boundary, known stakeholders, well-defined users, or customers. A product could be a service, a physical product, or something more abstract.*
>
> —Scrum Guide 2020

One of the keys to building a great product is to keep the customer in mind. Take that outside-in perspective and focus on customer problems, wants, needs, and jobs-to-be-done. When talking to many product people in the field, a common response is that they can't ask customers what they need—either because they "don't know," "don't care," "can't be talked to by the Product Owner," or "ask for solutions, and don't come up with problems." A common response from Product Owners is that they feel much like Henry Ford back in the day, thinking to themselves, "If I asked my stakeholders what they wanted, they would have said faster horses."

Instead of asking people what they want, Ford could have asked what people disliked about traveling by horse. Some likely answers could have been the speed, the smell, the stamina, the cost, the noise, and getting wet in the rain. Those would have been the problems that need to be solved for customers. So, when talking to customers, focus on their problems, their pains, likes, and dislikes about current solutions, but don't focus on the solution itself just yet.

It turns out that you can identify your product by looking at the five Ps of a product, being:

1. Does your product solve a **problem** for customers? Which problem(s)?
2. Is the problem **pervasive**? Are there enough people in the market who experience that problem? Is the market segment large enough?
3. Is the customer willing to **pay** for a solution? (This is usually proportional to the perceived "pain" of the customer.)
4. The **positioning**, does the product align with or extend the company brand in a way that makes sense? (For example, would you be buying running

shoes from Volkswagen? Would you buy an insurance or banking product from Red Bull?)

5. Is it **possible** to build the product (within a reasonable time and budget)?

Many Product Owners (and Developers and stakeholders) are triggered by question 5. Especially if you have a technical or engineering background, or if you have a lot of domain knowledge, you will probably love question 5 and dig right into it. However, please answer these questions in numerical order.

> *At one point, I was product manager for a real-time maritime surveillance network that could scale indefinitely. The engineering challenge was enormous, and we were immensely proud that we pulled it off. Once completed, however, we discovered it was impossible to sell in our market. Hence, start with question 1. The engineers will figure out number 5, trust me.*
>
> — Chris

What you will find when answering those five questions is that there is always a product. Every company, organization, and institution delivers products (or services) that solve problems, whether customers pay with their money, time, data, or otherwise. The products may not always be easy to identify, and they may not always be obvious, but they are there, and they need to be identified to be effective as a Product Owner.

Some characteristics apply to every product in addition to the five Ps. Every product has a **customer** who is one of the following:

- **User:** Someone who gets value from the product by using the product.
- **Buyer:** Someone who pays for your product (with money, time, data, or otherwise).
- **Both:** Someone who uses and pays for your product.

And every product has a **producer** who receives benefits by delivering the product (or service), usually in the form of

- Revenues
- Cost decrease or cost avoidance
- Time
- Data
- Societal benefit

# BUILDING CUSTOMER EMPATHY

## TALKING TO CUSTOMERS

Talking to customers is one of the most rewarding and interesting, yet scary, parts of being a Product Owner. To some people, it comes naturally, and they love talking to customers. To others, it's more difficult. But the key to the Customer Representative stance lies not within the four walls of your office. Talking with, listening to, and empathizing with customers is critical to the art of product management. As Calvin Coolidge once said, "No one ever listened himself out of a job." If problems occur when talking to customers, they generally occur when we open our mouths. They occur when we offer solutions to their problems, or when we make promises about products, services, or features that we currently don't have. So, how can we talk sensibly with customers? Let's find out.

## OBSERVING CUSTOMERS

A great way to learn about customer problems, pains, and needs is to observe customers in their natural habitats. It's powerful to watch people while trying to complete their tasks, activities, or jobs. A TV manufacturer did a research study a long time ago by observing consumers in their own homes. They asked their customers, "Can we watch you while you're watching television?" We know, it sounds creepy and weird, but apparently, some people were willing to participate in this study. The amazing discovery they made is that people had a recurring problem when watching television: many people lost their remote at some point in time and had to go searching for it in different places. This may not sound like a deep insight, but bear with us.

The study revealed some interesting patterns around watching a sports game, getting some refreshments, and leaving the remote in the fridge. Nobody blamed the television, nor would they think of the television as a possible solution. However, the TV manufacturer had the idea to add a button on the television that would make the remote emit a beeping sound. This helped consumers locate the remote. It is not something customers would have asked for, but something they needed. One student suggested removing the remote altogether and just putting the buttons on the television, which didn't make a lot of sense, because they already had that in the early days of TV.

According to a Logitech poll, when people lost their remote,

- 49% found it in the couch.
- 8% found it in the bathroom.
- 8% found it in a dresser drawer.
- 4% found it in the fridge/freezer.
- 2% found it outside or out in the car.

Source: Casey Chan, "50% of People Lose Their Remote in Their Couch," Gizmodo, March 23, 2011, https://www.gizmodo.com.au/2011/03/50-of-people-lose-their-remote-in-their-couch/.

As you see, observing the actual customers or users of your product is a powerful way to learn about customer behavior. Similar approaches are frequently used in software development as well—for example, by setting up usability labs or by eye-tracking systems and tracking users' clicking behaviors. These are powerful ways of discovering what customers do, see, and hear when interacting with the product.

# EFFECTIVELY DEALING WITH BIASES WHEN COLLABORATING WITH CUSTOMERS

Observing customers while they are solving their problems or trying to complete tasks, activities, or jobs is possible with your product, a competitor's product, or even a substitute solution. When you want to start observing your customers, there are some points to consider, as there are potential side effects of doing observations incorrectly.

The Hawthorne effect, for example, is a form of reactivity in which customers modify an aspect of their behavior, in response to knowing that they are being studied. Hawthorne studied whether different lighting conditions would improve productivity in 1924. The people he studied got quite nervous about a man in a white lab coat observing how they worked. Productivity soared, but not because of the light.

Another effect is the observer-expectancy effect. This happens when the customer is trying to "help" the observer to reach the desired result. Human nature (our willingness to help others, for example) is hard to ignore, but as Customer Representatives, we can at least be conscious to avoid communicating our desired outcome. This means that you don't want to communicate the desired or expected outcomes of your research with the people participating in the study.

It also works the other way around. Observer bias will make us pick up the clues of our desired outcome, ignoring other things that may transpire. This is especially difficult and one of the reasons why many observational studies are conducted in pairs. The second pair of eyes and ears will help to reveal insights that the other person's miss. Zen Buddhists use the word *Shoshin* (初心), which roughly translates into the "empty mind" or "beginner's mind." It refers to having an attitude of openness, eagerness, and lack of preconceptions, even when you might be very skilled. Approach the world just like a beginner would. Leave your ego and presumptions outside. Don't seek confirmation. Seek learning.

Imagine the following situation: You are at a car dealership, and you are looking around that dealership in search of a new car. As you peek through the windows of an appealing car to get a glimpse of its interior, a man comes up to you and says, "Hello, nice car, isn't it? Can I help you?" You exchange a look, and your eyes quickly scout his striped suit as they make their way down to his polished shoes. "No thank you, I'm just looking around," you mumble and hastily try to get away. Sound familiar? Why does this happen? You are looking for a car, and someone from the dealership comes up to you to help. This person probably knows more about all the cars in the showroom than you do. So, why not engage in a conversation with this person? "Well, he is from sales. . ." is the reply that most people would share in response to this question. "He is a salesman, and I don't want to get sold something. I don't trust them!"

We don't envy salespeople. It must be a hard line of work. But we (Product Owners or product managers) are not in sales! In our interactions with (potential) customers, we must ensure that the customer realizes that. We need to repeatedly communicate that we are not there to sell anything. You can do so right away in your introductions.

For example, "Hi, I'm Noa. I'm from Product Management, trying to build great solutions that solve peoples' problems. I'd love to learn more about how you do [a job or activity to be done]. I'm not here to sell you anything. I only want to learn about what products are solving your problems and challenges. Did I mention that I am not from sales?" Repeat the message about not being from sales at least three times in the conversation (preferably at the start) so the message is clear.

When talking to customers we want to learn about their problems, needs, fears, pains, and possible gains. *How* we might solve these is less interesting at this point. They are the expert on the problem, so typical comments you might make are "Can you show me that?" "That's interesting, tell me more," and "How would you solve that?" You can verify your observations with lines like "It felt like you. . ." or "I think I noticed that. . ." This allows customers to clarify or correct your interpretations. Prevent yourself from using phrases like "Why did you. . ." or "I noticed that you. . . ." Such phrasing makes it harder for customers to respond meaningfully. You're almost putting words in their mouths. Try to avoid using such phrases—you're trying to learn, not to confirm.

Even if the customer explains a certain problem or challenge and you think to yourself, "Hey, we have a solution for that," don't put on your sales hat! Don't mention to the customer that you have a solution to that problem! If you do, you risk making the customer think, "This person is from sales after all!" Instead, simply ask, "What have you done to try and resolve that issue?" The moment you put on your sales hat (even unintentionally), the customer's trust in you will be reduced. So, use the opportunity to find flaws in your marketing and sales approach rather than trying to make a single sale.

Another common pitfall is explaining how the product works. As Product Owners, we are usually knowledgeable about how the product works. We know about the problems it solves, we know about the features it has, heck, we might even know about all the possible configurations and settings. However, it is not our role to explain exactly how the product works! At least, not in the setting of talking to a customer to learn about them.

*I remember interviewing a customer in Hong Kong about their requirements for the next generation of our product. I was in Hong Kong primarily to learn more from one of our customers about the expectations and needs for that next-generation product. In one of the conversations I had, people from the customer side mentioned that they were experiencing some problems with the existing product. In all my youthful enthusiasm, I mentioned that I could probably find some empty spaces in my schedule of interviews to help them out. This drastically changed the way the rest of my time there went, and I ended up doing maintenance and educating the staff. Although it was fun, it was not my job. And more importantly, doing that work didn't help us to learn more about customer problems and needs. It robbed us of the opportunity to get the information that we needed.*

*— Chris*

In short, the best way to learn from and about customers, their problems, and their challenges is to get out of your office and connect with them. Make sure that (potential) customers understand that you are not from sales, nor from customer support, but that you are there to learn about them and their domain, and that you consider them to be the experts. The interview will take only 30 to 45 minutes of their time. Anything less is not a serious attempt at learning. Anything more requires them to commit too much time, making it harder to get them to agree to an appointment. Make sure to value their time and thank them for it!

Once you have talked to several customers you will spot patterns that allow you to create an archetypal customer. Do not select a particular individual but create a generic type that would match similar customers best. Try to capture your findings and learnings in a way for others to also understand your customers and their needs better. In other words, make sure to document your learnings, for example by using personas.

# CAPTURE YOUR CUSTOMER INSIGHTS VIA PERSONAS

## USER PERSONAS

In many organizations, people talk about creating value, building features, or delivering products and services to "the customer." But are all customers equal? Do they all have the same problems, needs, and wants? Do they have the same backgrounds? And what about their motivations for using your product or selecting your company in the first place? When talking about customers, you'll quickly discover that people in your organization will have different ideas about whom that customer is that you're talking about. Is it a user? A buyer? The people who maintain the product? The people who sell it? Store it? Ship it? Is it marketing? Sales? Our partners? Old users? Young users? People whom we want to turn into users? Or buyers? If you are not careful when talking about "the customer," you'll end up in a confusion of Babylonian proportions.

Alan Cooper wrote *The Inmates Are Running the Asylum*,[1] which is certainly a provocative title! But how often do we design products for ourselves rather

---

1. *The Inmates Are Running the Asylum: Why High Tech Products Drive Us Crazy and How to Restore the Sanity,* SAMS Technical Publishing, 2004.

than for the actual target audience of the product? Do the following exercise to find out whether or not your product is designed for your target audience.

Grab or log in to your product and start using it. The product characteristics are listed in Table 5.1. When using your product, see if you can tick these characteristics *as a user.*

**Table 5.1** Product Characteristics

| Is interested in me | Has common sense | Is well informed | Stays focused |
|---|---|---|---|
| Is deferential to me | Anticipates my needs | Is perceptive | Gives instant gratification |
| Is forthcoming | Is responsive | Is self-confident | Is trustworthy |

Once completed, count the number of boxes that you checked (the maximum score is 12). If your score is below 9, this might be an excellent time for you to start applying the Customer Representative stance more often. The next time that you are about to build new features or do Product Backlog refinement, limit your focus to designing or building a product for just a few user types (a few personas) rather than a product that tries to make everybody happy. As Seth Godin said, "Don't try to make a product for everybody, because that is a product for nobody."[2] Instead, focus on a clear, defined, and specific type of customer when building products. This leads to better products, higher quality, more real problems solved, and better sales for your company than if you develop a generic product to meet the needs of everyone.

## CREATING PERSONAS

Creating personas is a great technique for documenting and communicating customer insights as well as for supporting you in stakeholder management. It's helpful to collaborate with sales, marketing, and customer support in building personas, because these teams frequently interact with customers and are (or should be) conscious of customers' behavioral patterns. Ask them about "typical" customers and the problems the customers want solved. Ask

---

2. *Purple Cow: Transform Your Business by Being Remarkable,* Penguin, 2005.

what makes these customers typical. Interviewing your colleagues will help to reveal assumptions and hypotheses that they might have about customers, which you might want to test later. An additional benefit of talking to sales, marketing, and customer support about customers and personas is that it helps to generate their buy-in to the persona technique.

So, what is a persona? A persona is a narrative or story description about a customer or user that resonates with the team and the stakeholders (on an emotional level). Focusing on a clear target audience and using personas to reflect those target audiences ensures that you don't forget who your users are throughout the continuous development of your product. The process itself of creating personas is also beneficial because it requires you to really think from the customer's perspective as you build the persona and reinforces the customer's needs in your mind.

For example, for a personal navigation device product, one user persona could be a person who is passionate about ease of use and safety while car-pooling kids to unfamiliar locations all over the state for sports matches on a Saturday morning. It's easy to sense that this customer's needs are very different from the needs of a technical-savvy daily commuter.

> *When we launched a new e-commerce platform, we took wire-frames to the capital's main train station and interviewed people who matched our assumed profile in the context of our prototype. Then we revamped our design based on what we learned. You can tweak the persona to match the prototype or tweak the prototype to match the persona. It's a system with two variables, not one.*
>
> — Chris

As Chris's comment indicates, you may get the persona right but the product or prototype wrong, or the other way around. In other words, you will need to validate both your personas and your product. A common pitfall is that you create the wrong types of personas, so let's briefly highlight the different types of personas that can be used. Table 5.2 illustrates that there are different types of personas, where the user persona is based on usage habits and research, while the proto persona is based primarily on assumptions.

**Table 5.2** Types of Personas

| Marketing Persona | User Persona | Proto Persona |
|---|---|---|
| Demographic centered, to drive ad targeting | Behavioral, to drive product design | Behavioral, to drive product design |
| Aspirational, to drive messaging | Research based on usage habits | Represents what we know today |
| Research based on buying habits | Formal, high ceremony | Informal, easy to change |

The purpose of creating personas is to be able to empathize with them. Empathy should guide your product and design decisions. Here are two examples of customer personas in the context of World News (see Figures 5.1 and 5.2).

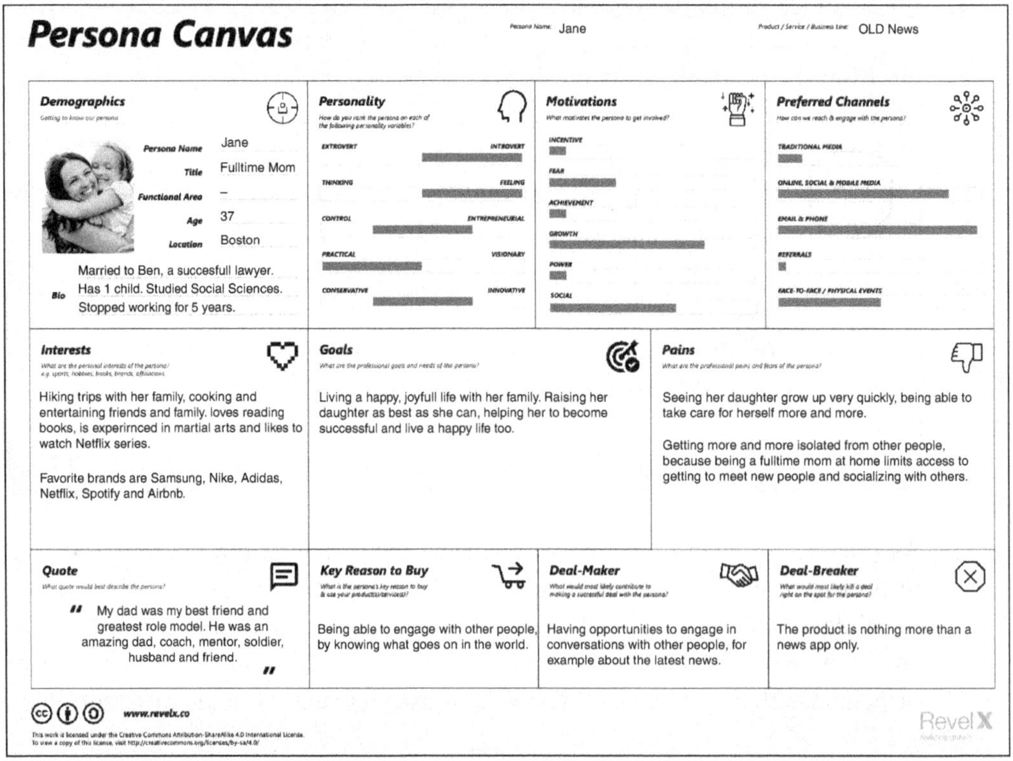

**Figure 5.1** Example persona: Jane

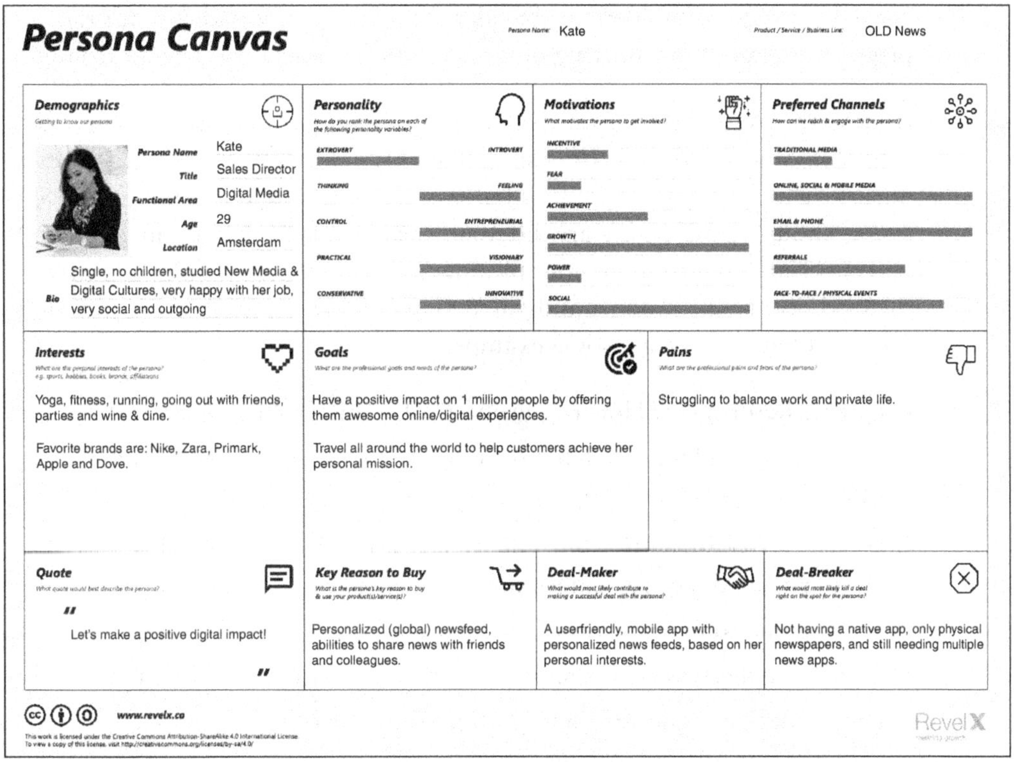

**Figure 5.2** Example persona: Kate

What do you think drives these personas, being Kate and Jane? They seem to be worlds apart, yet at the same time, they have similar needs. Typically, you end up with 3 to 12 different personas, which is a lot! Do you need to satisfy everybody? Well, maybe not. Many software-based products have menus for advanced settings or wizard-like functionality that helps one persona to have control over the behavior of the product depending on their needs.

Some Product Owners create a "negative" persona—a representation of a customer that is *not* our target audience. This practice is especially helpful for organizations that have pivoted to a different market. The desire to serve the requirements of the old segment is often deeply ingrained in the organization, and it is helpful to point at a persona and say, "What you are talking about makes sense for John, but remember that this product is not for John. How is it going to help Kate and Jane?" Rather than directly dismissing requests, you are redirecting stakeholders to consider the actual target audience for the product instead of considering other people who might also benefit from it.

Back to the examples of Kate and Jane. You may spot a desire to communicate with others and share or interact about the news. Whereas Kate wants to make an impact on her followers, Jane is more interested in making connections. Though their drivers are different, they have many things in common. Having clear insights about your product's customers can help you to drive the direction of the product and guide many of the day-to-day activities of a Product Owner. Here are some examples:

- **During Refinement:** How can we best solve this problem for Kate?
- **During Sprint Planning:** What meaningful increment can we create for Jane?
- **During Sprint Review:** What was the impact of this increment for Kate?
- **During a Roadmap presentation:** What problems will we solve first?
- **When going to market:** How can we reach Jane?
- **When offering financial forecasts:** How many Kates are out there?
- **During design sessions:** What did Kate think of this?

# IDENTIFYING AND EXPRESSING CUSTOMER VALUE

*Robert Lutz, the chairman of Chrysler, says that 80% of people in focus groups hated the new Dodge Ram pickup. He went ahead with production and made it into a best-seller because the other 20% loved it. Having people love your product, even if it is only a minority, is how you succeed.*

—Alan Cooper, *The Inmates Are Running the Asylum*

Perhaps the best description of the Product Owner accountability in Scrum is that of a "value maximizer." The value is typically out there but often hidden by a web of complexity. Scrum is merely a sword that allows us to cut through that complexity but does not guarantee that there is value on the other end. There is no greater waste than to build a product with great tenacity only to discover later that it should not have been built at all.

Where Robert Lutz found value in the eyes of the small group of users who loved his idea, we Product Owners often struggle to maximize the value of our products and services, in part because there is no universal language for value. There is no magic number that we can just measure and compare with other numbers. It's hard to quantify value, and thus there are many misconceptions about what value is and how to identify, express, measure, and maximize value.

In 2016, Eric Almquist, John Senior, and Nicolas Bloch wrote an interesting article about the elements of value.[1] Based on work done by Bain & Company, they created a pyramid containing various elements that contribute to the value that a customer perceives and receives from a product or service.

Much like the Maslow pyramid of needs, a product needs to satisfy some of the lower levels of the value pyramid before elements higher up in the value pyramids will be found attractive. For example, Maslow states that people will not work on things like respect and esteem when the physiological needs are not met. Depending on your culture, some layers may be swapped, but you get a general idea.

Value can be described in many ways, as the B2C value pyramid shown in Figure 6.1 illustrates. There are four levels of value: functional, emotional, life-changing, and social-impact elements.

---

1. "The Elements of Value," *Harvard Business Review*, September 2016.

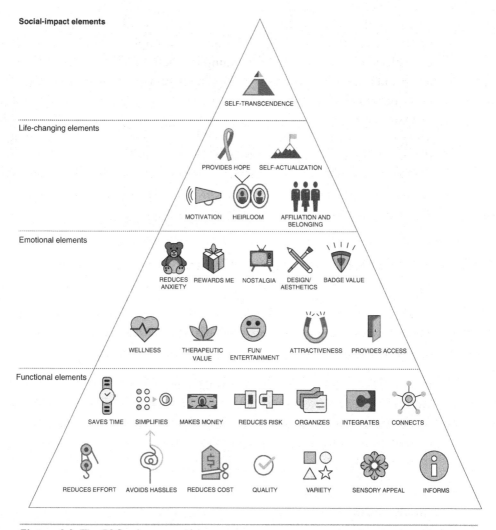

**Figure 6.1** The B2C value pyramid

# THE FUNCTIONAL ELEMENTS OF VALUE

Optimizing the value of a product or service all starts with the functional elements of value. Before customers or users will perceive the value of your product, a product should first cover the "table stakes" by providing value in the form of functionality, that is, providing the functional value. The product or service should solve the customer's or user's problem and fulfill their core needs. This can be done by making solutions simple, appealing, time saving, cost effective, or convenient, for example. These functional elements of value are found at the bottom of the B2C value pyramid. Numerous examples of how your product or service helps to deliver that value to your users will probably spring to mind as you go through the functional elements of value. You can consider these elements to be like seatbelts in your car. Without them, people won't buy your product. However, adding more seatbelts per seat will not make the car more attractive. In other words, saving people time or delivering more information to them alone won't help as such. You need to add additional value for your customers and users.

## EMOTIONAL ELEMENTS OF VALUE

The next level of the B2C value pyramid is emotional elements of value. In contrast to the functional elements, emotional elements do compound. Therefore, investing more time, money, and resources into improving the emotional elements will help to deliver more value for your product.

Polaroid, for example, leveraged nostalgia as an emotional element when it launched a modern version of its classic 1960 camera. If you look at the specs and features, that camera was on par with other cameras at the time. Maybe it was performing a bit below market average even. However, the camera rekindled old memories for many customers, making the product more valuable than competitor products.

Another example is that non-Apple (computer, tablet, or phone) users have pointed out that Apple's competitors often deliver cheaper products with better hardware specs. However, for Apple users, these competitor products are missing out on the design, aesthetics, and badge elements of emotional value.

## LIFE-CHANGING ELEMENTS OF VALUE

Products such as Fitbit (a smartwatch that helps you to maintain a healthy lifestyle) sell the value element of motivation. The product offers the motivation for a healthier lifestyle and a better chance of maintaining discipline. Another example of a company selling life-changing elements of value is Nike. Nike doesn't talk about its products in commercials. Its commercials are always about amazing sportsmen and women and about conveying the message that you can be just like them. Heirloom and a sense of affiliation and belonging are very powerful ways to add value for your customers and users, as humans are social animals by nature. Ever since we discovered that fighting with saber-tooth tigers alone is not a bright idea, we have wanted to be part of a group.

## SOCIAL-IMPACT ELEMENT OF VALUE

Finally, there is the social-impact element of value, called self-transcendence. This element aligns with Maslow's hierarchy of needs. Finding meaning in life is ultimately something everyone can relate to. This element is not so much about yourself as it is about improving the quality of life for others.

An example of this element of value is an institution in rural Ghana that enables women to access the world's market of shea butter. The women are able to make high-quality shea butter products. However, the effect and value that those products bring go beyond producing or having the product itself. Through these products, the institution makes the world a better place by improving the lives of women in rural Ghana.

Looking at how a product can add value for customers and users, the pyramids of value by Bain & Company can offer some great inspiration. Use the interactive value pyramids to identify what value your product or service is adding. Use the interactive B2B value pyramid or the interactive B2C value pyramid, or use both if you work on a B2B2C product/service.

Take another look at the example personas Kate and Jane. What elements of value would they relate to from the value pyramids?

# CONNECTING PRODUCT FEATURES TO OUTCOMES AND IMPACTS

### Connecting the Dots

Noa's head was pounding. She had just come out of what had arguably been the worst strategy meeting she had ever attended. It seemed like everyone had a different agenda, and everyone was using different language and jargon.

Trevon was advocating for content, which made sense because he was the head of editorial. Kemal had monopolized most of the meeting talking about what Google and Apple were doing but offered no practical guidance on how those strategies could be translated to a company with less than a hundredth of their resources. Shanice and Gijs had missed no opportunity to explain that most of the revenues still came from print. And Sandra from finance had explained—in a way that bored everyone to sleep—how bad the cash flow situation was. At some point, Dave intervened and postponed the discussion to next week, but Noa could tell that he was not happy about this meeting's outcomes.

On top of it all, Noa had gotten a flat tire this morning, so she was taking the metro home. *What a day,* she thought as she walked through the rain, which drizzled down in ever-increasing amounts. She concluded that the meeting attendees all had been talking about different things. Some had been talking about customer outcomes, things that make customers happy. Others had been focused on what the company impact of these proposals would be. If they couldn't connect the two, next week's meeting would be another difficult conversation.

When entering the metro station, Noa spotted a map near the entrance. It illustrated the whole metro network and all its lines and stations in the city, and she noticed that there were multiple routes to her destination. There was no right or wrong, but every route had pros and cons. In much the same way, everyone in the meeting was right to some extent, but nobody had the perfect answer. It gave Noa an idea.

Some people were talking about company goals, others about required results, and yet others about impacts for various customer segments. *How are these various elements connected?* Noa wondered. *Why would customers pay, or pay more, for our products? What would change their lives and behaviors, and how does that connect to the work that we are doing?"*

While Noa entered the metro toward home, she said to herself, "Tomorrow, I'm going to explore whether I can connect all these dots in one way or another. Perhaps that flat tire wasn't such a bad thing after all."

## CONNECTING GOALS, IMPACTS, OUTCOMES, AND FEATURES

Have you ever found yourself in a meeting where everyone was making good points but at the same time there didn't seem to be a connection between what everyone was saying? It's like watching a soccer match with your friends and one says, "They should be more active. They should pass the ball around more." The other one replies, "No, we need more shots at the goal. How are we supposed to score if we don't even try?" A third one points out that to win the cup, we need more points than the other teams, and a fourth one remarks that they have lost the interest of the audience. All valid remarks and seemingly unconnected.

Being Product Owners, we often find ourselves acting as translators. We're trying to translate the language of the developers to the language of the business, and vice versa, as if we were the fabled Babel fish from the classic cult novel *The Hitchhiker's Guide to the Galaxy*.

It is likely that a group of people in your company, such as executives and leaders, mostly talk about the company goals to be achieved. **Company goals** are often expressed in terms of market share, revenue, margin, costs, cash flow, or risk exposure, for example.

Other groups of people, from marketing, sales, customer support, or operations, for example, might be focused more on measurable results that affect the way the company is run. They seek to improve the **company impacts,** which include examples such as customer satisfaction, the number of new customers, retention of customers, incidents, and product usage.

Then we have our customers and users, who want to get their problems and pains resolved, satisfy their needs, and/or complete jobs and activities in better ways. These customer groups, perhaps being reflected as personas, seek to achieve certain **customer outcomes.**

And of course, the people who are involved in product development are typically focused on more hands-on stuff, like the roadmap, next steps, goals and objectives, and the next **features** to build.

Taking the stance of a Customer Representative Product Owner, you will often find yourself in the middle of all these different stakeholders and their perspectives. You will be thinking about how you can better impact the lives of your customers and perhaps how you might make them change their behavior to deliver value for both them and the other stakeholders. Figure 7.1 illustrates how you connect the needs of your organization and stakeholders (goal, impacts) with your target audiences (personas), their desired outcomes, and potential features to develop.

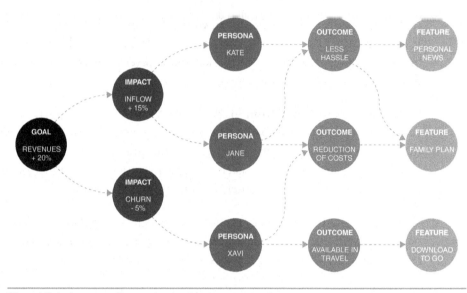

**Figure 7.1** A system diagram inspired by impact mapping

Imagine that the company's goal is to increase revenues by 20%. Quite an ambitious goal, for sure, but let's say that it is possible given the current market conditions, growth ambitions, and relative positioning.

There are at least two ways to achieve that company goal. One way is to simply get more subscribers, that is, get new product customers. In this example, let's say that we believe we can achieve 15% of the revenue goal by attracting more subscribers and 5% by reducing the churn rate of existing subscribers.

Note our use of the words *impacts* and *outcomes* here. There is no fixed definition of when to use *impact* and when to use *outcome*. Our convention is to use the term *company impact* when we are talking about *measurable results for the company,* and the term *customer outcomes* when we are talking about a *measurable change in customer behavior.*[1] We've seen these words used with various meanings and in various contexts, so it is good advice to communicate what they mean in your organization to avoid confusion.

---

1. This is in line with the Lean UX method.

Company impacts are ultimately a result of changes in customer behavior. In the World News case study, we focus on the two personas explored in Chapter 6, "Identifying and Expressing Customer Value," Kate and Jane. The third persona in the example, Xavi, is a persona for an existing print subscriber. We haven't shared the persona canvas for Xavi in this book, as we believe that having more examples doesn't add much value to the context. But it is important to keep other personas like Xavi in mind, as we don't want to lose our existing newspaper customers.

Going back to our user personas, we can find what they consider to be valuable and get an idea of how we could measure if that is the case. So, the next step is to connect your personas to the customer outcomes they seek to achieve.

Kate, for example, doesn't like it when apps are not self-explanatory. We can see if we are meeting her needs if she starts moving more swiftly through the app and spends more time consuming content. Jane on the other hand is more concerned with cost. Measuring how new signups are divided over the different plans and pricing schemes will tell us if they like our offering.

Where some behaviors amplify each other, others will have a negative effect. For example, more pricing tiers or a combination of ad-driven and premium versions may appeal to Jane. However, it might make the proposition more complicated for Kate. It's a game of balance.

Note that we haven't talked about the features yet. Features are a result of the change in behavior that you try to trigger in your personas. Just as with the customer outcomes, features can also influence each other, though that is typically a technical limitation that teams can overcome.

The purpose of a diagram, like the one created for World News, is to facilitate communication and create transparency. You can use it to explain to people how their (company, department, or personal) goals are achieved through a change in customer behavior. Following that you can connect the desired change to the work that we are doing. It is also a great tool to connect technologically oriented people with business-oriented people. It helps to explain and visualize how each feature to be developed contributes to the goal(s) of that feature. It helps to clarify what behavior change it is trying to accomplish and for which persona. Are there different and more cost-effective ways to achieve that change? Perhaps we can test some of our assumptions earlier by making this connection. Are we sure that this behavior change will lead to these business results?

Figure 7.1 works from left to right and from right to left. It functions as an invitation to a conversation. But it puts the customer at the center of what we do, and that is what the Customer Representative is all about.

# THE CUSTOMER REPRESENTATIVE

## SUMMARY

### KEY LEARNINGS AND INSIGHTS

This concludes Part II, in which you explored the Customer Representative stance. In this part, you learned how to identify and define a product, using the 5 Ps. You also learned how to develop customer empathy, how to capture customer insights using personas, and how to identify and express customer value. Finally, you learned how to connect all the dots, such as which features to build to deliver customer value and which impacts to achieve to reach your company goals and objectives. To create winning products in the marketplace, it all starts with a clear picture of the product's customers, their pains, gains, needs, and jobs-to-be-done. Product Owners and product managers need to talk to, observe, and engage with customers and users on a regular basis to understand their needs and problems to solve. Product Owners managing failing products often crank out as many features as they can, operating as feature factories. Winning products, on the other hand, solve clear customer problems for well-defined and well-understood target audiences.

## QUICK QUIZ REVIEW

If you took the Quick Quiz at the beginning of Part II, compare your answers to those in the following table. Now that you have read about the Customer Representative stance, would you change any of your answers? Do you agree with the following answers?

| Statement | Agree | Disagree |
| --- | --- | --- |
| People buy, hire, or absorb products to solve their problems, not for the features that products have. | ✓ | |
| If you ask customers what product they need, the only answer you get is "faster horses." | | ✓ |
| There is always a product, a customer, and a producer, but they are not always easy to define. | ✓ | |
| The best people to talk with to learn more about customers are sales, customer support, UX, and marketing people. They know best what customers really want. | | ✓ |
| The best way to express value for customers is in how much revenue they bring in for the company. | | ✓ |
| Visualizing user information (e.g., with personas or empathy maps) provides a better understanding of customer and user problems and needs. | ✓ | |
| Company goals, company impacts, personas, value for customers, and the features to be built are all interconnected in nonlinear ways. | | ✓ |

## WANT TO LEARN MORE?

Do you want to learn more about the Customer Representative stance? Well, a good way to get started is to create a persona.

From there you can explore the "The Elements of Value"[1] and the Bain Value Pyramid.[2] You can also use system diagrams or impact maps to summarize and connect the dots.

---

1. Eric Almquist, John Senior, and Nicolas Bloch, "The Elements of Value," *Harvard Business Review,* September 2016.
2. Bain & Company offer an interactive graphic at https://media.bain.com/elements-of-value/#.

Other relevant resources include *The Inmates Are Running the Asylum* by Alan Cooper (Sams, 2004), *Lean UX* by Jeff Gothelf and Josh Seiden (O'Reilly, 2017), and *What Customers Want: Using Outcome-Driven Innovation to Create Breakthrough Products and Services* by Anthony Ulwick (McGraw-Hill, 2005).

The customer representative domain is in constant shift. If you, as a Product Owner, want to know more about what your customers are experiencing, we highly recommend exploring the worlds of user experience design, user research, and/or user testing.

# THE VISIONARY
## III

*Big ideas almost always come in small words.*

— Jack Trout

## QUICK QUIZ

To connect to Part III, answer each of the following statements by checking the Agree or Disagree column. The answers are shared in the Part III Summary.

| Statement | Agree | Disagree |
|---|---|---|
| A product vision should inspire customers, users, stakeholders, and Developers. Communicating the product vision through storytelling is a great practice for sharing memorable stories that inspire people. | | |
| A Product Owner should have multiple Product Goals that are to be achieved for the product. | | |
| There are many ways to visualize Product Backlogs, such as by creating product roadmaps tailored to the stakeholders' needs and organizational context. | | |
| A clear definition of how to identify, express, estimate, and measure value (e.g., with Evidence-Based Management) helps to increase autonomy and improve decision making. | | |
| The Scrum Master and Developers in Scrum are accountable for time to market and innovation. | | |
| A Product Owner is not, and should not be, responsible for a product's pricing. Product Owners don't need to influence or define the pricing strategies and tactics to be used. | | |
| Releasing Done products is the only way to deliver value and measure progress toward business goals, product vision, and strategy. | | |

# CREATING AND COMMUNICATING PRODUCT VISION

## INTRODUCING: THE VISIONARY

 *When you think of it, the Product Owner is a kind of reverse Spider-Man. For Spider-Man, with great power comes great responsibility. But, for Product Owners, with great responsibility comes absolutely no power.*

— Chris

At times, a Product Owner should take the stance of being the Visionary. In Part II, "The Customer Representative," you learned more about how to take the stance of the Customer Representative, helping you get a solid understanding of your customers, their needs, and the product. After learning more about your product, your customers, and their needs, you may have gotten inspired, and you may have generated new ideas for your product. Representing those ideas, that vision about the product, and the goals to be achieved, is what the Visionary stance is about. Many Product Owners suffer from the reverse Spider-Man syndrome, meaning they have little formal power, but a great responsibility for the product, nonetheless. The result of not having that formal power is that you will need to create followers. These followers are people who are motivated to join the cause—*your* cause. Or in other words, they aren't following you just because of the person you are. Instead, they follow you because they are passionate about the vision, purpose, or goals you seek to achieve. But how do you create followers without formal power? How do you inspire people to follow your lead? Those and many others are exactly the questions to cover in this part: the Visionary.

A vision, mission, or purpose can be considered the North Star for your product. It explains where you are heading. When taking the Visionary stance as a Product Owner, you focus on the future. You look forward and imagine where you, your product, and the company are heading. Taking this stance is all about challenging the status quo. So, forget about those bugs for a moment. Forget about the technical debt in your product. Forget about the latest complaint by that very important customer. When you are in the Visionary stance, you don't focus on the now, you focus on what could be in the future.

Being future-focused (not all the time, but at least regularly) is important to avoid a catastrophe before it happens. Being future-focused helps you to plan for increases in staffing, production, customer demand, and rising and new target audiences, for example. Having and communicating a clear vision to the people around you will help to prepare for what might happen in the future. Having a clear vision keeps a Product Owner on course during hard times or when experiencing unexpected setbacks.

Communicating a clear vision helps you to build a unified force amongst your team(s) and stakeholders, and it also has a positive impact on your organization's effectiveness. Having an inspiring, ambitious, and clear vision inspires action. It ignites a spark, passion, and motivation. A strong vision pulls in ideas, people, and other resources to achieve it. When people understand and buy in to the vision, it brings them together. It creates the energy and willingness to make change happen. It inspires individuals and organizations to commit, persist, and give their best. It focuses and aligns efforts, so everyone is working towards the same understood direction.

A clear vision also acts as a guide for employee actions and decision making. It functions as a practical guide for creating plans, setting goals and objectives, and coordinating and evaluating the work on any initiative, whether it is small or large. For example, if there is a decision to be made about undertaking a new initiative, or if a decision is needed on how to complete a task, stop and ask yourself, "Is what I am doing—or what I am about to do—consistent with the vision?" If it is, that's great, go ahead and move forward! If not, or if there is any doubt that the idea aligns with the vision, now is a time to pause, evaluate, and if necessary, realign the action or decision with the vision. Or if it doesn't fit the vision, forgo it completely. The vision will provide the guidance people need to make the right decisions.

Possibly the most significant benefit of having a clear vision is that it can be motivating and inspiring for people around you. When an individual understands and aligns with the core values and vision of the organization, they can readily commit to, and engage in, the organization's efforts. Engaged and inspired personnel can go a long way in helping the organization achieve its goals. Having a clear and inspiring vision helps to keep organizations focused and together, especially when working on complex initiatives, and during stressful times. If people have a solid understanding of the vision, the teams will be able to build a better product or service. If everybody is aligned around the product vision, the dream, the goals, and the objectives, your chances of "building the right thing" are much higher.

Apart from building a better product, teams usually become more self-managing when the vision and strategy are clear to them. They will be able to make more day-to-day decisions themselves, and they will be able to contribute to the vision and strategy by sharing their knowledge and insights. This increased self-management of the teams allows the Product Owner to spend more time on other responsibilities, and the team members' contributions will improve the vision and strategy.

Research has proven many additional benefits of having a clear vision. Through experience in practice, we mostly learned that regularly taking a Visionary stance as a Product Owner will lead to improved product usage, increased revenues, an improved total cost of ownership, and increased customer satisfaction. So, what's holding you back? Time to take the Visionary stance!

Let's summarize what great Visionary Product Owners do:

- **Personal belief in the vision:** Visionary Product Owners are personally bought into the vision. It is as if the vision is inside them. The vision is theirs and they are the vision. They are connected to the vision; they live it and breathe it. If you don't believe in your personnel, product, or company vision, how can you be the visionary and inspirational (product) leader to follow?

- **Think of what might be, forget about what is:** Great visionaries are optimistic about the future. They are also consumed with making tomorrow better than today. These visionary and hopeful leaders never settle with today being good enough. They always strive to make tomorrow even better. It is this focus in combination with a relentless challenge of the status quo that makes great visionary leaders so successful.

- **Visionary Product Owners are imaginative and focus on the bigger picture:** Visionary people can visualize things easily. They have great imagination and visualization skills. It is as if they can see the future. Visionaries can imagine future possibilities in their minds and then explain what they have imagined. They can explain it so clearly, it is as if they have already been there.

- **Apply storytelling to your vision:** It starts when we're just little children, and it never ends. We all love great stories! Whether it was listening to our parents reading us stories when we were kids, playing video games with a great storyline, or binge-watching a new Netflix series, we all love stories. And great visionaries know this. Great visionaries not only can define, create, shape, and visualize a vision, they also are awesome storytellers, which makes the vision memorable.

- **Visionary leaders are inclusive, not exclusive:** Great visionary leaders share and communicate their dream/vision. One sign of working with a Visionary Product Owner is their willingness to share the vision with the world. Great visionaries don't keep their vision to themselves because they know that they cannot get to the destination alone. Visionary leaders however are also accepting of the change. They are open to inviting others to join in their vision, but also to add to it and make it their own.

- **They are never afraid of failures:** As mentioned earlier, true visionaries see what others cannot see. They see the big picture. They see the links among different events. They see possible obstacles. Great visionaries know that Winston Churchill was right when he said, "Success is walking from failure to failure with no loss of enthusiasm."

## CONNECTING THE PRODUCT VISION TO THE COMPANY MISSION, VISION, AND VALUES

Before diving into the topic of vision, let's pause for a moment to clarify some terms. What we often find is that there are many definitions and interpretations of what "vision," "mission," "purpose," and "strategy" mean. Different people have different definitions of these terms. So do many organizations. Let's start with some definitions so that you'll know what we refer to in the context of this book.

The **vision** usually describes a problem to be solved, and the **mission** describes how the company will contribute to solving that problem. The mission is typically defined based on the vision and is often also considered to be the **purpose** of the organization. The mission describes what a company seeks to achieve, what it seeks to contribute to the world, and how it wishes to do so.

For some companies, the mission will be about generating knowledge through research. For others, it might be about building bridges and connecting people. Both statements should not describe business results, goals, objectives, or deliverables. Instead, they should describe how the company makes the world a better place.

Let's explore the following mission and vision statements, read them slowly, and imagine what the company could be about:

- The mission is to entertain, inform, and inspire people around the globe through the power of unparalleled storytelling, reflecting the iconic brands, creative minds, and innovative technologies that make ours the world's premier entertainment company.
- To make people happy, especially children.

To which company do you think these mission statements belong? The correct answer is that these statements are from the Walt Disney Company. Which sentence is most inspiring to you? The mission or the vision? It's likely that the second statement (the vision) is more inspiring to you. Vision statements are usually shorter and more inspiring, while mission statements are longer and offer more details on how to achieve the vision.

Most organizations also define **company values.** These values describe the core behaviors, values, and principles that the company and its people operate from. The company values should not change often, as they form the heart of how the company and its people behave. Company values should be more than just a description, though. Some companies write down beautiful statements of their values; however, when taking a closer look, you don't see people behaving that way. We believe that company values are not so much defined by how you describe them on paper, but by the behaviors that people display. People should display the company values consistently, as they are the deep-seated core values at the heart of the organization.

As mentioned before, the company vision is a, usually brief, description of the future state of the world. It often describes the complex problem to be solved, or the ambition/purpose to be achieved. The vision describes what ultimate value a company seeks to deliver, and it guides the company on its journey to get there. If a vision changes frequently, it becomes difficult for companies and their people to deliver coherent products and services that serve as stepping stones towards that desired vision.

Here are a couple of examples of vision statements for your inspiration:

**Facebook:** Connect with friends and the world around you.

**LinkedIn:** Create economic opportunities for every member of the global workforce.

**Teach for America:** One day, all children in this nation will have the opportunity to attain an excellent education.

**Alzheimer's Association:** A world without Alzheimer's and all other dementia.

**The Nature Conservancy:** To leave a sustainable world for future generations.

After the vision comes **strategy** as the next step. Strategy is a description of *how* the company is going to achieve its vision. It's a measurable, actionable form of planning, and usually contains goals to be achieved. You should be able to explain the strategy of a company based on the products it creates and how those products get created. After all, what is the strategy trying to achieve if not the company mission? And what is the mission if it is not an embodiment of the vision?

> *Strategy without tactics is the slowest route to victory. Tactics without strategy is the noise before defeat.*
>
> —Sun Tzu

Some organizations add additional layers of goals, objectives, key results, and others between the company vision and the product portfolio. So, the terminology used in this book might be slightly different from how your organization implemented these terms. Regardless, having and developing products and services should serve as evidence of the strategy a company has. A product is more than a collection of features, components, tools, and technologies.

In Tables 8.1 and 8.2, you will find vision, mission, and strategy examples for inspiration.

**Table 8.1** Example Vision, Mission, and Strategy: Alzheimer's Association (July 2022, alz.org)

| Vision | Mission | Strategy |
|--------|---------|----------|
| A world without Alzheimer's and all other dementia. | The Alzheimer's Association leads the way to end Alzheimer's and all other dementia—by accelerating global research, driving risk reduction and early detection, and maximizing quality care and support. | • Providing and Enhancing Quality Care and Support—The Alzheimer's Association engages with communities on national, state, and local levels to ensure access to quality care and support for everyone affected by Alzheimer's and all other dementia. |

| Vision | Mission | Strategy |
|--------|---------|----------|
| | | • Accelerating Research—The Alzheimer's Association leads and accelerates research worldwide to advance risk reduction, earlier detection, and more effective treatments to end Alzheimer's and all other dementia. |
| | | • Increasing Concern and Awareness—The Alzheimer's Association is the leading global voluntary health organization advancing Alzheimer's disease and dementia awareness in all communities. We have successfully built our brand and extended reach to increase awareness, reduce stigma, and increase the public's knowledge of our support resources and advances in Alzheimer's and dementia research. |
| | | • Strengthening Diversity, Equity, and Inclusion—The Alzheimer's Association strives to be a leading organization in diversity, equity, and inclusion. We seek to create a culture where staff, volunteers, and constituents are empowered to share their voices and perspectives to create an environment of inclusion, growth, positivity, belonging, and change. This culture is embraced by all parts of the Association and partnering organizations. |
| | | • Advancing Public Policy—The Alzheimer's Association and the Alzheimer's Impact Movement will advance our mission for all communities through the pursuit of federal and state policy to provide broad, timely, and equitable access to effective treatment, comprehensive education, care, services, and support, and research funding to meet the growing needs of all affected. |

| Vision | Mission | Strategy |
| --- | --- | --- |
| | | • Increasing Revenue—The Alzheimer's Association will increase revenue through the mobilization of all communities by engaging individual constituents, corporations, and organizations to accelerate progress and maximize mission impact. |

**Table 8.2** Example Vision, Mission, and Strategy: Carepay

| Vision | Mission | Strategy |
| --- | --- | --- |
| We believe that mobile has the potential to transform healthcare in Africa by orchestrating access to good quality healthcare with great member experience with lower out-of-pocket contributions. | We give everyone the power to care. | 1. **International Scaling,** multi country, multi payers platform setup<br>2. **Extreme Loyalty,** gamifications positively benefit health eco-system<br>3. **Lowest Transaction Costs,** member-controlled click-and-play health eco-system connectivity platform |

# A PRODUCT VISION ALIGNED WITH THE COMPANY MISSION AND VISION

A Product Owner should be able to influence the company strategy (at least to some extent) by finding new and innovative ways to create value for customers, the company, and society. Of course, Product Owners should be thinking about the company mission and vision and how their work contributes to achieving the mission and vision. The main concern for a Product Owner is the product or service itself, and that this product or service solves customer problems and generates value.

Product Owners play a key role in the bridging of a vacuum (as illustrated in Figure 8.1) that often exists between company vision and strategy, and the daily work and operations that teams perform. This vacuum is called the *product management vacuum,* and Product Owners play an important role in resolving it.

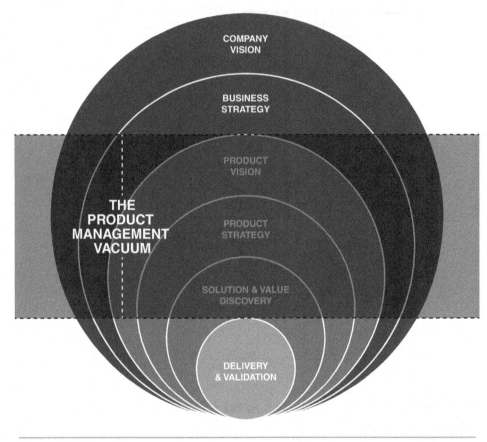

**Figure 8.1** The product management vacuum

Think of your organization. How well are the teams in your company aligned to what the executives want to achieve? How well are the executives informed about what is *really* happening on the work floor?

Chances are that there is not enough alignment. It happens quite often that the executives are not aware of what really happens. And it is quite common that employees do not exactly know what is to be achieved and how they can contribute to that. This phenomenon of misalignment is often referred to as "watermelon reporting."

Watermelon reporting describes the phenomenon where things *appear* to be green on the outside (like a watermelon). In other words, the status reports and management dashboards are displaying green lights and little to no issues. However, like with a watermelon, once you slice it open and delve a bit deeper into those status updates, dashboards, and reports, you will find that most of the stuff is red. It is not going well, and serious issues might be present. Watermelon reporting often happens in organizations where fear, stress, and anxiety rule. It also happens often if there is a disconnect between the company strategy (what C-level management aims to achieve) and what happens on the work floor (what employees and teams do daily).

Product Owners play a crucial part in resolving the product management vacuum. Their effectiveness in resolving this vacuum determines the influence they can exert on the company strategy itself. The more alignment from top to bottom in the company you can create, the more people will notice your contributions, and the more influence you will gain over time. Let us look at some of the ideas that put the Product Owner in a position for resolving that vacuum. *The Agile Manifesto* makes no literal mention of vision or mission. However, vision has a key role if you can read between the lines:

1. **"Our highest priority is to satisfy the customer through early and continuous delivery of valuable software."** If our highest priority is to deliver value early and often, we should have a good understanding of what value is for our customers, which means that we need to have a clear vision of this.

2. **"Welcome changing requirements, even late in development."** Agile processes harness change for the customer's competitive advantage. If one of our goals in Agile is to enable a competitive advantage for our customers, that means that we should have a clear understanding of our customers, their problems, needs, and goals. But we should also try to obtain a good understanding of their vision, strategy, goals, objectives, and business model, right?

10. **"Simplicity—the art of maximizing the amount of work not done—is essential."** To maximize the amount of work not done, and to try to keep the product as simple as possible. Stick to the core of the product and its customers' needs. We need to have a clear understanding of the product's purpose.

In summary, Product Owners need to connect company mission, vision, and strategy to product vision and strategy to solve the product management vacuum. Defining and communicating product vision and strategy effectively helps create focus, inspire people, create alignment, and build better products. But how do you create and communicate your product vision effectively?

## ELEMENTS OF AN INSPIRING PRODUCT VISION

A product vision can be looked at from many angles, and each angle offers a different perspective on how it represents the strategy. Table 8.3 lists various tools, canvases, and formats for capturing your Product Vision.

Many tools for creating a vision can be used. There is a wide variety of tools and canvases available, some even for specific products and contexts (like hardware or marketing). We recommend you search the web for these tools, including how-to guides and explanations. There are various helpful how-to guides for creating your product vision (like on our blog: www.medium.com/the-value-maximizers), which is why this isn't included in this book.

**Table 8.3** Examples of Tools Used by Product Owners/Managers for Visioning and Strategizing

| Format | Emphasis on | Useful For |
|---|---|---|
| Business Model Canvas | How the product fits into the business | Discovering financial flows, channels, key assets |
| Value Proposition Canvas | How the customer is affected by the product | Describing the outcome the product is trying to achieve |
| Lean Canvas | Finding product-market fit | Young products trying to spin growth |
| Lean UX Canvas | Hypotheses and the user | Validating assumptions and making them transparent |
| Product Box | Buying behavior of the customer | Discovering the unique message |
| Product Vision Statement | Standardizing your description | Comparing product propositions |
| Empathy Mapping | Describing the problem of the customer | Finding deeper drivers for the customer |

What all these tools have in common is that they connect the customer problem(s) to solve to the business impacts to be achieved, while also sketching a picture of what the future could look like. What worked very well for us in the past is to make vision-creation a collaborative exercise. Although you could create a product vision on your own, it is often more interesting, more fun, and more valuable to create the vision together. Also, remember that taking the Visionary stance doesn't mean that you need to come up with everything yourself! Leading and facilitating people in creating the vision is also important. So, don't worry if you don't have a big and ambitious vision (yet). Bring the right people on board to help create it.

Creating a vision is just the first step though. Once you have defined the vision, including the target audience, problems to solve, revenue and cost streams, and the unique value proposition, the actual work is about to get started. Creating, defining, or documenting the product vision is typically not the biggest challenge you see. The bigger challenge is to communicate the vision effectively and to get people to buy into that vision. Even more so, it is about getting people to support the vision, and communicate it themselves.

So, what do you do next? Well, it's time to start communicating your vision! Once you have discovered the crucial elements of your product vision, you should start communicating and pitching the vision. What you'll probably learn by doing so is that different audiences require different approaches. Some are more interested in the value a product offers, others wonder about the changes required to create the product, and some might be afraid of what this means for their products or services. In the next chapter, we'll explore how to communicate vision through storytelling. But before doing so, Table 8.4 shows some do's and don'ts to consider before you start communicating, pitching, and storytelling your vision.

**Table 8.4** Do's and Don'ts for Communicating Product Vision

| Do/Show/Communicate | Don't Do/Show/Communicate |
| --- | --- |
| Passion | Not believing the vision yourself |
| Energy/enthusiasm | A long list of features |
| Visual | Bullsh*t bingo |

| Do/Show/Communicate | Don't Do/Show/Communicate |
| --- | --- |
| Appealing | Technical |
| Short | Buzzwords |
| Clear core message | Rattling/not making a clear point |
| Interactive | Boring/monotonous |
| Appeal to morals/feelings | Being unclear what you are asking |

# COMMUNICATING THE PRODUCT VISION EFFECTIVELY

One of the most important characteristics of a great vision is its ability to capture the imagination of the recipients. Great visions tend to tell a story, but what does that mean and what are some ways that we can create such a narrative? Let's start with the fact that there is no one type of story. Nor is there one perfect story for your product, to be used in the same way for every stakeholder. Instead, think of storytelling like people do and did in the past when sitting around the campfire. People were, are, and will forever be trading different stories. It's not about repeating the same story over and over again.

Looking at most of the stories that Product Owners communicate, you will find that they can be connected to one of the following categories, each having its clear objective from the storyteller's perspective:

- A story to inform the audience (e.g., "How do you operate the product?")
- A story to create a connection (e.g., "Did you ever notice that. . . ?")
- A story to inspire (e.g., "The world of X will never be the same.")

The goal you seek to achieve helps you structure your story. For example, to build a connection, you may want to start your story with a thought-provoking question. When listening to stories from other people—for example, TED

Talks or Disney films—you will find that many great stories follow the path of the so-called hero's journey (see Figure 9.1).

The hero often starts their adventure in the known world. Then they come across somebody important, such as a mentor.

At a certain point, they cross a threshold and leave the known world for a new adventure. During this adventure, they overcome various challenges, find a partner, and learn new skills. And, just when things seem to be going well, death and rebirth happen. A tragedy must be overcome, and they can overcome it.

Finally, changes start to happen, the world is becoming a better place, and the main purpose is achieved. Then they return to the normal world as changed people (or animals) and live happily ever after. So, what can we learn from the hero's journey? What is it about these stories that makes us remember them?

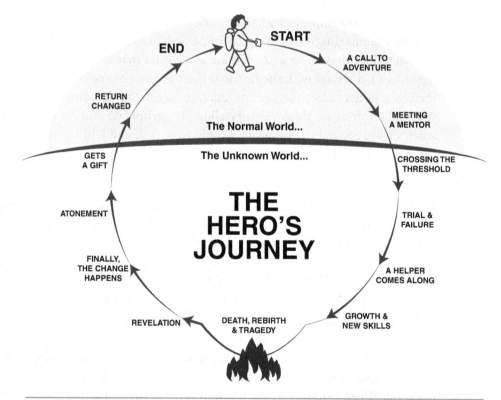

**Figure 9.1** Hero's journey

# THE 3×3 STORYTELLING FRAMEWORK[1]

When communicating or pitching your vision, you usually get about two to five minutes of people's attention. If it is much shorter than that, people probably won't understand the vision. If it is much longer than that, you may not be very clear and spot-on in your pitch, and people will likely lose interest. So, to make those couple of minutes count, you should be able to communicate your product vision in a concise, clear, relatable, yet also comprehensive way.

After analyzing many great and highly valued TED Talks, we have learned that there are a couple of elements that the speakers include in their stories and presentations. Through this analysis, we have identified nine elements that are included in almost all those great talks. This led to the creation of a framework for building your own great stories, which is referred to as the 3×3 storytelling framework. Table 9.1 shows what it looks like.

**Table 9.1** The 3×3 Storytelling Framework

| Status quo | Observations | Story |
|------------|--------------|-------|
| Insight | Opportunity | Analogy |
| Solution | Advantages | Ethos |

The top row of boxes helps you to build a "hook" with the audience. The purpose of communicating the status quo, observations, and story is to get your audience connected to the topic and to gain their empathy. The first thing to start your story with is a description of the status quo in the market or industry. It is typically something that is or has been going on for some time already. You could say that it is a pattern that you've noticed in the market, company, the product, across a target audience or industry. Although there are many ways to describe the status quo, many different openings to use, and many sentences to speak, a frequently used phrase that works well for the status quo is, "There is a problem in the industry today." It is almost too simple, yet it seems to work across time and industries.

---

1. See also Chris Lukassen, *The Product Samurai: A Product Manager's Guide to Continuous Innovation*, 3rd ed., Product Dojo, 2021.

Just saying that there is a problem in the industry isn't enough, though. The next step is to prove that the problem exists. This means that you'll be adding information to your statement by sharing some (usually two to four) of your observations about the market, company, product, or industry. This builds a connection with the audience, who hopefully recognize the symptoms and observations that you are describing.

With this increased understanding of what's going on, it's time to share a story. People love stories. Stories are the things we remember. Stories, practical examples, and experiences from real life tend to strike us the most. The magic of storytelling goes back to the stone age, when we sat around a fire, sharing the stories of our ancestors. Stories from people we know build stronger connections and make the audience pay attention. You could share a story from a customer, for example, or a colleague who is experiencing challenges. Set the scene for the rest of your story and don't forget to explain the crazy number of tasks that customers need to complete, how inefficiently they need to spend their time, or how much frustration they experience. Build up the tension for the rest of your pitch.

Then, share the insight that you have obtained. Share the great discovery that is your new product, service, or feature set. The insight is usually a short and simple sentence. Something like, "This gave us an insight; people need X and are craving for Y" usually works well. It doesn't have to be a long list of insights. Just share one or two of the most important.

After the insights is a description of the unique opportunity that your idea presents to change the world. The opportunity describes two or three real improvements that could be made to improve people's lives. It describes some of the benefits that this idea will bring to the audience. The opportunity is part of the arc, where we are opening the minds of the audience that there is a way out of this situation, and you are taking them along on the journey.

The analogy is the part of your pitch where you connect the given situation to something that the listener is already familiar with. Analogies appeal to how the human brain works. They trigger a familiar path of neurons, so the listeners' brains will presume a similar outcome. You can compare your solution to a famous company or product, for example. Although you might want to explain in more detail, you can use something like, "This is exactly how Google started!" or "This strategy worked very well in hospitals, so it might just work as well for general practitioners." There's a big chance that your listeners don't want to miss out on an opportunity to be as successful as Google!

Once you've gained empathy with your audience, and once you have used an analogy to create insights, your audience is primed and ready for your solution. This is when you talk about that solution. Well, at least a little bit. You may not even need to go into great detail. You don't need to describe exactly how the product works. Assume that it just does. People are not necessarily interested in how their needs are met. They don't necessarily care about the details of your solution. They're interested in knowing that you know what problems and needs they have and that your product will solve those problems and fulfill their needs.

Your listeners might be more interested in the advantages that your product offers. What is the value your product will add for them? How does it compare to other solutions on the market? How does it compare to alternatives, perhaps not being products (yet)? Tell them why you believe in your solution. What makes it so awesome? If you don't believe that this product is the best thing since sliced bread, then why would anyone else care about it?

The final piece of the puzzle is ethos. In this context, *ethos* means "for the benefit of mankind." It's the ultimate purpose of building the solution, which transcends the needs of the company or the individual. Because the problem is so widespread in the industry, and your solution is so impressive, it must be worthwhile to invest in it. It is for the greater good.

Now it's time for a complete example of a story designed with the 3×3 storytelling framework. World News's mission statement is, "We globally leverage cutting-edge technology to develop world-class real-time news to customers while enabling advertisers in an ever-changing marketplace."

This mission statement, although not particularly exciting, is a decent mission statement. It describes the high-level product: news. It describes some of the how: technology. It doesn't describe the main target audience very well, though: newsreaders in general. And it describes that they want to enable their core customers: advertisers. So, the statement is okay, but will it make people get out of bed in the morning for an exciting day at work? We don't know.

So, what if our protagonist, Noa, created her pitch as follows:

(**status quo**) There is a problem in the industry today: smartphones are eating a lot of our time.

(**observations**) You see it all around you: people switching between multiple news apps on their smartphones to get a good overview of all the news (left, right, local, international, social, etc.).

(**story**) Last week, I spoke to a coworker, and she told me how shocked she was to discover that she spends four hours each day on her phone via the new "screen time" feature. The time spent was mostly in news apps. Imagine spending four hours, a quarter of your non-sleeping time, going through news apps.

(**insight**) This gave us an insight: news needs to be personalized and centralized.

(**opportunities**) You will need only one app. It adapts to what you like, and you can limit the amount of time you spend in it. We will bring all the local, global, social, left, and right news together in one place.

(**analogy**) Much like Facebook, where the stories of your friends and family are brought together, we will present the local news from all over the world in one convenient place.

(**solution**) We have a solution for this problem.

(**advantages**) The solution does not require you to go through all those apps, figures out what you like, and saves you time.

(**ethos**) In the end, if we can improve the lives of our customers by giving them more time with their friends and family, we are not just delivering news but changing the world for the better.

What does your product pitch sound like?

# THE POWER OF REASONING

Being a Product Owner, your purpose of pitching, presenting, or sharing stories is likely that you want to convince other people of your ideas. When convincing people of your ideas, an important aspect is the ability to reason well. To make good arguments for your case and ideas. Your audience needs to be able to follow your reasoning and check the validity of your arguments. The study of rhetoric offers a simple-to-remember metaphor that might help when you are trying to make a point. The metaphor is to use your hand as a reference when reasoning with people. This is how it works:

**The problem:** The problem is represented by the palm of your hand. It is the largest area and ultimately what we are trying to convey. If you are not sure what you want the recipient to remember, then it will lead to an incoherent story. In the example before, the problem was the amount of time that people spend on their phones.

**The core message:** The core message is your thumb. It's a snappy and short description of the problem. Often, it is a sound bite, a phrase that catches the attention and is easy to remember. Rather than saying, "Computers have become increasingly complex and difficult to operate, leaving the average user frustrated about why certain software and hardware refuse to cooperate and dumbfounded on possible remedies," Apple said, "It just works."

The core message is enforced by three arguments (representing the index, middle, and ring fingers). Why does your solution work? What advantages do you offer over existing solutions? Three is the magic number, fewer and people are still critical, more and people have already forgotten about the first argument.

The index finger represents a counterargument. Yes, you read that correctly. By labeling the counterargument yourself you control the narrative. The index finger is small, so the counterargument should not derail the entire solution of course, but rather point out that you are aware that there are consequences to this idea, and you have thought about them. This is a really important step! Research around how customers buy or buy into products has proven repeatedly that conversion rates (actual purchases from customers) increase if there are some negative evaluations of—or arguments for—a product among many good evaluations or arguments. Especially negative evaluations or comments that are not relevant, important, or critical to the product's functioning help to drive buy-in.

Don't close your story on a low note, however! Though the index finger might be the last finger on your hand, it is better to insert the counterargument between the first and second positive arguments so that by the time we reach the third the audience is on a high.

## MAKE IT SEXI

*I recall giving a presentation in the UAE on cross-mobile development platforms. Ignorant of the hero's journey, my presentation focused mainly on what our product could do, what functionality it offered, and how it compared to other platforms. Truth be told, it was not a very sexy subject.*

*At some point, I noticed the customer pulled out his Blackberry and started typing. Initially, I thought, "Great! He is texting his colleagues about this awesomeness." This was not the case, though. Shortly after he stood up and left the room without a word. A few minutes later his secretary showed up, and joined the presentation to take notes and create an abstract for the customer. He was not going to spend time on a presentation that didn't capture his imagination. Looking back, I can't say I can blame him for it.*

— Chris

How can you create memorable, and captivating, presentations? Of course, the 3×3 storytelling framework will get you a long way. Communicating with passion and enthusiasm will contribute for sure. But there is more! This is how you make a presentation SEXI.

SEXI in this context means that for each Statement, you will create an EXplanation and an Illustration to support it. Instead of listing features and benefits in bullet points, you can turn them into a statement. For example, "This platform allows you to battle the fragmentation in the smartphone market," or "This book will help you to become the Product Owner you want to be." Then explain why your product does that and what it looks like. But don't ever again use bullet points in PowerPoint to communicate something that people should get excited about (like your vision). Instead, tying it back to the smartphone example, use an image of all the Android phones that were released that year.

A picture paints a thousand words. It's a cliché, but it's true. Use images to have the audience connect the facts that you narrate to what they see. Avoid making your listeners read and listen at the same time. People have loved stories since the dawn of time, but they still can't process two inputs simultaneously. So, keep it simple, and make it visual!

# CRAFTING PRODUCT GOALS THAT ALIGN STAKEHOLDERS AND TEAMS

# 10

In November 2020, Jeff Sutherland and Ken Schwaber released a new version of the Scrum Guide. Many changes, small and large, were made, and the Scrum Guide was greatly simplified to support even more teams and industries. One of the more notable changes in this new version was the introduction of a new concept, Product Goal:

> The Product Goal describes a future state of the product which can serve as a target for the Scrum Team to plan against. The Product Goal is in the Product Backlog. The rest of the Product Backlog emerges to define "what" will fulfill the Product Goal.
>
> . . .
>
> The Product Goal is the long-term objective for the Scrum Team. They must fulfill (or abandon) one objective before taking on the next.[1]

What's important about that Product Goal? you may wonder. The concept of goal setting in product management is not new. It's not new for most companies, right? Setting goals for companies, products, services, and teams is done

---

1. Ken Schwaber and Jeff Sutherland, *The 2020 Scrum Guide*™, November 2020, https://scrumguides.org/scrum-guide.html.

in various ways. Approaches such as objective key results (OKRs), key result areas (KRAs), key performance indicators (KPIs), management by objectives (MBO), and goal-driven development (GDD) all strive for the same thing: to provide a clear goal to work toward.

Why is this concept introduced in the new Scrum Guide? Well, Scrum's purpose is to provide a framework to solve complex problems and to discover and deliver value in complex environments. It seeks to generate value in situations where more is unknown than known. Defining goals, Product Goals in this case, serves as a steppingstone in that river of complexity. They help you to define a (big) step toward your vision. In addition, the Sprint Goals serve as smaller steps toward your Product Goal. Remember the product management vacuum in Chapter 8, "Creating and Communicating Product Vision"? Creating alignment between the product vision, Product Goal, Sprint Goal, and the product features to deliver is an important accountability of the Product Owner for closing the product management vacuum.

## WHAT IS A PRODUCT GOAL?

> *A goal is not always meant to be reached; sometimes it serves simply as something to aim for.*
>
> —Bruce Lee

Product Goals can be considered as the next objectives to be achieved. They align with the product vision and strategy and provide focus and context for the Product Backlog. Product Goals create alignment around shared objectives and improve the commitment of the Scrum team to collaborate toward those objectives. When Product Goals are shared openly, the Scrum Team's commitment is transparent to the rest of the organization, making it possible to align ideas and initiatives with the Product Goals, park those ideas for later, or reject them (for now) by saying no.

Another way to think about Product Goals is that they are manifestations of the product strategy. Product Goals connect the product vision to solutions and value discovery, to delivery and validation, as illustrated in Figure 10.1.

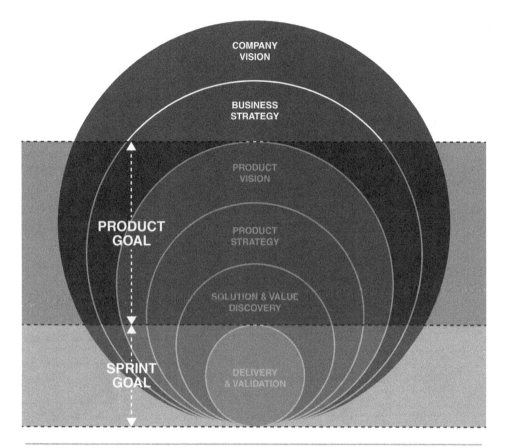

**Figure 10.1** Product Goals reside on various levels; some are huge, others are more achievable.

Whereas the company vision is often holistic and describes a moonshot, the company strategy serves to describe how to get there via clear goals and objectives. Common questions to be answered through the product strategy are: How are we going to achieve our vision? What are the goals for the next quarters? What do we aim to achieve in the next quarter? What does success look like? Many companies use a form of OKRs, KRAs, or KPIs to track progress toward their Product Goals and business goals.

Setting clear goals for a product—and having one active Product Goal to pursue right now—provides measurable guidance toward achieving the product vision. If your company has only a single product or service, these will be very much alike. A Product Goal connects the work on the product (as recorded in the Product Backlog) to the product vision.

Table 10.1 shows some examples. Notice that the good examples present concrete, measurable goals, whereas the bad examples are vague and subjective.

**Table 10.1** Good and Bad Examples of Product Goals

| Good Examples | Bad Examples |
| --- | --- |
| Increase product usage by 10% before December 31 | Build the best product in the world |
| Optimize website conversion by 2% before April 1 | Make our customers and users happy |
| Improve product quality by 10% before the end of the year | Reduce operational costs |
| Improve customer referrals by 5% before May | Eliminate technical debt from the product |
| Reduce hassles for persona Kate by 10% before end of the year | Deliver the complete project scope before the deadline |
| Improve customer-complaints-handling efficiency by 20% before June | Increase revenues by 10% |
| Offer news readers a coherent user experience across devices and platforms by November | Deliver the complete product design |

## CHARACTERISTICS OF GREAT PRODUCT GOALS

When reviewing the Product Goals that Product Owners create in practice, we often notice that these goals are either very fluffy or unattainable. Neither fluffy nor unattainable goals help to achieve great things. So, what are some characteristics that make a Product Goal a *great* Product Goal?

- Great Product Goals are defined clearly and communicated transparently. There are various practices for doing so. Commonly used techniques include making Product Goals SMART[2] or INVEST.[3]

- Product Goals function as the steppingstones toward the product vision. The Scrum Teams and stakeholders should be able to easily see how they connect.

- Product Goals are preferably market driven or customer driven, not Product Backlog driven. Product Goals are a result of responding to emerging market conditions rather than an abstraction of work. Define the Product Goal first and define the work to be done to achieve the goal after—not the other way around.

- Product Goals should be ambitious, yet achievable. This is where many of the OKR goals go off the rails. Stretch goals (meaning the company is typically satisfied when achieving 80%) are a great way to stimulate growth and stretch people, but often, teams simply don't see themselves getting there. Make sure your goals can be achieved.

- Product Goals are measurable. There are many ways to make goals measurable and many measures and metrics that can be tracked. The evidence-based management framework (see also Part III, "The Visionary"), for example, provides excellent measures to track. Alternatives include pirate metrics (AARRR)[4] or Google's HEART[5] framework metrics.

- Goals for a product should be ordered. Aim to achieve goal A first, then work toward goal B. The Scrum framework goes one step further and prescribes having only one Product Goal at a time.

- Product Goals should communicate intent, not a solution. It is better to talk about problems to solve, value to deliver, or a new state to reach than to clarify what scope is to be delivered or what work is to be done.

---

2. Specific, Measurable, Achievable, Realistic, and Timely.
3. Independent, Negotiable, Valuable, Estimable, Small, Testable.
4. Acquisition, Activation, Retention, Referral, Revenue.
5. Happiness, Engagement, Adoption, Retention, Task Success.

## HOW TO CREATE PRODUCT GOALS

There are various ways to create goals for a product. If you asked us how to do it, we would likely answer, "In any way that works for you and your product." That said, some things work well for other Product Owners, so they might work well for you. Here are some tips for creating Product Goals:

- Set Product Goals together with your customers, stakeholders, and/or team(s). Leveraging the collective knowledge of a group never hurt anyone. In addition, collaborating on goal creation creates alignment, buy-in, acceptance, and communication and understanding of the goals to be achieved. If you find it difficult to facilitate such (creative/brainstorm/ collaborative) sessions, then we recommend you learn about Liberating Structures (a toolkit packed with facilitation techniques and working structures) or, even better, ask your Scrum Master or Agile Coach for support.

- Make sure you communicate and create transparency about the product vision before talking about the Product Goals. Make sure that all people involved in the goal setting have the same North Star to work toward.

- There is no fixed time within the Scrum framework for creating your Product Goals, unlike the Sprint Goal, which is created during Sprint Planning, for example. So, when do you set a Product Goal? Well, it could be at any point in time. You could collaborate about Product Goals during refinement activities. You could talk about them during the Sprint Review. There is no fixed time as such. What could help, though, is to align your Product Goals with quarterly business reviews (if you have them). Though goals could be shorter or longer, it makes sense to maintain a cadence that allows for alignment with changes in the business while maintaining a focused mission for a longer period.

- Focus your discussions about the Product Goals around important product management questions, such as, For whom are we building this product? What problem does it solve for them? What proof or evidence do we have for this? Why do we care about this objective or problem? What assumptions do we have? How will we measure a change in our target audiences' behavior?

It's not easy to define great Product Goals. It will probably take some time to learn the skill of goal setting. When creating Product Goals collaboratively (especially with different groups of people over time), you may want to use a question-based approach. Some example questions you could ask your Product Goal co-creators include the following:

- If we have many items in the Product Backlog that don't contribute toward the Product Goal, do we have the right Product Goal?
- If we aren't going to have another release after this one, what would be a Product Goal to support and drive the current release to return optimal value?
- If we were paying for this product with our own money, what Product Goal would give us the highest chance to get that money back?
- When we achieve this Product Goal, what has changed or improved from the perspective of customers?
- Is the least amount of work required to achieve our Product Goal feasible?
- With our current Product Goal, can we reduce the possibility that we abandon it later?
- Does our Product Goal excite us and our customers with opportunities?
- Can we use the Product Goal to prevent increasing risk or wasting time and money?
- Given our current Product Goal, what would indicate that we should abandon it?

## INSPECT AND ADAPT PRODUCT GOALS

When developing or managing products in the complex domain, where more is unknown than known, it is usually difficult to define "the truth." Achieving goals and delivering great results are often the result of discovery and emerging patterns. Hence, goals are often achieved through frequent inspection and adaptation of transparent Product Increments. So, you might wonder, this means that you should regularly inspect and adapt the Product Goal as well, right?

Well, yes and no. If a goal is no longer attainable, it can be abandoned, and a new one can be formulated. For example, due to changed laws and regulations in the Netherlands, it was no longer possible for Uber to achieve its Product Goal. Likewise, if we discover that the goal was misunderstood, we can refine and update the Product Goal to create a better understanding.

Ultimately, a Product Goal is an active mission for the Scrum Team to achieve. You would expect the Scrum Team to be committed to the Product Goal, so changing it frequently would be unsettling and wouldn't provide much focus. Think of the commitment to a Product Goal as you would to the commitment of marriage. Renegotiating what commitment means halfway through is bound to cause problems.

## HAVING MULTIPLE PRODUCT GOALS: IS THAT AN OPTION?

Can a team work on more than one Product Goal at a time? Well, perhaps. It is easy to see that a single team pursuing 25 Product Goals has set itself up for failure—as humorously illustrated in Figure 10.2. Those Product Goals won't help to create focus, that's for sure! However, if you have multiple teams working on the same product, it might make sense. Alternatively, you could consider aligning all the teams around the same Product Goal. In some circumstances, that might help to achieve the goal faster or at least learn about it faster.

On the other hand, the Scrum Guide is clear on what you should do, which is select one active Product Goal at a time. Focus and commitment toward a single objective often pays off, so for a single team, it doesn't make sense to have multiple goals at the same time. However, if you have multiple teams, you can achieve multiple goals simultaneously. If you find yourself chasing multiple goals at the same time, you might want to evaluate whether they should be done in parallel or could be pursued in order. Alternatively, consider whether you are working on a single product or on multiple products at the same time. And if you are working on multiple products at the same time, how much focus are you then providing to the teams?

**Figure 10.2** Focus!

# Creating the Right Product Roadmap for Your Audience

## Introduction to Product Roadmaps

Let's say that the product vision and strategy have been established. You have defined the purpose, the North Star for your product, and a couple of steps to work toward that North Star in the form of Product Goals. However, that doesn't mean that you're done. A lot of the work to be done for a Product Owner continues from this point onward.

Some of that work relates to identifying, defining, and communicating what work needs to be done on the product. In other words, you'll want to identify the key features and capabilities that your product should provide for customers and users. You'll want to create a Product Backlog. To create and manage a Product Backlog, various techniques can be employed. Think about techniques such as story mapping, event storming, value-stream mapping, impact mapping, and jobs-to-be-done, for example. These techniques help you to get a clearer picture of your product's important features. In addition, you will probably need to do some estimations of value and effort with your team and stakeholders.

All this work done on the Product Backlog to prepare work for future iterations (Sprints) is commonly referred to as *Product Backlog refinement*. To put these techniques and pieces together in one picture, look at Figure 11.1, which walks through a typical refinement process.

**(INCOMING)
NEW ITEMS**

**SPLITTING BIGGER ITEMS
INTO SMALLER ONES**

**POTENTIAL TECHNIQUES**

Stakeholders pitch their ideas

5-minute Q&A

T-shirt size estimation by the team

Say "Maybe" or "No"

**POTENTIAL TECHNIQUES**

Impact mapping

Story mapping

System diagram

Magic/silent estimation

**CREATING "READY FOR
SPRINT" ITEMS**

**(BUSINESS) VALUE
ESTIMATION**

**POTENTIAL TECHNIQUES**

Adding details such as description,
order, value, effort, visual designs,
mock-ups, paper prototypes, sketches,
technical design, data-flow diagram,
high-level architecture design
Planning Poker

**POTENTIAL TECHNIQUES**

Business Value Estimation workshop
with stakeholders

**Figure 11.1**  The different forms of Product Backlog refinement

Figure 11.1 shows that teams often use different forms of Product Backlog refinement. Although there are many more practices available for doing refinement, some techniques work particularly well for adding new items to the Product Backlog, such as doing a pitch, a timeboxed Q&A, and a t-shirt size estimate. Some techniques are more suitable for splitting big items into smaller ones, such as story mapping, impact mapping, and event storming. The techniques for refining items into "ready for Sprint items" vary greatly across organizations. However, many teams want to clarify items to a level of detail that is insufficient (not complete or extensive enough) for them to pick up the work in a Sprint. And finally, there is the estimation of value, which we'll get back to in Chapter 12, "Identification of Company Value and Impact."

Summarizing, many techniques can be employed for refining the Product Backlog and its items. They can be used; it isn't mandatory that they be used.

When talking about "agile" or "agility" in organizations, people often make jokes such as "We have Post-it notes and we do stand-ups, so we are very Agile." Although humorous, there is some seriousness in such comments. People often have a false understanding of what Agile is about. It's not about doing stand-ups, Planning Poker, or any of the refinement techniques discussed. It's rather about maximizing value for customers through continuous collaboration, a focus on working products, and responding to changes in the marketplace. Let's not go into the essence of Agile or agility, though. There are plenty of books written about that already.

Using some of the refinement techniques may "feel very Agile." There is no guarantee, however, that stakeholder ideas will contribute to the Product Goals. It's also not a guarantee that those ideas function as steppingstones toward the product vision. What will happen if the stakeholders lose interest? What will happen if it takes too long (in their opinion) to deliver on the ideas they proposed? What will happen if they discover a new area of value, problems to solve, or ideas that might contradict the product vision?

We don't know what will happen. However, you will probably need a connecting element between the product vision and the Product Backlog. This connecting element in the middle will communicate your path toward the product vision. This element is usually called a *product roadmap*. Product roadmaps are especially useful for communicating the intended direction of the product. They communicate how the product is *likely* going to evolve. In many organizations, though, roadmaps are applied and understood as a fail-proof prediction of the future. They are often used as set-in-stone plans with hard deadlines. Applying roadmaps that way doesn't help and can sometimes be a detriment.

> *I have trained and coached Product Owners in many organizations. Common challenges they face are stakeholder management, forecasting, and dealing with deadlines. After I had been working in a company for some time, I introduced the concept of a roadmap, which they liked. However, they were still afraid about the deadlines. I then used a simple sentence to describe the roadmap, being: "This is the plan to deviate from." People liked that simple sentence, and although I hadn't worked with marketing and sales at that point, I kept hearing that simple sentence from more and more people, including people I hadn't worked with. To me, that was a great example of good use of roadmaps. People started to understand the essence of agility and how to properly use product roadmaps.*
>
> — Robbin

So, product roadmaps are *not* set-in-stone plans but rather are "a plan to deviate from." Roadmaps are an actionable plan to communicate how the product is likely going to evolve. You must communicate that uncertainty along with the roadmap itself. Especially for (management) stakeholders who are used to getting a plan and sticking to it, deviating from a plan seems counterintuitive. So, make sure to explain it.

*I coached a coffee brewer (company, not the device) some time ago that was facing a culture clash between the operations, management, and engineering departments. They had been making coffee for nearly 200 years. It had become a highly predictable process after decades of lean process management. They simply could not understand why the e-commerce part of the business had such difficulties with deadlines. It was even worse: delays in the software domain would now influence this well-oiled machine and affect their predictability.*

— Chris

Accepting that things may change is perhaps one of the most difficult parts of being a Product Owner—or Agile product manager, if you will—but it doesn't mean that we should stop trying to develop a plan. In addition, we create a plan in the first place so that we know (and learn) what and where we deviated from. Not having a plan isn't an option. Not having a plan is also not Agile. Having extensive plans and not deviating from them, even though new insights might suggest doing so, also isn't very Agile—or very smart.

## TYPES OF PRODUCT ROADMAPS

Hopefully, you are convinced of the relevancy and usefulness of having a product roadmap. But what does a product roadmap look like? Can you use one roadmap for every situation? Can you use the same roadmap for every target audience? It turns out there are many formats and ways to create product roadmaps. What we learned is that great Product Owners don't get stuck on a single roadmap format. What they do is consider their target audience and the purpose or goal of presenting the roadmap to them. Based on their audience and the goal to achieve, they adjust the type of roadmap used to get the best results.

In this chapter, we discuss five commonly used product roadmaps (though many other types exist). We explore when each roadmap might be helpful, when you should avoid it, and for which audiences they work well and don't work well. These results are based on a study of well over 500 Product Owners using these roadmaps; however, keep in mind that you'll need to discover what works best in your specific situation.

## ROADMAP 1: THE GOAL-ORIENTED ROADMAP

The goal-oriented (GO) product roadmap (shown in Figure 11.2) was created by Roman Pichler. It focuses strongly on the goals to be achieved for the product rather than offering a long list of features. It is a lightweight template that can be modified to align with your needs as a Product Owner. It contains various elements, including dates/versions, goals, key features, and metrics. A GO product roadmap is suitable for many audiences. Product Owners in practice have reported, though, that they find it a bit too high level for the developers to work with daily. It lacks some details, making it harder to use during a Sprint. On the other hand, it works very well to align stakeholders and other teams to make your product a success.

| | Q1 | Q2 | Q3 | Q4 |
|---|---|---|---|---|
| **DATE / VERSION** | BRONZE 01-01-2020 | SILVER 01-04-2020 | GOLD 01-07-2020 | PLATINUM 01-10-2020 |
| **GOAL** | LAUNCH MVP WITH AT LEAST 1000 EARLY ADOPTER USERS | IMPROVE EARLY ADOPTER USER SATISFACTION TO AN 8+ ON AVERAGE | CONVERT 50% OF EARLY ADOPTERS TO A PAYING MEMBERSHIP WITH AT LEAST A BASIC SUBSCRIPTION | INCREASE USER BASE WITH AT LEAST 1000 MORE PAYING SUBSCRIBERS (AT LEAST BASIC MEMBERSHIP) |
| **KEY FEATURES** | HOMEPAGE WITH TOP 10 MOST READ ARTICLES<br><br>SHARE WITH YOUR FRIENDS VIA SOCIAL MEDIA | SAVE ARTICLES FOR LATER READING<br><br>LAUNCH IN-APP CUSTOMER FEEDBACK FUNCTIONALITY | PERSONALIZED SEARCH FUNCTION<br><br>MIGRATE CURRENT USER BASE TO NEW APP VERSION<br><br>LAUNCH FIRST THIRD-PARTY API'S | LAUNCH MARKETING CAMPAIGN IN USA<br><br>INTEGRATE VIDEO SUBSCRIPTIONS IN THE NEW APP<br><br>INTEGRATE QUICKNEWS |
| **METRICS** | # APP DOWNLOADS<br><br># REGISTERED USERS<br><br># SOCIAL MEDIA MENTIONS | IN-APP CUSTOMER SATISFACTION SCORE<br><br>CUSTOMER SATISFACTION SURVEY | IN-APP CUSTOMER SATISFACTION SCORE<br><br>% PAYING USERS OF ALL USERS<br><br># REGISTERED USERS | IN-APP CUSTOMER SATISFACTION SCORE<br><br>% PAYING USERS OF ALL USERS<br><br># REGISTERED USERS |

**Figure 11.2** The goal-oriented product roadmap

The first element you'll notice in the GO product roadmap is the date or version element. Dates, as any Product Owner knows, are somewhat dangerous. People think of deadlines instead of forecasts when they see or hear dates, so it's good to be careful in roadmap communication.

If an organization is not particularly Agile, do not use dates. In other words, if people interpret a date as a deadline, then don't use dates in your roadmap. Stakeholders may not be used to working in or managing products in a complex domain. They may not be used to not knowing everything up front. They may not be used to the fact that more is unknown, uncertain, or unstable than is known, certain, or stable. These stakeholders are likely to treat dates as deadlines and commitments. And they will likely get angry if you prove to be "unreliable" as new insights and deviations to the plan emerge. If this is the case in your situation, we encourage you to replace the quarters shown in the roadmap illustration with something else. For example, use Now, Next, Later instead of Q1, Q2, Q3, Q4. Your stakeholders may not understand or like this approach at first. But think back to the coffee brewer example: you are trying to change the mindset of people in a company where dates and deadlines may have been the "right" way of thinking for a long time.

If people understand that you are creating plans to deviate from and that dates are forecasts rather than deadlines, it may be perfectly safe to use dates in your roadmap. As these stakeholders have embraced uncertainty and understand that things change, they won't be surprised that the roadmap changes now and then due to new insights. They will expect it and perhaps even encourage it.

The second element of the GO product roadmap contains the goals to be achieved. The goals are the leading and most important element of this roadmap. Our recommendation is therefore to start with the goals and identify the dates later. The goals are also more important than the actual work to be done (the features to be built). Although the GO product roadmap predates the introduction of Product Goals in the Scrum Guide, it relates to the same idea. Thus, the goals in this roadmap should align with the Product Goals for the product.

The next step is to add the key features to be delivered. The idea is that these key features are the most important features to deliver to achieve the goal for that date or period. This means that you should *not* define a long list of features here. It's a small list (typically three to five features) for each column. It is also likely that features defined for earlier dates are smaller than the features defined for later dates. Again, make sure to communicate that these features are *likely* going to be built to achieve the goal. More will be learned over time—remember, this is the plan to deviate from. So, focus on value steering (steering on goals and outcomes) instead of steering on work packages (steering on output). If you want to list features, then list only the high-level features that will help to achieve the goals, thereby highlighting the most valuable work.

Perhaps you are aware that principle 10 from the Agile Manifesto is "Simplicity—maximizing the work not done." Because the template doesn't offer much space to write down a long list of features, you will need to focus here. A roadmap helps to provide focus. And providing focus helps in stakeholder management as well. Many Product Owners in practice end up with endless Product Backlogs that contain many small items. They often struggle when a large new initiative needs to be added. Using the GO product roadmap format allows you to focus on the most valuable work; the small things will follow and do not need to be communicated in the product roadmap. Just make sure that the teams save some time each Sprint to process those small changes if needed.

## ROADMAP 2: THE NOW-NEXT-LATER ROADMAP

The Now-Next-Later product roadmap exists in many formats, but the one we see most often is of the roadmap with expanding circles, much like water ripples when you throw a rock in a pond. The water ripples are a useful analogy in this context. The initial splash is clear to see. The first ripples are too. However, the ripples fade out as they move farther from the spot where the rock hit the water. Although all the ripples are connected, this connection might fade at some point. This often happens in practice as well because of all the background noise and distractions. The Now-Next-Later roadmap functions in a similar way. What happens in the Now area of the roadmap is usually clear to see and understand. The current iteration (or Sprint) will have a clear goal to be achieved and clear work to be done. Perhaps you'll have a pretty good idea about what comes in the next iteration as well. A few Sprints further into the future, however, things are less clear.

A Now-Next-Later roadmap, shown in Figure 11.3, can mimic the ripple effect by using various colors in the roadmap. These colors can be used in various ways, for example, by representing themes or by connecting features and goals that have a relationship. The roadmap reveals in one glance how far into the future a particular theme extends. If designed correctly, the roadmap should display very limited space in the Now area. This limited space helps you to squeeze in only a couple of ideas to work on. Hence, this helps you to provide focus to the team and stakeholders. It is also likely that these items are smaller and clearer for everyone.

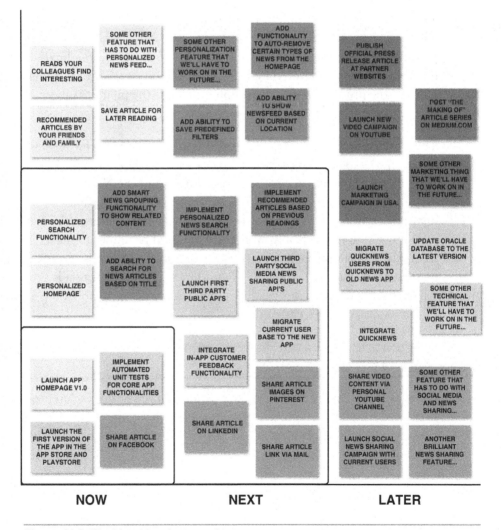

**Figure 11.3** The Now-Next-Later roadmap

The Next area in the roadmap is somewhat bigger than the Now area, meaning that you can position multiple ideas to be worked on next. It doesn't mean that all of those ideas will be worked on next but should rather be considered a preselection of all the other stuff to be done from the Later area. The items in the Later area often have an even bigger level of granularity. There may be some big new feature sets or Epics to work on if time allows in the future. Don't make these items too small, too soon. Refinement and clarification of future work, if done too soon, often result in waste, as items might be discarded at a later stage.

The Now-Next-Later roadmap is usually suitable for situations where your audience is not familiar with an Agile mindset and or where dates are interpreted as set-in-stone deadlines. The absence of dates in a roadmap can be a lifesaver. It shows that you have thought of the future and that you have a plan for the product. But it also emphasizes that the plan is likely to change on the basis of new insights and learnings.

The Now-Next-Later roadmap is often used during the Sprint Review. It reveals trade-offs due to the limited physical space in the roadmap. Supporting departments and Developers often find the Now-Next-Later roadmap too vague to do any actual planning against. If your job is to set up a distribution network and get into negotiations with resellers, then "later" is probably not going to help you. If there are hard deadlines to make, be sure to highlight them on those tickets. Perhaps prioritize them in the roadmap to increase your odds of making those deadlines. If every ticket ends up getting a hard (legal, for example) deadline, then you should probably have a conversation about deadlines early on.

## ROADMAP 3: THE USER STORY MAP

Ever since Jeff Patton published *User Story Mapping*,[1] this technique has been used for many purposes (see Figure 11.4). It is often treated as a magical cure for all kinds of problems. Truth be told, it tends to deliver on those perceptions.

---

1. Jeff Patton, *User Story Mapping*, O'Reilly, 2011.

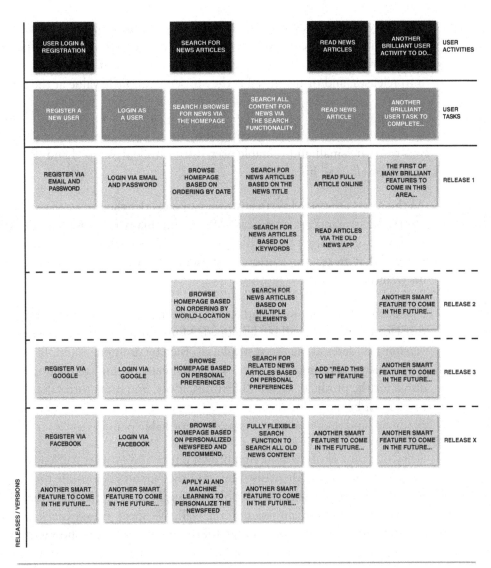

**Figure 11.4** The user story map roadmap

The user story map, or story map, is a great tool to refine big ideas into small ideas by looking at the product from a user perspective. The story map reveals the activities or tasks a user must perform to complete their job. It also reveals all the options or alternatives that a user has to complete that job. Detailing all those activities and options makes the story map a great tool when you are developing a new product or when working on a new initiative.

The story map creates an overview of all the features that people can think of for the product and connects those features to the user's journey. Once all the brainstorming is over, the feature ideas (the stories) can be ordered, grouped into releases, and/or discarded if they provide too little value at the time.

The story map is a user-centric technique. It provides an overview of all the user activities that need to be covered by the system, which in turn enables you to create small and valuable user stories to be developed and delivered incrementally and iteratively.

As the items are sorted vertically, you can consider their necessity, value, effort, performance, security, ease of use, and many other factors. Ordering the user stories allows you and your stakeholders to think in incremental releases that create momentum for a user and allow you to capture feedback on your assumptions.

The downside of the story map is that it creates the illusion that all the features for the product will be developed. Many Product Owners use releases, versions, or dates along the vertical axis, thereby grouping multiple user stories into a release. The goal, however, is not to create a complete plan or breakdown for the product, so not all features, ideas, and user stories that were identified must be built. The story map is another form of creating a product roadmap, and thus it is, once again, an actionable plan to deviate from.

Story mapping is often done in a brown paper and Post-its workshop. Before (or after) completing the workshop, find the person responsible for cleaning the offices or for the clean-desk policy, if applicable, and explain that the story map should remain fixed on the wall. We speak from experience: the morning after we had run a successful story mapping workshop with the management of a major car brand, the cleaner approached us and said that next time, we had to leave a meeting room as we had found it, and surely not with all that paper still stuck to the wall. You can guess what happened to the story map. **Don't make this classic mistake!**

## ROADMAP 4: THE VISUAL ROADMAP

Looks great, doesn't it? At least, that is what most Product Owners say when looking at the visual product roadmap, shown in Figure 11.5. It is a simple, visual roadmap. It doesn't contain a lot of information, and that's the idea of it. A visual product roadmap should be simple to understand and shouldn't contain a lot of information. Its purpose is to convey a core message. The visual product roadmap is often used in situations where Product Owners communicate with management-level stakeholders or customers about goals and broad timelines. It is often used to offer stakeholders a sneak peek into the high-level plans for the product. It is not designed to contain a lot of details, and thus you won't use this roadmap for all your different target audiences.

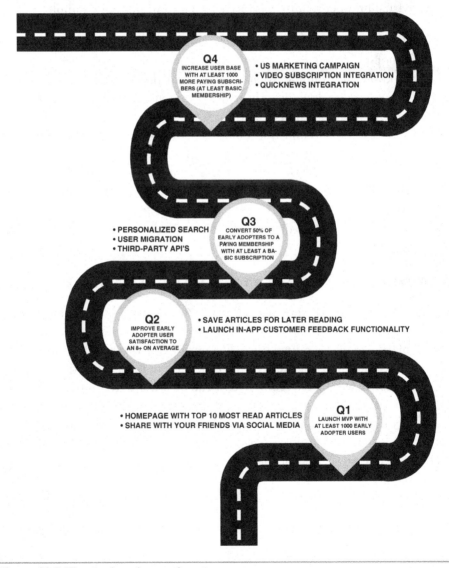

**Figure 11.5** The visual product roadmap

A typical visual roadmap contains a few milestones, releases, versions, or dates, usually no more than four. It illustrates the goal to be achieved for each milestone or date and sometimes lists one to three key features to be delivered. Out of all product roadmap formats, this one contains the fewest details. Consequently, it works well when addressing large audiences or when communicating asynchronously, such as when sending the roadmap as part of an information packet rather than discussing or collaborating on it. The visual product roadmap is often used as a poster, for example.

The lack of detail in the visual product roadmap also has some downsides. It is not an ideal basis for planning with teams or stakeholders, who may need to know, for example, what the impact of the releases is in terms of metrics or work to be done. It is difficult for stakeholders to see from the roadmap exactly what you are going to work on. It is also difficult to see what features will be delivered, and when. This is a downside for the stakeholders because they won't be able to come banging on your door with the roadmap under their arm. It makes it hard for them to hold you accountable for the deadlines they came up with. But is that a downside for you? Or is it creating some room to maneuver? Isn't it more supportive for iterative and incremental development of the product? Doesn't it look more like a plan to deviate from?

## ROADMAP 5: THE GANTT CHART ROADMAP

The Gantt chart, shown in Figure 11.6, was initially designed between 1910 and 1915. It is a roadmap that has lived in companies, initiatives, and product management for a long time. The purpose of this roadmap is to highlight which initiatives or areas of the product will be developed and how long each initiative will take to complete. It can be a useful roadmap for discovering the critical path in a project as well as the elements and dependencies that might derail the project. Moving critical-path work to be done forward in the project increases the odds of successful project delivery. Doing so also removes the pressure on the rest of the project's work.

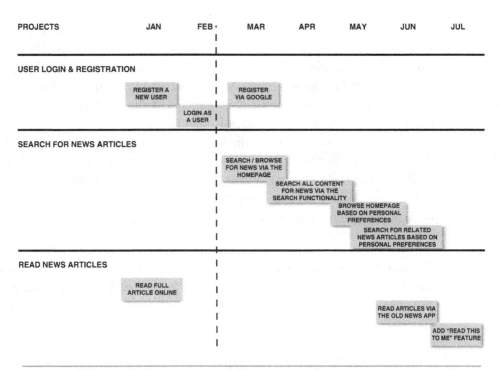

**Figure 11.6** The Gantt chart

The Gantt chart is particularly popular among project managers for tasks such as project planning, resource allocation, and dependency management. However, when using this roadmap for product management and product development, two main issues must be addressed.

The first issue is that a Gantt chart invites a form of horizontal Tetris, trying to fit all the moving parts into a fixed frame. Tasks to be performed in the far future (perhaps 1 year from now, perhaps 5 years from now) are all estimated on a high level, but they aren't very clear for the people who'll do the job. The effort estimates aren't very accurate, and the work packages often don't include enough detail. Detailing the work packages isn't helpful, though, because the details are likely to change a year or 5 years from now. Creating a plan like the Gantt chart offers a false sense of certainty to the stakeholders, which often leads to nasty surprises during the project.

The second problem is that the Gantt chart is optimized to manage dependencies. It does so by sequencing *all* the work to be done. Sequencing all that work, identifying all the dependencies and risks, and trying to get them resolved might be a giant puzzle. All this puzzling keeps us planning and analyzing rather than delivering small increments of the product to the customer. It delays the chance to get feedback from customers, which is the only way to learn what customers need and the best way to learn from and improve the effort estimates. Rather than try to identify and manage all the dependencies up front, try to remove them. Dependencies might become impediments, blockers, or deal-breakers at some point, so try to solve them structurally. Break work into releasable increments. Perhaps simplify the product. Don't make it a monolithic system or product. Make it small and simple.

The Gantt chart was initially designed at a time when most of the work people did was more predictable or repeatable. It often included the fabrication or production of goods. Most of the costs of initiatives were the construction materials or raw resources to be used. Work may have been difficult, but the environment in which the work took place was often complicated but rarely complex.[2] Avoid using this roadmap format for product management in complex environments.

## ELEVEN TIPS FOR ROADMAP CREATION

Product Owners frequently struggle with roadmap creation and communication. If you are one of those Product Owners as well, then here are some additional tips for you to get started.

1. **Start with the product vision.** Make it visible on the roadmap, or communicate the product vision first, before digging into the product roadmap.

---

2. *Complicated* environments can be compared to a game of chess. Chess (played on a professional level) is extremely difficult and requires a great player to win a professional tournament. As hard as it is, though, all the potential moves a player can make can be calculated. It may require some help from supercomputers, but all potential moves can be calculated.

   *Complex* environments, in contrast, are like a game of (professional) poker. You don't hold all the cards. There are more cards in the deck or in other players' hands than on the table. So, there is no way of calculating all the possible moves and picking a move that guarantees success. In other words, there is more unknown or uncertainty than there is known or certainty.

2. **Describe and validate your product strategy.** Focus on the critical capabilities of the product to achieve the product vision.

3. **Set clear goals, outcomes, and benefits** (e.g., SMART or INVEST) and communicate them to the stakeholders.

4. **Tell a coherent story** about the likely growth of your product. Communicate the goals once more. Communicate how features and capabilities contribute to achieving the goals. Don't talk about features that aren't connected to the goals, strategy, or vision.

5. **Keep it simple!** Don't add too many details to the product roadmap. The details can be found in the Product Backlog or story map.

6. **Actively collaborate** with stakeholders to ensure buy-in.

7. **Have the courage to say no** to ideas, features, and deadlines. A roadmap is a high-level plan to communicate how the product will likely evolve. It doesn't have to contain all future ideas.

8. **Think twice** about adding timelines, dates, or deadlines to your roadmap. If you do, consider adding the date as an "at best before" or "not sooner than" date.

9. **Make sure your roadmap is measurable.** Make sure you have some clear metrics in the roadmap and a dashboard—or at least in the back of your mind.

10. **Create a rough value and effort estimate** for each feature to assess its viability. Do these estimations together with stakeholders (for value) and the Developers (for effort).

11. **Review and adapt** your product roadmap regularly. Inspect and adapt. Remember: it's the plan to deviate from.

# IDENTIFICATION OF COMPANY VALUE AND IMPACT

## UNDERSTANDING COMPANY VALUE AND IMPACT

Have you ever been in a situation where your boss or a stakeholder said: "Sounds like a great idea! Do you have a business case for it?" If so, you are not alone! Business cases sometimes seem like a thing of the past. Many Agile teams don't create a business case for new products, services, or features. However, a common business case does ask you to answer relevant questions that need answering in a business context. So, how do we connect the product vision and product strategy to value?

Remember that the purpose of a Product Owner is to maximize the value of the product. This means that you should connect the product vision to the potential value to be delivered. This is what we will explore in this chapter. How to define value? How to identify and express value? What areas of value measurement should you focus on? And how to measure value?

## It's All in the Numbers!

Noa looked frustrated. She finally managed to find a working dongle to connect her laptop with the projector in the boardroom. Seriously, you can put a man on the moon nowadays, and perhaps soon on Mars as well, but getting a projector to work out of the box seems to be outside the realm of possibilities.

The quarterly meeting had gone well up to this point. The board liked the product vision, and Noa managed to align everyone on the roadmap and Product Goal. It was tough convincing everyone that they needed focus and that they shouldn't pursue so many topics at the same time. It wasn't easy to gain their trust that Noa would handle the ideas in a sensible order, which automatically implied that some things would come later.

The next topic on the agenda was the forecasts and the numbers. Noa had been struggling to align all the different perspectives that the stakeholders had. Dave was looking to increase revenues fast. Shanice from circulation wanted to improve the net promoter score (NPS). Kemal wanted to know how much she was investing in new markets. Aiko voiced concerns about accumulated technical debt. And Trevon wanted to know why the heck everything took so incredibly long to complete.

Noa started the second part of the meeting with a story. It was a story about a company that had issued a bonus for all Developers who could find bugs in the software. And she told how this decision had led to a drastic drop in quality. With the drastic drop in product quality, the company started to punish the people who created the bugs in the first place. This led to some massive changes in people's behaviors, as they became very skilled at hiding all those bugs and not reporting any new ones. Moral of the story: be careful what you steer on. Defining key performance indicators (KPIs) and then adding targets, rewards, or punishments based on those metrics will lead to strange, unexpected behaviors. Product management is partly a numbers game, but with the wrong metrics or the wrong "rewards" and "punishments," you will get weird and unexpected behaviors.

World News had mainly steered on internal metrics up till now. Noa proposed to change this way of steering the company as well as product management. Rather than looking at how productive everyone was, she wanted to focus on the impacts that were generated for the company. Noa realized that two things would make this a hard sell: first, it would be hard to measure impacts, and second, no one likes to be told that they have always been doing it the wrong way. She sighed and flipped on the projector as the group returned from getting coffee.

A typical product development process starts with an idea. It may come from customer feedback, it may be a technological breakthrough in the industry, or could be an insight gained from a stakeholder. The idea gets iterated on, but ultimately it gets refined, designed, and built in.

The next step is to release the product to (a part of) its intended users. It is time to put the product in the hands of (potential) customers. Sometimes the product is released to the entire customer or user base. Other times, it is released to a subset, a selection of that customer or user base. In other cases, you may feel more confident releasing to a group of people such as your colleagues—the employees of the company you work for. Xing, for example, is a German company that develops enterprise social networking software that releases its products first to its 1,600 employees. The company uses this beta release to make sure that Developers don't run into surprises when they release the product to customers. When TomTom was secretly developing a sports watch for Nike, a surprisingly large number of employees started wearing long sleeves to cover their wrists. Guess what they were hiding from the competition?

There is only so much feedback that you can get from your fans—the people who already love your products, your company, or your brand. A great way to discover if a product is impacting the behavior of your customers is to provide them with the product. This situation puts us in a bit of a conundrum. You want to release something that works for your customers, but the only way to learn whether it works for them—and whether it is valuable and useful to them—is to ship something to those customers.

One way to limit the risks associated with releasing is to roll out your changes gradually and to make sure that you can undo the changes in case of unforeseen side effects. Many companies have improved and optimized their (software) release processes for these purposes. A great example of such a company is Suitsupply, a Dutch company that rolled out its ideas country by country while measuring the effect of changes for their customers. If Suitsupply learns that a change doesn't work well, it can undo the change by rolling back to the previous version of the product.

There is another variable to influence, though. Some products and changes have a positive impact on customers but have a low impact on the bottom line of the company. Sometimes there is a strategic misfit, or other products simply perform better. Intuit, for example, experimented with a service that would match accountants to people who had a life-changing event. Although its flagship product, QuickBooks, could handle those situations well, many of its potential customers preferred human contact and interaction over the use of the software. Once Intuit's new human-powered service became popular among customers, it created friction with the QuickBooks product. The company decided to shut down the new service before it could mature and create an impact for the company.

As you've seen in the "It's all in the numbers game!" story about Noa and World News, there are many ways to steer a company and its products. Some metrics are more valuable and relevant than others. Measurements and metrics often have a relationship with each other. Sometimes they build upon each other, and sometimes they offer more details for analysis. Some measures are more valuable than others. The pyramid in Figure 12.1 highlights how internal metrics can be a proxy for value metrics. They provide insights into activities and outputs; however, these internal measures do not replace the value measures to steer on.

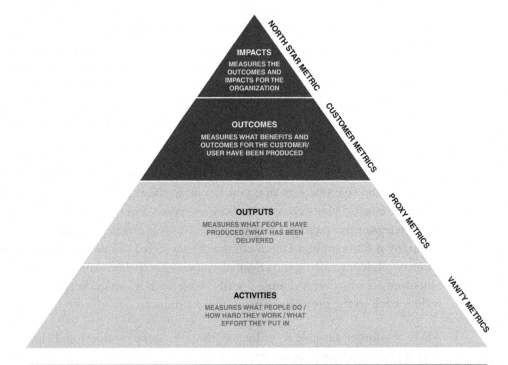

**Figure 12.1** What do you measure?

Let's explore the use of different metrics for a soccer match. Many measures could be tracked, such as meters run, number of passes won and lost, number of shots taken, shots on goal, ball possession, and many more. These are all **activities** that the players put into the game. The activities are important, sure. However, optimizing ball possession or the number of shots taken is helpful yet not decisive. Without these activities, a team is unlikely to win the match. Activities, though, do not equal results, or in other words, value. Famous ice hockey player Wayne Gretzky's advice was: "I skate to where the puck is going to be, not to where it has been," and that is a great way to maximize results while minimizing activity.

The next type of metric that many organizations focus on is **output**. In a soccer match, those outputs would be the number of goals. Again, these outputs are important. Without output, we cannot change the status quo. However, scoring a goal does not guarantee winning the match. Both output and activity are easy to measure for most teams, and therein lies a pitfall. Organizations tend to focus on these metrics while spending less energy on collecting data about the more important metrics: **customer outcomes** and **company impacts.**

Measuring changes in customer behavior is typically done by applying practices such as A/B testing[1] or canary releases.[2] It requires substantial effort to put these practices into place, and they might result in the Hawthorne effect (refer to Chapter 4, "Building Customer Empathy"), meaning that customers might change their behaviors because they are aware of being observed. Often, the data obtained from such experiments is difficult to interpret well, and it often takes some time to obtain and analyze enough quality data to draw conclusions.

Figure 12.2 is the result of an A/B test in which user traffic was sent to three different versions of a recommender tool. This tool helped people to find the right products, for example, by showing products that other people also liked.

---

1. A test in which viewer participants are shown a different version of a testing variable—for example, a website—to measure how each version influences viewers'/users' behavior.
2. A test in which a new version is first released to a subset of the total audience to measure customer response.

Each version of the recommender was used by a part (a percentage) of the total website visitors. By distributing the site visitors among the different versions of the recommender, the company was able to measure which version worked best. The results of the various implementations were measured, including the conversion rate (CR). Based on the conversion rate, the company was able to determine which recommender version was the best one to use.

| | Sessions | Orders | CR% | Win?** |
|---|---|---|---|---|
| Control A | 48511 | 609 | 1.26 | 1% |
| Variant B | 45713 | 607 | 1.33 | 10% |
| Variant C | 44610 | 642 | 1.44* | 88% |
| Total | 138834 | 1859 | 1.34 | |

\*) Speculative extra revenue/month: € xxx,xxx,-
\*\*) Given the data, the probability that this variant is the best (>95% is significant)

**Figure 12.2** Translating an A/B test to business language

But wait! What if variant C wasn't the best option, despite having the highest conversion rate? What if variant C was just lucky? What if all the people who wanted to buy a product anyway were served that variant? And perhaps all the people that were just looking around on the website ended up with the control variant? It's possible but unlikely. How unlikely? Well, that could be calculated using Bayesian statistics. This isn't covered in this book, so look it up if you are interested. However, to get more certainty about the validity of the data, a certain volume of traffic is needed to ensure that the results are significant.

Take another look at Figure 12.2. Focus on the last lines on the screenshot. The numbers in the image seem very technical and likely require more explanation. So, the team explained the image to their stakeholders as follows: "We might earn XXXX dollars extra per month if we roll out this feature. We are 88% sure that we are right about this feature." By adding this explanation, the team translated their vision in very tangible terms, which facilitated faster decision making and supported them in stakeholder management.

Optimizing a single metric is often rather easy. If you only want to improve conversion rate, for example, just drop your prices below that of competitors, and you will likely get better conversion. However, that is not often what we want, right? So, what if you need to optimize a set of measures or a system of measures? What if the measures relate to and influence each other? What different angles would you consider if you want to steer on (value) measures? How can a comprehensive set of measures for company impact be created? Find out in the next section.

## EXPRESSING COMPANY IMPACT

Expressing what "value" a product or service adds for a company is simple on the one hand, yet also difficult on the other. It is rather simple because, for most commercial companies, value boils down to making money, increasing profits, increasing revenues, increasing margins, and saving costs. For most commercial companies, increasing their financial position is the ultimate form of expressing value. However, it is rather difficult to express company impact because . . . Is it just about the money? Shouldn't other aspects of business, like employee wellbeing, customer satisfaction, and making a positive impact also matter? In addition, it's not only about generating value and impact for the business today but also to generate value for tomorrow. It's about delivering value right now but also ensuring value is added in the future.

A 2016 study[3] found that companies need 12 years on average to recover their initial and subsequent investments. That's quite a long time, isn't it? To reach the break-even point, you need to look at the speed of innovation as much as the cost structure in the industry. It is not enough to look at the market value; you also need to balance out the organizational capability to achieve it.

A framework that may help you to express company impact for these different dimensions is Evidence-Based Management (EBM)™.[4] This framework covers both the market value and the organization's ability to capture that value

---

3. WonKoo Park, KwangSook Lee, SeoYoung Doo, and Sung-Soo Yoon, "Investments for New Product Development: A Break-Even Time Analysis," *Engineering Management Journal* 28, no. 3 (2016), 158–67. https://doi.org/10.1080/10429247.2016.1199747.

4. https://www.scrum.org/resources/evidence-based-management-guide

from the market. In other words, it helps you to measure the value delivered for the company, customers, and the market, as well as the organization's ability to deliver that value. The framework offers four key value areas (KVAs): current value, time to market, ability to innovate, and unrealized value (see Figure 12.3).

**Figure 12.3** Evidence-Based Management™

Each **KVA** focuses on a different aspect of value: the actual value (to be) delivered or the organization's ability to deliver value. The **current value** area aims to measure how much value an organization delivers at present; that is, how much value is being delivered today. This is an important area to track for most organizations. However, an organization should also be able to respond to changes in the marketplace quickly to deliver value to their customers. That's where the **time to market** area comes in. In addition, it's not just about being fast. It's not just about shipping bug fixes or small improvements to customers. Instead, companies should be able to sustain innovation over a longer period. Therefore, you want to measure the **ability to innovate**. And finally, organizations want to make progress toward their long-term goals and objectives. They want to capture new markets, target audiences, or unlock new value for customers. The final part is **unrealized value,** which tracks the potential value to be gained in the future.

Each KVA is explained in more detail, but first, let's take a moment to clarify some terms related to measuring value. Two terms that often come up when discussing value are *leading indicators* and *lagging indicators*. Leading indicators are usually the more actionable measures to steer on because they can be measured, tracked, and steered on (usually) before something happens. Lagging indicators, however, are "lagging" in reality. They can often be measured only after an event has already occurred. In most cases, lagging indicators are easier to measure, but their value generally isn't realized until a similar event occurs.

For example, companies often have lagging indicators such as revenues, costs, and margins. However, the actual revenues can only be measured once the books are closed for the month. Leading indicators for revenues, for example, might be the number of calls by sales, the number of proposals sent, and the percentage of deals won. The airbags in your car are a lagging indicator. They will open after a crash has occurred. It's useful to have those airbags, but perhaps you want some proactive collision avoidance measures (and thus leading indicators) as well.

## KEY VALUE AREA 1: CURRENT VALUE

Current value (CV) considers the value that an organization delivers to customers, stakeholders, and society **at present.** The current value area considers only what value exists right now, not what value might exist in the future. Various measures and perspectives are considered in this KVA, but we usually find that companies and Product Owners are familiar with the measures in this KVA.

The following list shows various examples of measures that could be tracked in this KVA. It is not a complete list, and there are many other measures that could be tracked to gain more insights into the current value a company delivers.

- **Revenue:** How much money is earned with the products and services of the company? How much money is being extracted from the market?

**EBITDA:**[5] How much of the revenues are turned into margins?

**Product-cost ratio:** How do products and costs evolve? What is the margin gap between income and expenditures? What are the trends?

**Headcount:** How many people are working for the company and product? When combined with the previous two, headcount offers insights into the competitiveness of the company.

**Customer satisfaction or happiness:** How satisfied are customers with the products, services, brand, image, or reputation of the company? How is customer satisfaction evolving? This metric can be used as an early indicator for buying behavior.

- **Product usage:** How much or how often is the product being used? Products that are being used frequently (given their purpose) are more likely to add value for customers.

- **Employee satisfaction or happiness:** How satisfied are employees with their jobs, the company, and their leaders? Energized employees often produce better results.

- **(Internal) investor satisfaction or happiness:** How satisfied are stakeholders and investors with the way the company is run? How satisfied are they with the results achieved? This metric is an indicator of the financial runway and/or the patience that the stakeholders or shareholders may have.

So, where should you start? Which measures should you track? And how? As an example, the net promoter score (NPS) is a widely adopted metric. It tracks how likely customers are to recommend your product or company to other people. It is a valuable insight to gain, but NPS has been facing some issues as well. One of the issues is that customers are simply asked for their opinion about the product or company. You may have experienced this yourself as well, being overwhelmed by all those companies that ask you to fill in a customer satisfaction survey. It's becoming a bit too much, perhaps.

Another challenge around NPS is that many companies apply it the wrong way. What we've seen in various companies is that they use a red and green

---

5. Earnings before interest, taxes, depreciation, and amortization (EBITDA) is essentially the net income of the company (or earnings) including interest, taxes, depreciation, and amortization added back.

color scheme in the survey. A 9 or 10 is colored in green, meaning it's a good score. Any number 8 or lower is colored in red, meaning the services weren't too good. To us, this is a great example of how to *not* measure customer satisfaction. If you only want to get 9s and 10s from your customers to make you feel good, then why are you asking for feedback in the first place?

In addition, the data is questionable. Customers are asked to fill in a survey or NPS score because their opinions might change by the day or context. Whether they reach out to you with a question, to report a problem, or to buy a product will influence the customer's opinion. Therefore, it is wiser to get feedback about the specific thing that you interacted with a customer about rather than ask broad questions such as whether they would recommend your company to others. And perhaps it would be even more valuable to track what customers do rather than what they say.

So, tracking customer behaviors could be the best way of getting feedback. In software, this is easy. Customer behaviors can be tracked via clicks, downloads, signups, time spent on a webpage, sharing, and many other elements. Before tracking all of this activity, make sure to connect with the security and privacy experts in the company, of course. E-commerce companies often track the number of items purchased per visit, the number of visits per user per month, and the number of referral codes redeemed, for example. These measures help them to get an idea about customer loyalty and purchasing behavior. When working in a business-to-business context, though, you could consider conversion rates from sales leads to actual customers, the number of products sold per customer, or the number of positive reviews, for example.

*If you have to start somewhere, start by creating one fan per day.*
—Jos Burgers

## KEY VALUE AREA 2: UNREALIZED VALUE

Unrealized value (UV) is the **potential future value** that **could** be realized if the organization meets the needs of potential customers. Notice the words *potential* and *could*. It is not a guarantee that future value will be delivered.

Quite the contrary. Companies need to discover what potential value could be delivered, and then they need to experiment their way toward obtaining that potential value.

*A long, long time ago (long before Scrum was as widely known as it is today), I worked for a company that built software products for the healthcare industry. We built software-as-a-service products for making our customers' lives easier when it came to doing work around HR, salary payments, capacity planning, and other administrative duties that take place in healthcare institutions. These were rather time-consuming and expensive back then, so we helped them to automate their processes.*

*One of the new products we were developing was a business intelligence solution that offered the company insights to better lead and manage its institutions. We saw a massive gap in the market. We noticed many problems to be solved with this solution. It was going to be huge.*

*When we finally shipped the product to the market after 1.5 years of Scrum-ish (SINO) development, it turned out that we were wrong. The product was developed in short sprints. All the Scrum roles and events were present. However, the product was never really released to customers. We did demos, for sure. We got great feedback for improvements (which we made), and customers were excited. However, throughout those 1.5 years, they couldn't use the product in their own company and their work.*

*Half a year after releasing the product to the market, it was unfortunately shut down. The problems that customers had still existed, yet we weren't able to sell the product to them. It was a massive disappointment, but also huge learning. I will never be building products anymore in a waterfall-ish or Scrum-ish way. And I will never again assume that the potential value that we see is the value that we'll obtain. I at least learned from this experience that assumptions need to be validated first, before building anything big.*

— Robbin

As the example shows, we cannot take potential value for granted. It is *potential,* not *certain,* value, and we obtain it (hopefully) by taking small steps. Visionary Product Owners, though, focus on obtaining unrealized value to maximize the value of the product over time. When customers experience a gap between their current experience and their desired experience, an opportunity presents itself. The difference between current experience and desired experience is what is measured in the unrealized value area.

Lagging measures for unrealized value are market share and the customer satisfaction gap, for example. Companies are often used to measuring their current market share (to be tracked in the current value area). If those companies can also size up their total potential market, they could estimate how much more market share there is to gain (being the unrealized value). If they can also size up the market share of competitors, they might be able to identify from which competitor to obtain more market share. People who already have a working solution to their problem via one of your competitors are likely to care about switching costs. Switching costs are the time and money it takes to switch from one company to another. People who do not yet have a solution are often easier to persuade to buy your solution, as they don't need to overcome their switching costs. The challenge with these potential customers, though, is that you'll need to convince them that they have a problem to solve in the first place.

Various example measures can be tracked in the unrealized value area:

- **Potential market share:** How many people or organizations exist that have a problem that your product solves? How many of those people are your customers, and how many more are available in the market? How many of them could become your customers in the future?
- **Potential EBITDA improvement:** How can the margins on the products and services be optimized? Can value be generated by optimizing costs? Can revenues be increased? Can the number of paying customers be increased? There are many ways for improving margins.
- **Potential product usage:** How much is your product being used currently, and how does that relate to how often you'd like your product to be used? Should people be spending more (or less) time using the product?

- **Customer or user satisfaction gap:** What is the difference between a customer's or user's desired experience and their current experience?
- **Desired customer experience:** What would your customer like to experience with your product?

Many other measures could be tracked to gain insights into potential future value. It's not so much about the number of measures, of course, but rather about finding the right ones for your product. It is also important to track all four KVAs from the Evidence-Based Management framework. Think of the company SpaceX, for example. A product it created is the Falcon 9 rocket. When this product was introduced to the market, it had a low current value because an early version of the product was being used to test the market, technology, marketing, and sales of flying to outer space. There weren't a lot of customers, sales were low, and the first product wasn't great. However, the market potential was huge, and thus the unrealized value was very high. Massive investments were done in the product and company, given the potential future returns, even though the current value was low.

Conversely, you'll likely remember Nokia and Blackberry having products that delivered high current value. They had a huge market share, there were no nearby competitors, and they had very satisfied customers. Investing in those products didn't make much sense because the unrealized value was low. There wasn't a lot more potential value to gain. Looking back, it would have been more beneficial to invest time and money into unlocking new value, rather than optimizing products with low unrealized value.

Both current value and unrealized value are commonly used product management value areas to track. Both areas focus on the actual value to be delivered for the company, its customers, its stakeholders, and the wider society. There is more to be measured and steered on. To deliver value today or tomorrow, companies need the right capabilities of delivering that value in the first place. Companies need to be able to ship products to the market fast enough, and they need to be able to innovate. Such capabilities are often being steered on with engineering or software development. Many Agile Coaches and Scrum Masters also focus on time to market and getting feedback quickly to learn. But why? If a Product Owner is responsible for the long-term value of a product, then why not measure and steer on the capabilities of delivering on that outcome? Let's explore how a Product Owner can measure and steer on the capabilities of delivering value in the next part.

## KEY VALUE AREA 3: TIME TO MARKET

The KVA time to market (TTM) represents how quickly an organization can deliver new value, capabilities, services, or products to the market. Being able to create, deliver, and ship value fast is often considered a strategic advantage. Especially when operating in a complex domain, with competitors trying to beat you in getting to market, being able to ship and learn fast is an advantage. Without active measurement and management of the time to market, the ability to sustainably deliver value in the future is unknown.

When Toyota entered foreign markets in 1957, it had little chance of competing with giant car manufacturers like General Motors and Ford, especially in the volumes of cars produced. The huge volumes of cars these companies were able to produce offered them economies of scale advantage. They were able to distribute fixed costs across the huge volume of cars being produced. Therefore, they were able to price their cars lower and win more customers.

Although Toyota applied many strategies to grow and expand, one of them could be described as a common Judo tactic when facing a larger opponent. When facing a larger, bigger, or stronger opponent in Judo, the inertia of a larger opponent can be used to your advantage. The bigger opponents may be strong, but the smaller ones are often fast. Toyota applied this principle as well. The company focused on time to market. Toyota was a smaller and more nimble company, and it was able to introduce new models, colors, and variants much more quickly than the competition. This allowed Toyota not only to respond to changes and customer demands faster but also to influence them. The large car manufacturers struggled to respond because their strategy limited changes and deviations.

There are many measures to track in the time to market KVA. A significant number of those measures can be tied back to the ideas of Toyota. Some frequently used measures in this area include the following:

- **Release frequency:** How often are new products or versions being released? Can the release frequency be improved to get a competitive advantage? As an example, Amazon was well-known for deploying a new version of its product every 11 seconds in 2016.
- **Release stabilization period:** How much time is spent between solving reported problems in a release, the point in time where the Developers say it is ready to release, and the point in time where it is released to customers?
- **Mean time to repair:** What is the average amount of time it takes for an error, once detected, to be solved?
- **Time to learn:** What is the total time needed to sketch an idea or improvement, build it, deliver it to users, and learn from their usage of the product?
- **Build and integration frequency:** What is the number of integrated and tested builds per period? For a team that is releasing frequently or continuously, this measure is superseded by actual release measures.
- **Time to remove impediment:** What is the average amount of time from when an impediment is raised until it is resolved? It is a contributing factor to lead time and employee satisfaction.

Xiaomi is a Chinese smartphone manufacturer. It releases 100,000 phones[6] every Tuesday at noon. Within hours—not days, weeks, or months—it collects feedback from customers. That feedback is delivered to the engineering teams within hours. Remember that these phones are physical devices, not software-only products, each with exactly the same code and performance. Releasing physical products has a huge impact on the supply chain, production, distribution, shipment, and logistics. The ability to ship, get feedback from customers, and learn quickly was the result of a strategic choice to invest in time to market that gave Xiaomi an edge over its competitors. Its investment ensures the company can deliver value fast today *and* tomorrow.

---

6. Datapoint from 2020.

# KEY VALUE AREA 4: ABILITY TO INNOVATE

The fourth and final KVA is the ability to innovate (A2I). The issue that many organizations face often seems to be a lack of resources. However, lack of resources isn't the biggest challenge; often, what the company is doing and how it's doing it is what hinders progress. An example was clarified by the CEO of a large, fast-moving electronics goods company, who said: "Never before have I seen so many people work so hard, and yet see so little of that work end up in the hands of our customers." Clearly, he was worried about the ability to innovate.

Most Product Owners in practice are aware of the ability to innovate area. They experience that a part of the Developers' capacity is spent on keeping the lights on, part of their time is spent on managing the installed base, part is spent on fixing bugs, and so on. All this work is necessary and important, but it doesn't create new value. It only keeps the current products and services in operation. Decisions are often made on different levels in the organization. Companies aren't always able to hire, develop, retain, and inspire talented and passionate people who might improve the ability to innovate. So, what can we measure and steer on as Product Owners?

Once more, many measures can be tracked:

- **Defect trends:** Is product quality getting better or worse? A defect could be anything that reduces the value of the product for a customer, user, or organization. How are defects evolving? What's causing those defects, and how can the company improve quality and reduce defects structurally?
- **Installed version index:** An installed base is a measure of past success, but maintaining many versions strains the organization's ability to innovate. How many versions or variants of the product are in production? How many different versions require operations, maintenance, and support? Can installed versions be updated to reduce the variety of products being supported, leading to an improved ability to innovate?
- **On-product index:** What percentage of time do teams spend working on the product and working on value? How many people are dedicatedly working on the product?

- **Technical debt:** How much extra development and testing work arises when quick and dirty solutions result in later remediation? Technical debt, a well-known concept in software products, creates an undesirable impact on the delivery of value and an avoidable increase in waste and risk.

- **Innovation rate:** How much effort or cost is spent on creating new product capabilities, value, or features? The total product effort or cost is divided by that number to determine the percentage spent on innovation. The result provides insight into the capacity of the organization to deliver new product capabilities.

Most of these measures are lagging indicators that can be measured after the work has been done or the time and money spent. Tracking and steering on leading indicators are often perceived to be more difficult. An example measure that could be used is to track the percentage of time that people can work on the product (on-product index). What we observe is that in eight out of ten Scrum Teams, Developers work on multiple Sprint Backlog items simultaneously. They're working on multiple features at the same time, or even worse, they're working on multiple projects or teams at the same time. This causes a lack of focus, reduced efficiency and effectiveness, and task-switching costs. Even more important, it is devastating for the teams' ability to create something valuable fast. A Product Owner can (and should) help the Scrum Team to apply focus in their work, for example, by communicating vision, the Product Goal, an ordered Product Backlog, and by saying no to stakeholders. Product Owners need to say no to good ideas and focus on great ideas. Focus is key to improving the ability to innovate. It's one of the five Scrum Values, so embrace it.

A common pitfall for people and organizations is to add more people to a project to speed things up. Adding more people won't speed things up. Projects often slow down even more because the new crew needs to be brought up to speed, adapt to the new team and culture, and learn about the product, customers, and market. Although most people are aware of this, it never hurts to share a story, so here we go:

> *A manager confronted a Product Owner, saying that he wanted to add four more developers to the Product Owner's team. The Product Owner wasn't interested in adding more people to his team to speed things up, as he knew that this would only slow him down. So, the Product Owner went out to*

*buy four copies of Fred Brooks's The Mythical Man-Month for his manager. He brought the books to his manager and explained that he had purchased four copies so that the manager could read it four times as fast.*

If this story doesn't trigger you, then surely this quote will:

*No matter how great the talent or efforts, some things just take time. You can't produce a baby in one month by getting nine women pregnant.*

—Warren Buffett

Enough about focus and people. Let's talk about technical debt. Technical debt is a well-known concept in the software development industry but also applies to most other products. Technical debt is often created by taking shortcuts, by not delivering high quality, and/or by not maintaining and operating products correctly. Although it is often referred to as "technical" debt, the debt itself doesn't have to be technical. It could also be related to design, maintenance, operations, documentation, and so on.

Consider the windows in your house, for example. The wooden window frames around the glass need to be sanded and repainted about every 5 years. If you do this well, your window frames will last a very long time. However, if you don't paint them for 10 or 15 years, the wood will start to rot. The result is that you'll need to replace the window frames completely. Buying paint, sanding the window frames, and painting them costs time and money. However, it won't be nearly as much as replacing the window frames completely with new ones.

As the example shows, the word *debt* is quite important to understand. It is called technical debt because we need to pay interest for taking shortcuts or for not doing our maintenance properly. Technical debt tends to grow over time, just as interest does. So, if you want to improve your ability to innovate, make sure to create high-quality products, don't take shortcuts, avoid creating technical debt, and if you must, make sure to pay off the interest quickly by getting on par with quality standards.

Product Owners often struggle with technical debt because it is not always visible and transparent. "I feel like the Developers flag their code as technical debt as soon as they have finished writing it" is a frequently heard remark. However, there are many stories about products that have been rushed to the market as experiments or minimum viable products (MVPs) that have become nightmares to maintain and operate. Technical debt can be a result of poor quality or engineering standards or of pressure from management or customers to release a product. It can also, however, be a result of new insights.

> *Uber, for example, started with an infrastructure that could handle only one city at best. During its hypergrowth, many of the assumptions made in the original design needed to be refactored to meet the new and emerging demands from the market.*
>
> — Chris

How fast your teams run—or, better said, how fast they can perform a certain type of change—is an unbiased metric that should be part of your decision-making process. Don't ignore technical debt, but also don't refactor a product for the sake of refactoring. The same applies to the KVAs time to market and ability to innovate. You don't always need stuff like continuous delivery, continuous integration, or the ability to release with one click. You don't always need to be the most innovative, most disruptive, or to produce the highest-quality products. You need to build products with the speed and innovation that matches the market and your customers, or just be a little bit ahead of them. It's much like Tim Ferriss once said: "If you're getting chased by a lion, you don't need to run faster than the lion, just the people running with you."

# Maximizing Value through Effective Pricing Strategies and Tactics

## Introduction to Product Pricing

Warren Buffett said it best: "Price is what you pay. Value is what you get." The difference between value and price has a lot to do with the problem your product solves for customers. Whether your product is paint sold in a web shop, your interior design skills, or guitars manufactured by your company, it's all about the problems to solve for customers. Classic guitars, for example, are a combination of wood and strings. When you ask owners of Fender and Gibson guitars about what value is to them, however, you'll likely get many different ideas and opinions. These two brands offer and sell different experiences, although both sell a similar product. The same could be said for the Harley-Davidson brand. It doesn't just sell motorcycles; it sells a way of living.

"So what? Why does it matter?" you may wonder. Well, let's take the product water as an example (see Figure 13.1). Plain and simple tap water is a fine way (in most countries) to resolve your thirst. It's also a very cost-effective solution to resolving thirst. The price of tap water in the Netherlands, for example, is around 0.60 to 0.70 cents per 1,000 liters. The pricing strategy used by water companies is cost-plus pricing, meaning that all the costs for the product are calculated, a small margin is added, and that's the price for customers.

With such an affordable product on the market, why would there be a need for a competing product? Well, there are plenty of competing products when it comes to water. Mineral water, for example, is sold in bottles at roughly 40 times the price of tap water and has a mind-boggling market cap of $350 billion.[1] Prices from various suppliers are within a close range, between $1.20 and $1.60 per bottle. The pricing strategy used is market pricing.

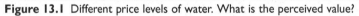

**Figure 13.1** Different price levels of water. What is the perceived value?

Another sector of the drinking water industry is reserved for sparkling water and distilled water. This represents roughly 20% of the total market size in terms of revenues but only 10% of the market in terms of the number of bottles sold. Companies like Perrier focus on this part of the market specifically. They apply the pricing strategy of market skimming or price differentiation with their exclusive bottles of water. This price "skimming" of the market originates from the processing of milk. The best, fattest, and creamiest part of the milk rises to the top of the milk churn during milk processing and is then skimmed off to be sold at a higher price than the rest of the milk.

The last commonly used pricing strategy is value-based pricing. With value-based pricing, there is no direct correlation between the actual costs and the

---

1. 2021 estimate from Grand View Research.

price of the product. It is often difficult to apply value-based pricing to a commodity market or product. However, if there is no alternative available, the value is determined by the pains and gains of the customer, and their willingness to get those resolved.

> *Fun fact: The average product manager spends 13% of their time pricing.*
>
> —Product Focus Survey 2017[2]

What we often find is that Product Owners don't have anything to do with pricing. Pricing products and services is often done by the pricing department or by sales and marketing, who define the prices for all products and services of the organization. This is strange to us. If Product Owners are supposed to maximize the value of a product, shouldn't they also think about the product's price? Isn't price a lever that can be adjusted to deliver value (e.g., revenues and margins) for the organization? Let's find out.

## THE PRODUCT PRICING PROCESS

Let's define product pricing first:

> *Pricing is a process where a business sets the price at which it will sell its products and services. In this process, the organization considers the costs of time and materials for producing the products or services, supply chain costs, marketplace, competition, market conditions, brand, and quality of the product.*[3]

An important piece in the definition is that pricing is a process. Processes are usually a series of activities or jobs that occur regularly, at least more often than once. In other words, pricing is a process that should happen regularly. The pricing process activities are illustrated in Figure 13.2. Whether this

---

2. https://www.productfocus.com.
3. Wikipedia, s.v. pricing, 2022, https://en.wikipedia.org/wiki/Pricing.

regular basis is yearly, quarterly, monthly, weekly, daily, or even hourly, depends on the company, its products and services, and the industry, amongst other factors.

In some organizations, pricing is a manual process, where individuals or groups of people set prices for new products, and where they inspect and adapt prices regularly. In other organizations prices are set automatically. For example, think about websites where you can book a hotel or a flight. Such companies typically change their prices automatically, based on predicted demand, availability, and the season amongst other factors. When taking a high-level view of a typical pricing process, the following steps can be identified:

- Inspection of various inputs, sources, documents, and numbers
- Inspection of current company goals
- Selection and setting of the pricing strategy
- Selection and setting of the pricing tactics
- Adaptation of product prices, including supportive tools, and communicating changes

| INSPECT | COMPANY GOAL | PRICING STRATEGY | PRICING TACTICS | ADAPT |
|---|---|---|---|---|
| Win/Loss Analysis | Increase Revenues | Cost-Plus Pricing | Charm Pricing | Market Communication |
| Competitor Offering | Increase Margins | Competitive Pricing | Anchoring | Internal Communication |
| Cost (of creation) | Increase Marketshare | Value-Based Pricing | Tiers | System & Software Changes |
| Predicted Demand | Reduce Churn | Price Skimming | Bundling | Price Calculation Tools |
| Product-Market Fit? | Achieve Survival | Penetration Pricing | Unbundling | Market Feedback on Price Updates |
| Value Proposition | | | Variable | |
| | | | Luxury | |
| | | | Dynamic | |
| | | | Personalized | |
| | | | Subscription | |
| | | | Others... | |

PRICING IS A PROCESS. APPLY INSPECTION & ADAPTATION.

**Figure 13.2** The pricing process

As the definition shows, pricing is a process. But more important, as you'll notice in the steps illustrated in Figure 13.2, pricing is an empirical process.

This is important to notice because it means that the pricing process and its outcomes need to be inspected and adapted regularly. To optimize the value delivered, feedback from customers, competitors, and the market is needed to validate prices and learn if they're right. But what makes a price "right"? We explore the pricing process in more detail in the rest of this chapter and share practical advice and examples. Hopefully, this will enable you to bring some great ideas to the table the next time prices are being updated in your company.

## STEP 1: INSPECTION OF INPUTS

The first step in the pricing process, before setting or changing product prices, is gathering information. Information about the marketplace, information about competitors, and information about costs of time and materials, for example. You can also think of other sources, like how many products were sold, or how many deals were made, and why those deals were successful or not. Let's explore some commonly used sources of information in this first step of the pricing process:

- **Win/loss analysis:** If you work for a commercial company, there is likely a sales team or department in the company. This team's job is to get new customer orders and assignments, and make deals for the company. They probably create quotes for customers to get those orders in. There's also a chance that the company participates in tenders (Requests for Proposals) now and then. Tenders and quotes can be great sources of information during the pricing process. Analyze them and try to learn why the organization has won or lost certain tenders/quotes. Why did prospective customers decide to work with your company? Why did they select one of your competitor's products or services? Was their decision based on prices, or did they believe they got more value from the selected party?

- **Competitor offering:** Another great source of information that can be found outside of the company: your competitors' offerings. If you want to set or change the prices of your products or services, then you better know what your competitors' offering is. Learn more about their pricing model, if possible, but also make sure to understand where they differ from your company. Create a Strategy Canvas, for example, to compare products and services. Find your unique differentiators and know about your competitors' unique selling points.

- **Costs:** Think of the costs of designing, building, maintaining, servicing, and improving products and services. Consider the costs of raw materials, labor, transportation, shipping, and more. As a Product Owner, you should know what the total cost of ownership of the product is. Once you do, you will also know how much revenue or cost savings your product should produce at minimum to have a positive balance.

- **Predicted demand and availability:** Predicted demand and availability of alternatives are also big influences on a product's price. It's basic supply and demand. Obtaining insights about market trends, product usage, sales trends, customer trends, and other market information is useful. Seek to understand how demand and supply are likely to change.

- **Value proposition:** Another source to inspect is the value proposition. Does the value proposition still align with customer needs? Are key customer problems still being solved? Do these problems still exist? What alternatives are available? You can use, for example, the 5Ps (Problem, Pervasiveness, Pay, Position, and Possible) to validate the value proposition. You could also use various canvases like the Business Model Canvas, Lean Canvas, or Product Canvas. The thing is, if there is a mismatch between your product and customer needs, or if there is only little value in solving the customer problem, that will influence the prices.

## STEP 2: INSPECTION OF CURRENT COMPANY GOALS

Every organization has goals to be achieved. Products also strive to achieve certain goals, such as improving revenues, reducing costs, or increasing customer satisfaction. The company and product goals usually influence product prices. Therefore, when setting your product's prices, consider what goal needs to be achieved. Following are a few typical examples of goals:

- **Increase revenues:** For many products and organizations, there is a goal of increasing overall revenues. When managing your product, this can also be your Product Goal. Increasing revenues can be done in many ways, including bringing in new customers, improving customer churn, and up-selling and cross-selling products.

- **Increase margins:** When the company and product goal is to increase margins, organizations often focus more on reducing costs, optimizing processes, and improving overall efficiency. Alternatively, prices can be increased, which tends to be more difficult to explain to customers.

- **Increase market share:** This company goal is mainly focused on getting new customers in, which may contribute to increasing revenues at present and/or in the future.

- **Reduce churn:** This company's goal is about keeping the customers that the organization has. It is usually more difficult and costly to attract new customers than it is to keep current customers.

- **Achieve survival:** Achieving survival is not the ambitious and inspiring goal that organizations want to be chasing, of course. No company or person wants to fight for survival. However, companies sometimes end up in a crisis. Sometimes they lose customers, and sometimes a disruptive innovation comes along, putting them in survival mode. If this is the situation a company is in, it will most likely influence their pricing strategy.

### STEP 3: SELECTION AND SETTING OF THE PRICING STRATEGY

The objectives of setting the price of a product are typically to maximize profit, meet target sales, and market share targets, and maintain a price that is stable in relation to competitors' prices. There are many factors (internal and external) that influence a product's price. Internal factors include the cost of creating the product, marketing strategies, product specifications, distribution, production plant capacity, and promotion, for example. Some external factors influencing the price include market competition, legal factors, target audiences, data, personalization, and of course, supply and demand.

There are various pricing strategies you can employ. We explain five common ones:

- **Cost-plus pricing:** Cost-plus pricing is a pricing strategy in which the selling price is determined by adding a margin or buffer to a product's costs. This means that an organization must deliberately maintain a product cost breakdown, to prevent selling the product below cost price.

Cost-plus pricing is a common pricing strategy for government contracts, utilities, and single-buyer products that are manufactured to the buyer's specifications.

A taxi runway of Schiphol Airport in the Netherlands crosses one of the Dutch highways via a flyover. This airport used to do maintenance on this bridge and the tarmac every four years, to keep it safe and in good condition. This maintenance work was very costly, so the airport asked one of its vendors to develop a software product to calculate the wear and tear of the bridge and tarmac. Inputs for this included the actual tonnage of planes that crossed it. The vendor calculated how much it would cost to build the product and they added a nice margin to that cost. They then delivered a quote to the airport, which seemed very profitable. Sometime later, the project was executed, the product was delivered, the customer was happy, and bottles of champagne were opened to celebrate. When the Product Manager asked the client, "It's great to learn that maintenance can be done every six years rather than every four. But, just out of curiosity, how much money does this save for the airport?" The answer to this question was a factor of 1,000 of the price he had calculated! Perhaps it would have been more beneficial to have chosen a different pricing strategy.

- **Competitive pricing:** Competitive pricing, or competition-based pricing, is a pricing method in which the price of your product is based on competing products in the market, which function as a benchmark for your products' prices. Typically, your product is then sold at a price just above or below the benchmark of your competitors.

  Setting a price above the benchmark will result in higher profit per unit but might result in fewer units sold as customers would prefer products with lower prices. On the other hand, setting a price below the benchmark might result in more units sold but will cause less profit per unit. In competitive markets, selling organizations have little control over their prices, which are mostly determined by supply and demand.

  One of the advantages of competitive pricing is that no complex calculations are required. Selling organizations follow the common market price or a price set by market leaders. In addition, in competitive markets, the burden of price-based marketing is lifted. However, other forms of marketing efforts might be needed.

The downside of competitive pricing is that when most competitors adopt roughly the same prices, price is no longer a differentiator. This means that organizations typically must make additional marketing efforts to attract customers. Additional marketing efforts might include aggressive advertising, better customer support, market saturation, and others.

- **Value-based pricing:** Value-based pricing is a pricing strategy wherein prices are based on the buyers' perceived value. Value-based pricing is a strategy that is often used by companies that offer unique or distinguishing products or services in comparison to competitors.

Value-based pricing is rarely used for commodity products but is more applicable for products and services such as attorney fees, architectural design, car customization, and other custom products and services. Another form of value-based pricing is to take a small percentage of the costs saved or extra profits made by the customer (e.g., a consultancy company taking 5% of the cost savings that a company gets after helping them with their Agile transformation).

The following example from Accountingverse illustrates value-based pricing:

*Mr. Davis wishes to have his car, a 1969 Cadillac Coupe, restored. It has been sitting in his barn for a while and rust has eaten most of its parts. He approaches KustomKars Company to do the job. Based on the value it would give the owner, the company quotes an all-in price of $30,000. Mr. Davis agrees to the price as he believes that it is a fair measure of the benefit he will receive.*

*KustomKars now must work within a budget and make sure that the total cost it will incur will be within $30,000 if it wishes to make a profit. If the company wishes to earn at least $2,000, then target costs must be set at up to $28,000. However, the satisfaction of the customer must not be sacrificed. The perceived value must be met.*[4]

---

4. https://www.accountingverse.com/managerial-accounting/pricing-decisions/value-based-pricing.html.

- **Price skimming:** With the price skimming strategy, selling companies set high prices after the initial launch of the product so that they can quickly recover a large part of the costs made and generate large profits quickly. Price skimming is a common strategy in technology markets, such as games, videos, mobile phones, gaming consoles, and laptops.

  The idea with price skimming is that once the upper-class market has been served (product units sold are decreasing), the price is lowered to also attract another target audience and increase the customer base. This is interesting for the groups of potential customers who were not able to afford the product or were not willing to pay the higher price after the initial launch. Price skimming results in a larger market share and continuous sales.

  The biggest advantage of price skimming is that the organization generates higher profits in the earlier stages of the product's lifecycle. This is useful because R&D and development costs for technology products are high. By setting high prices, these high expenses can be recovered quickly. Another benefit of high prices is that customers often associate high prices with high quality.

  The downside of price skimming is that organizations will limit their sales volume because prices may be too high for the majority of the potential market. Another disadvantage of this strategy is that when the prices are reduced, later customers might not be as happy as the initial group of people, who bought the new product right after the launch.

- **Penetration pricing:** Penetration pricing is the exact opposite of price skimming. With this strategy, the company first sets low prices for the new product, intending to quickly capture market share. The goal is to attract customers away from competitors by initially offering low(er) prices. After the product has been accepted and adopted by customers, and once it becomes an established brand in the market, prices may be increased. Many people are enticed by low(er) prices, and it is an incentive for many people and organizations to switch between suppliers.

The benefits of penetration pricing are typically a high volume of sales, getting many new customers quickly, and therefore quickly getting more market share. Another benefit of setting low prices is that possible startups will be discouraged to enter the market and current competitors may be forced to leave if they cannot keep up with low prices.

The downside of this pricing strategy is that the margins and revenues per product unit sold are quite low and might cause customers to question the quality of the product. Also, customers may not be willing to extend contracts or repeat purchases when the prices are increased.

## STEP 4: SELECTION AND SETTING OF PRICING TACTICS

Pricing tactics differ from pricing strategies in the sense that they are easier to change and can often be combined. Simply said, pricing tactics help you to communicate how you will support the pricing strategy, and it will help to improve pricing effectiveness. The ten most popular pricing tactics are as follows:

1. Charm pricing
2. Anchoring
3. Tiers
4. Bundle
5. Unbundle
6. Variable
7. Luxury
8. Dynamic
9. Personalized
10. Subscription

As you scan the tactics illustrated in Figure 13.4, you'll probably recognize most of them and that a combination of various tactics is used for your product.

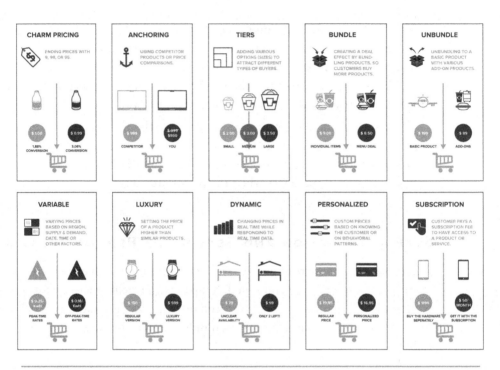

**Figure 13.4** The ten pricing tactics

## STEP 5: ADAPTATION OF PRICES, TOOLS, AND COMMUNICATING CHANGES

Many people don't realize that pricing is a process and that setting great prices may be complex at times. As illustrated in this chapter, setting prices for products and services is much more than picking a random number. Pricing doesn't end just after selecting the strategy, applying the tactics, and setting a number. Setting or changing prices often requires a lot of adaptation in the organization. Here are some examples of what is typically needed to set or change your products' prices:

- **Market communication:** Newly set or changed product and service prices need to be communicated to the market. Customers need to be made aware of price changes before the actual price change happens, which probably means communication to customers via a printed letter, digital newsletter, advertisements, or other forms of communication.

- **Internal communication:** Besides customer communication, your internal colleagues need to be aware of the price changes as well. For example, think of sales, account management, marketing, website, or web shop team, developers of calculation/quote tools, and so on. Your colleagues will probably need some time to process the price changes, so make sure to communicate this in time.

- **System changes and tools:** In most organizations, we use all kinds of tools and systems that help us to do pricing. For example, price calculation tools, price explanation tools, websites and web shops, invoicing software, financial systems, and more. Organizations use a lot of different tools; we've encountered some organizations that had up to 20 different finance-related tools, all of which were influenced by every price change made.

- **Market feedback on price:** When all the adaptation is done, the Pricing process still isn't over. This is when it starts all over again. Because the market might respond to your new prices in unexpected ways. Customers might start complaining about the new prices or maybe they even want to leave you and go to a competitor. Of course, it is a great idea to do price experiments. Don't wait for feedback from stakeholders and the market until all the work is already done and all communication and tools are adapted.

# THE VISIONARY

# SUMMARY

## KEY LEARNINGS AND INSIGHTS

This concludes Part III, in which you explored he Visionary stance. In this part, you learned about product vision and why it's so important to connect the product vision to the business strategy. You learned how to communicate that product vision effectively through the art of storytelling and why that approach is so powerful. You learned about creating Product Goals for your product, helping you to achieve strategic product objectives. You also explored how to visualize your Product Goals, product features, and Product Backlog items in various types of product roadmaps. You explored how to identify, express, and measure company value with Evidence-Based Management. Finally, you explored product pricing, learning about the product pricing process, various pricing strategies, and different pricing tactics to be used. To create winning products in the marketplace, Product Owners and product managers need to create and communicate a clear vision and strategy for the product's future. Many failing products and services are driven by (internal) stakeholder wishes, targets, and needs with complete disregard for whether those changes are what the product really needs. Winning products always solve a clear problem in the marketplace for a defined target audience.

In other words, Product Owners need to develop themselves into effective developers, communicators, and advocates of the product vision and strategy.

## QUICK QUIZ REVIEW

If you took the Quick Quiz at the beginning of Part III, compare your answers to those in the following table. Now that you have read about the Visionary stance, would you change any of your answers? Do you agree with the following answers?

| Statement | Agree | Disagree |
|---|---|---|
| A product vision should inspire customers, users, stakeholders, and Developers. Communicating the product vision through storytelling is a great practice for sharing memorable stories that inspire people. | ✓ | |
| A Product Owner should have multiple Product Goals that are to be achieved for the product. | | ✓ |
| There are many ways to visualize Product Backlogs, such as by creating product roadmaps tailored to the stakeholders' needs and organizational context. | ✓ | |
| A clear definition of how to identify, express, estimate, and measure value (e.g., with Evidence-Based Management) helps to increase autonomy and improve decision making. | ✓ | |
| The Scrum Master and Developers in Scrum are accountable for time to market and innovation. | | ✓ |
| A Product Owner is not, and should not be, responsible for a product's pricing. Product Owners don't need to influence or define the pricing strategies and tactics to be used. | | ✓ |
| Releasing Done products is the only way to deliver value and measure progress toward business goals, product vision, and strategy. | ✓ | |

# WANT TO LEARN MORE?

In this part, you learned about the Visionary Product Owner stance. Various topics, tools, techniques, and concepts will help you to strengthen your Visionary stance.

If you want to improve your Visionary stance, consider creating a Business Model Canvas, Lean Canvas, or Product Canvas as a start. In addition, create a couple of stories to be told, using the Pitch Canvas or 3×3 framework for storytelling.

If you want to learn more about the Visionary stance, consider reading one of these books: *Start with Why: How Great Leaders Inspire Everyone to Take Action* by Simon Sinek (Penguin, 2011), *The Product Samurai* by Chris Lukassen (2nd ed., Xebia B.V., 2018), or *The Evidence-Based Management Guide* (https://www.scrum.org/resources/evidence-based-management-guide).

# THE EXPERIMENTER

*The one test of innovation is the value it brings us, the result. Anything else is just . . . showing off.*

— IBM TV Ad

# Quick Quiz

To connect to Part IV, answer each of the following statements by checking the Agree or Disagree column. The answers are shared in the Part IV Summary.

| Statement | Agree | Disagree |
|---|---|---|
| New business models are always emerging as others fall out of fashion, never to be heard of again. | | |
| Experimentation is the only way to discover if your business model innovation is going to work. | | |
| Successful scaling of product development is achieved by applying a proven framework such as Nexus or LeSS. | | |
| A company is either innovative, or it isn't. A Product Owner can use little to no influence to promote innovation. | | |
| Making decisions around bundling or unbundling products is the responsibility of a Product Owner. | | |
| Product management responsibilities and tasks should be performed solely by the Product Owner. | | |
| The team of Developers should include skills such as sales, marketing, business analysis, design, and product management if required for the product. | | |
| The main question to be answered when it comes to scaling is, How do we organize all our people into teams? | | |

# DRIVING INSIDE-OUT PRODUCT INNOVATION

## INTRODUCING: THE EXPERIMENTER

A challenge of the digital age[1] is that enormous amounts of information are available to us. With so much knowledge and information at our fingertips, it is harder than ever to make the right decisions. What information should we use? What insights are useful? What insights are true? How do we separate the facts from assumptions and opinions? The overload of information isn't the only challenge, though. We must research, talk to, and empathize with customers; we must learn as much as we can to guide us toward the right steps and approach with our products. However, we can't be sure of taking the right steps if we base those steps solely on research and conversation. We must conduct experiments and validate our results.

Product Owners are frequently confronted by strong-minded stakeholders who might face a similar dilemma. Conversations between Product Owners and stakeholders regularly result in a battle of wills. One party tries to convince the other it is right only to be overthrown with facts, figures, big customer name dropping, or otherwise. Most Product Owners do not aspire to battles of will. Thus, they need ways to work around these situations.

---

1. The digital age is also referred to as *industry 4.0, information age,* or the *age of software.*

The Experimenter stance might be a way out. Taking this stance as a Product Owner helps you to acknowledge that you don't know everything but that you might know enough to define the right hypothesis, do experiments, and learn more.

Experimentation can be done in many ways, with various sources, approaches, tools, techniques, and results. In this chapter, you learn about various sources of innovation. How does innovation typically work in organizations? Experimenters are market data-driven, but where do you find that information? What conclusions might be drawn from that research? How can innovation be done around the business model? How should assumptions and hypotheses be tested? These are some of the questions we explore in this part of the book.

An unusual aspect of the Experimenter stance concerns scaling. Most people don't think about scaling and experimentation as a good combination. Most organizations take a process-driven approach to scaling. They tend to focus on the mechanics of making product teams work at a larger scale. They tend to focus on implementing a framework rather than learning about what works and what doesn't work. Scaling a product or scaling an organization introduces many new variables, such as dependencies in people, knowledge, skills, technology, order of things, and others. Rather than talking about scaling the process[2] via so-called scaling frameworks, this book focuses on how you might scale the product.

Following are some characteristics of great Experimenters:

- **Great innovators are brilliantly lazy.** It's like Bill Gates once said: "I choose a lazy person to do a hard job. Because a lazy person will find an easy way to do it." Gates could substitute "a lazy person" with "an innovative person" because great innovators will find the best and easiest way to get a project done. Many great innovators live by the saying, "Work smarter, not harder."

- **They pursue multiple options.** Elon Musk has Tesla, SpaceX, and SolarCity. Marcus Lemonis is chairman and CEO of Camping World, Good Sam Enterprises, Gander Outdoors, and The House Boardshop as well as an investor and shareholder in dozens of companies. What we can learn from their examples is that various interests overlap and feed off each

---

2. The book: The Nexus Framework for Scaling Scrum is a great resource for that.

other. Having multiple projects breaks the psychological bottleneck and pressure of succeeding in one single venture. It also expands your breadth of knowledge and overall business acumen.

- **They embrace paradoxical thinking and keep themselves updated.** A good experimenter never stops learning. And a great one would never remain uninformed about the discoveries and advances. Great innovators do not see the world in black and white. While many people come to either/or conclusions, they strive to see both/and. F. Scott Fitzgerald, a great American novelist, said it best: "The test of a first-rate intelligence is the ability to hold two opposing ideas in mind at the same time and still retain the ability to function."

Here are some positive outcomes and benefits that we observe when Product Owners take the Experimenter stance:

- **Improved productivity and reduced costs:** In many organizations, process innovation is about reducing costs. This might be achieved by improving the capacity and/or flexibility of the business to enable it to exploit economies of scale.

- **Better product and service quality:** By definition, high-quality products and services are more likely to meet customer and user needs. Assuming that these products and services are effectively marketed and sold, this should result in increased sales and high profits for the organization.

- **Building a larger product and services range:** A business with a single product or limited product range would almost certainly benefit from innovation. Having a broader range of products and services provides an opportunity for increased sales and bigger profits and reduces the risk for shareholders.

- **Innovation contributes to handling legal and environmental issues:** Innovation might enable the business to reduce its carbon emissions, produce less waste, or perhaps comply with changing product legislation. Changes in laws often force businesses to innovate when they might not otherwise do so.

- **More added value:** Effective innovation is a great way to establish a unique selling proposition (USP) for a product—something for which the customer is prepared to pay more and that helps a business differentiate itself from competitors.

- **Improved staff retention, motivation, and easier recruitment:** These improvements are not an obvious benefit, but they are often significant. Potential good-quality recruits are often drawn to a business with a reputation for innovation. Innovative businesses have a reputation for being inspiring places in which to work.

- **Increased chances of discovering the Next Big Thing:** When pursuing multiple options, running tons of experiments, and taking every stakeholder request as an assumption and hypothesis, we see that our chances of building the Next Big Thing increase.

Although there may be other benefits as well, regularly taking an Experimenter stance as a Product Owner will hopefully lead to improved time to market, time to learn, ability to innovate, and new ground-breaking products that boost revenues and have an amazing customer satisfaction score.

### An Enlightened Moment

Noa had been with World News for several weeks now. She found her way around the company and worked with most of the people. She loved the people. All in all, she was happy to be working for this news company, though most of her friends thought that it was a boring business.

The roadmap looks okay now, after some hard work and negotiating. Some concept goals for the rest of the year are identified, and an inspiring yet achievable Product Goal was defined. Although some good steps were taken, something just kept nagging in Noa's brain. It felt like something was missing. *I'd better get some coffee,* Noa thought.

Noa noticed Seiko, the Scrum Master, was in the coffee corner as well. While she inserted a Nespresso cup into the machine, a thought crossed her mind: "It's great coffee, Seiko, but the price of those cups is ridiculous. It must be at least twice as expensive as ground coffee."

He looked at her and smiled. "You realize it is an old product management trick, don't you?" His eyes twinkled. "Did you know the Standard Oil Company sold very affordable lighting lamps back in the 18th century? It created a continuous demand for its lamps."

*Seiko is probably right,* Noa thought. The coffee company has a similar business model to inkjet printers and bargain razors with replaceable blades. It occurred to her that many companies follow the same model to capture value. "Why are we using a subscription service model?" she asked Seiko. "I mean, there must be other ways to run our business, right? With the current approach, it feels like a race to the bottom price with all the other news companies. What if Nespresso was running our business? What would they do?"

Seiko looked a bit puzzled. "Sounds like a real Product Owner question to me!" he said, as he hastily exited the coffee corner.

"That's right, and I'm going to find the answer to it," Noa said to herself.

## INSIDE-OUT INNOVATION SOURCES

Most organizations recognize the need for innovation. However, when looking at the actual time spent on innovation, it seems like it doesn't get much priority. It's easy to say that innovation is important. It's easy to say that you need to work on innovation. However, it's just as easy to get lost in day-to-day activities. Trying to keep the product running smoothly can easily take up more time than you have available. Product Owners must set time apart for innovation. Time needs to be reserved for the growth and evolution of the product. If you don't prioritize innovation, stakeholders will assume that role and start steering the product for you.

There are two types of innovation: inside-out and outside-in. Both have their merits and drawbacks. Most organizations apply an inside-out approach that typically leads to sustaining innovation rather than radical innovation. So, where do you get your innovative ideas from when applying inside-out innovation? What are typical sources of innovation? In this chapter, we explore inside-out innovation and discuss various sources of ideas being sales, customer support, account management, R&D, executives, and the market.

### SALES

Salespeople can be a great source of innovative ideas. After all, they talk to customers all the time. Salespeople are usually aware of some of the latest developments in their customer segment or market, and they are often the first people to be confronted with changes in the competitive landscape. The sales team knows what customers ask for and can quickly learn if the offered quotes and proposals seem to match their needs.

It typically pays off to engage with sales early on in your role as a Product Owner. It also pays off to train and inform your sales colleagues about the product. What is the product vision? What are the goals and objectives? What is the high-level roadmap, the plan to deviate from? Also talk about the product's capabilities: What is it capable of, and what can it not do or be used for? A tool we've used for sales teams in the past is competitive battle cards. They are simple to use and make sales teams' lives easier while focusing the message on the direction you have in mind.

Salespeople have a front-row position regarding talking to customers. It's usual for salespeople to come up to a Product Owner with a special request such as, "Can we develop feature X for customer Y? All my big customers are telling me the competition performs better in Z. If we just develop this one feature for X, Y, Z, that will help us to do more business." Such ideas driven by sales are not necessarily bad ideas, but they tend to be fluid. Because salespeople are typically focused on closing a deal, they tend to skip over the long-term effects of a certain innovation or the impact of not doing something else. Great ideas can be derived from sales, but always consider the long-term impact on the product, its value, total cost of ownership, technical debt, and potential future maintenance.

## CUSTOMER SUPPORT

Customer support is another department that usually has short communication lines with Product Owners. It's unfortunate, though, that very few customers call customer support to congratulate the company on the amazing product that was delivered. Customers call more often to ask questions about the product, how to change something, how something works, and so forth. They're even more likely to call when something happens that they didn't expect or didn't like. With all these questions and complaints coming in, customer support is a great place for any Product Owner to spend a couple of days, especially when they are new to the product or new to the job. Listening in on customer support calls can be a very cleansing experience because you can learn what customers experience while using the product. Some calls may be about obvious mistakes on the company's part. Others might be more obscure or corner cases, but they remain your company's—and thereby, in some cases, your—responsibility to handle well.

Thus, collaborating closely with customer support is very helpful. However, you don't want to focus on the current version of the product only. Just fixing bugs, responding to questions, and solving complaints isn't maximization of value for the product, per se. It would lead to a very single-sided approach to "innovation." Customer support may suggest innovations such as this: "These are the top ten things customers hate about our product. When will we fix theme?" "Every time they do this, that thing happens." "Yeah, they call about that issue all the time—they just don't get it." "I've given up on reporting that issue in the system—that bug has been around for ages." Such questions and comments touch on the quality aspect of your product. Some of them may be about technical quality (does it work the way it was designed?), and some may be about product quality (does the customer appreciate the way it was designed?). Generally speaking, quality should not be compromised. Compromising on quality often has serious long-term impacts. Not compromising quality doesn't mean creating gold-plated solutions, though. The quality of the product (technical or functional) should be good enough. Voltaire said it well: "The best is the enemy of the good."[3]

## ACCOUNT MANAGEMENT

Account management is typically found in business-to-business (B2B) companies. In contrast to business-to-consumer (B2C) companies, not all customers are equal in a B2B company. It is quite common in B2B companies that 80% or more of the revenue is generated by three to five key customers. Losing such a customer or a souring relationship with such a customer can have a direct impact on the cash flow and liquidity of the organization.

---

3. Robert Watson-Watt, who developed early warning radar in Britain to counter the rapid growth of the Luftwaffe, propounded a "cult of the imperfect," which he stated as, "Give them the third best to go on with; the second best comes too late, the best never comes."

Account managers are aware of this. They know that their big clients are important to the company and its financial future. They are usually not afraid to wield that power within the organization. You may have been confronted with statements like the following yourself: "I know we have other customers, but this one is simply more important" or "That is not a direction that our top customers want to take." This is a difficult situation to deal with for many people. You don't want to be the person who might screw up the deal with this big customer, right? But you also don't want to be the person changing the product based on one customer's needs! It's a tough spot to be in, and an important choice must be made here: What kind of company does your company want to be? And how does that affect its products and services?

One option is to be a company that delivers generic products or services to customers. This setup means that every product is essentially the same. Perhaps there are some options to choose from or settings to adjust, but the base product is identical. An example of such a product is Trello. It's a simple tool for creating lists, such as a Product Backlog or Sprint Backlog. The tool allows you to adjust some settings or options, but Trello accounts and boards are (except for the contents) very similar. Designing, developing, and shipping standard, generic products make a lot of things simpler.

Another option is to tailor the product or service implementation to customer needs. Such products often come with a product implementation phase. Examples of such products include Jira, ProductBoard, and Aha! These tools are standard solutions but offer a huge range of options and possibilities in the implementation to tailor to customer needs. In essence, the software is the same, though.

The final option we discuss here is custom work. In this case, a customer usually pays for the development of a feature, functionality, or capability. This is a custom feature, solely for this one client. Such developments always seem nice up front. A big customer willing to pay big bucks for a feature often seems like easy money, especially for startups and scaleups. The effect of these choices, though, is that companies are often forced to maintain different versions of the product. This results in maintenance in multiple locations, bug fixing in multiple locations, reduced focus, not being able to sell the feature to other clients, and so on. Although it is a business model that allows for some quick cash in the short term, it's often harmful to products, time to market, and ability to innovate in the longer term.

## RESEARCH AND DEVELOPMENT

It seems like innovation is done more often and faster than ever. A huge number of innovations have come in the past 20 years. From the early days of the Internet to all the possibilities of today, innovation has swept through our lives at an incredible pace! Technology especially is evolving at a high pace, forming problems and challenges. Ask any front-end developer what development framework they favor, and their answer may vary before and after lunch. Okay, maybe that is an exaggeration, but the average lifecycle of a JavaScript framework, for example, is less than two years from peak adoption to decline. It means that there is always another way to solve the problem.

Combine these high-pace technology changes with the dynamics that occur when a product starts to take off. A fast-growing product often imposes scaling challenges, sometimes on architectures that weren't designed for such usage. The desire to rebuild or redesign a product often follows swiftly.

New technologies may offer new capabilities that allow the Product Owner to create a product to overtake the competition. Technology sometimes is a two-edged sword. That being said, new approaches, frameworks, technologies, hardware, software, models, data, and many other innovations are usually found in the R&D part of an organization. Building bridges and relationships with such teams may prove to be useful for a Product Owner. Learning about trends and new opportunities can be helpful if you want to boost your product's innovation.

## EXECUTIVES

Board members are often found in different circles than Product Owners. Executives often have additional roles, positions, or interests in other parties. It's not uncommon to be a board member of a company and chairman for a foundation, institution, or overarching industry initiative at the same time. Although these board members may be disconnected from the actual product development, they are often keen to know what is happening at the top of other companies. They often meet other board members in the industry and pick up on trends, innovations, and industry developments quickly. The result may be that a board member approaches Product Owners with a comment such as, "I hear company XYZ is moving their proposition to the cloud. We should do the same thing." This also happens quite often regarding startup culture, for example: "We should be more like company XYZ. We need the spirit of XYZ." Sometimes companies acquire startups to make the enterprise more innovative. Though the desire makes sense, it doesn't necessarily lead to a very effective way of changing the culture, innovation rate, or people.

## MARKET ANALYSTS

Some firms specialize in market analysis, trend analysis, and reporting or publishing. They discover what the industry is doing by talking to many people about a certain topic, specialty, or domain. They seek to identify where general trends are heading and who might be thought leaders in a particular domain. Such firms often have access to a wide array of companies, allowing them to take a broad view. Getting informed by such companies may be helpful if you want to identify patterns and trends in your industry.

Unfortunately, the articles and reports of information and trends are available to everyone (sometimes at a price). Think of companies like Gartner, Forrester, and McKinsey, for example. Gathering insights about the industry is useful. It's useful to know what your competitors are doing. However, perhaps moving in the same direction as everyone else isn't the best place for your company to be.

Imagine the market being like a pasture with cattle, as Figure 14.1 illustrates. The cows represent the organizations in your market. Each cow is looking for some tasty grass to eat, just as the companies are looking for potential customers to attract. Cattle are usually found together, in a herd. Suppose now that one cow (an innovator) becomes detached from the rest of the herd. At first, it might think, "Shouldn't I go where all the other cows are? Surely the grass must be greener there?" Well, it's not. You can imagine what the grass looks like after a herd of cows has trampled over it. The grass surely isn't better in a place where everyone else is, although it might look that way from a distance. Thus, a big mistake would be to engage in strategic herd behavior, following everyone else. This is a mistake, of course, only if your purpose is to be innovative.

**Figure 14.1** A lovely view of the market

# Driving Outside-In Product Innovation

## Outside-In Innovation Sources

The inside-out sources of innovation discussed in the previous chapter are useful, yet they tend to lead to incremental innovations. They generate enhancements or improvements to existing products. You might have been aware of some of those ideas already, and maybe some were generated by the various sources discussed. However, most of those ideas won't help you to launch disruptive new ideas, new cash cow products, or conquer the market. An outside-in approach to innovation is often better when chasing such objectives.

When taking an outside-in approach, you'll gather your knowledge, information, insights, data, and observations outside the walls of your company. Activities for gathering outside-in innovation ideas vary, but common practices include online market research, competitor analysis, customer interviews, customer panels, and focus group sessions. None of these examples involve talking to your internal colleagues only. Focus on listening to and observing people outside the company, customers, prospects, users, and competitors. How can you approach outside-in research? Which groups should you study? Let's explore these questions in this chapter, starting with market segmentation.

## MARKET SEGMENTATION

Market segmentation is the process of dividing a target market into smaller, more defined categories or segments. Market segmentation helps to group customers and audiences that share similar characteristics such as problems to solve, needs, demographics, interests, or locations. There are many elements and characteristics that can be used to identify market segments. Which elements to use depend on the product or service, the total market size, the rough size of each segment, and other factors. In general, it helps to identify various rather specific market segments, because it will help you and your teams and stakeholders understand the market better. Following are five commonly used methods of segmentation:

- **Demographic** segmentation is one of the most popular and commonly used types of market segmentation. It refers to statistical data about a group of people. Characteristics for B2C products often include biographical details such as age, gender, income range, living area, work area, goals, passions, marital status, and many others. For B2B products, characteristics often include company size, industry, number of products, type of products or services, distribution channels, et cetera.

- **Psychographic** segmentation categorizes audiences and customers by factors that relate to their personalities and characteristics. Examples of these factors include people's values, attitudes, interests, and lifestyles, as well as their conscious and unconscious beliefs.

- **Behavioral** segmentation focuses on people's behavior. In other words, it focuses on how the customer or user acts. Common characteristics include purchasing habits, user status, brand interactions, brand engagement, product engagement, average spend per purchase, and average product usage.

- **Geographic** segmentation categorizes customers based on geographic borders. For example, based on their zip code, country of residence, the climate they live in, or their country of origin.

- **Problems to solve** segmentation is a way of categorizing customers by considering their motivators. You might consider what it is that drives customers to do certain things. You might consider their key problems to be solved, their jobs to be done, their needs, and, therefore, what they are trying to achieve. Characteristics to consider include the various use cases they need, their satisfaction with a job to be done, or any alternatives they could employ to get to a solution for their problem.

Each approach offers you different insights into your current or potential customer or user base. Those insights will likely be of high value during the development and delivery of your products and services to the marketplace. The "problems to solve" approach is typically the most difficult approach for customer segmentation. However, it often delivers the most valuable insights. Let's look at an example.

*Let's say you want to create a golf ball as your product. Many brands in the market are perfectly capable of producing great golf balls. You don't want to start a race to the lowest price but deliver a high-quality product for a clear target audience. So, for whom could you design this product?*

*Will the product mostly be targeted towards men or women? What are the age bandwidths for this product? What kind of jobs do people in this target audience have? Where do they typically live? Some questions are often asked from a demographic segmentation approach. But will these insights prove to be valuable during the product's development? Will you be able to design a better golf ball knowing that a woman called Sally lives in the desert near Las Vegas, is 47 years old, and works in a casino? Maybe. . . .*

*It will be more useful, though, to know how often Sally plays golf. Does she play once a day, week, or month? Does she play in matches or just for fun with some friends? Does she want to improve her game, or just have some fun? What is her average swing speed? What shots does she struggle with most? Answers to these questions are likely more valuable than demographics.*

— Robbin

The answers to the problems to solve questions typically offer the most valuable insights and help to design a good product. You may remember "the five Ps" that make a viable product, which were introduced in Part II, "The Customer Representative." One of those Ps represents the pervasive market. This is your market segment. The market segment should be large enough to be worthwhile for your company to build the product. Defining and focusing on your market segment brings many advantages.

Knowing what problem to solve for customers not only allows you to develop a better product. It also helps deliver the right marketing message to potential customers. Generic, vague, or unrelated language for the broad public should be avoided. Instead, direct messaging can be applied. It should speak to the problems, needs, wants, and unique characteristics of your target audience.

Being specific about your value propositions and messaging also allows you to stand out from competitors. Instead of blending in with other brands, you can differentiate your brand by focusing on specific customer needs and characteristics. This distinct value and messaging leads to stronger bonds between brands and customers and creates lasting brand affinity.

Most of all, it will help you stay focused. There are many customer problems to solve in the world and targeting everyone usually means targeting no one. So, get to it, and identify the characteristics of your potential customers!

## PEOPLE WHO BOUGHT YOUR PRODUCT

Let's get back to the topic of gathering innovative ideas by using an outside-in approach. Once the market segment is identified, it becomes easier to find the people in it. Some people in this target segment are smart. These smart people realized that they had a problem, and they went out to find a solution for it. These people are the buyers and users of your product. (That's what makes them the smart ones, right?) Considering various options, they picked your product. This group of people, your customers, can offer insight. They have been using the product, potentially for some time already, so they can explain how well the product is solving their problem. Perhaps they can also explain their perspective on the buying process; and they might be able to tell you how they experienced product orientation, product selection, and product adoption. Acquiring their insights may be a great source of innovative ideas.

The people who went out and bought your product are easy to access. You may need to collaborate with sales, marketing, customer support, or account management, but ultimately these people are close. Customer support may have some insights about potential clients to learn from. Perhaps you can arrange an interview to find another way to make observations. Alternatively, you could do a win/loss analysis, simply by picking up the phone and calling a customer. What made this customer buy your product? What made them choose a competitor's product? What were the key arguments to make this decision? Such insights are valuable to have and can help you improve your product and drive innovation.

## PEOPLE WHO BOUGHT A COMPETITOR'S PRODUCT

Another part of your target segment can be found in the group of people who bought a solution from your competitor. These people are not as smart as the other group, but they are smart enough to realize they had a problem to solve. Typically, this group is more difficult to reach, because your competitors won't be happy about you talking to them. However, it's possible. These competitor customers might also not be interested at first, as they might worry that you'll try to restart the sales process. So, if you want to talk with them, make it clear that you are not there to sell them anything. Explain that your company has accepted the loss of this customer, but that you want to learn from them.

What we've often witnessed when working in B2B companies is that there are trade shows, events, and associations where many potential customers show up. Being present at such events is a great way for any Product Owner to learn more about customers. Positioning yourself strategically near the coffee counter can lead to great conversations and contacts to follow up on.

If you want potential customers to choose your product more often in the future, or if you want to acquire customers from your competitors, you should be aware of switching costs. People who use a competitor's product generally care about switching costs. They have a working solution to their product already, so why would they switch vendors? The fact that your product may have more features, better features, better usability, or a more scalable architecture won't likely convince them to switch. Ask iPhone users why they won't switch to Android and vice versa. Sure, some people have clear opinions and can't be convinced to switch anyway. However, a big group of people would probably say that the other brand doesn't deliver a bad phone, it's just such a hassle to move your pictures, contacts, apps, and other stuff over between brands. In other words, the costs of switching are too much to even consider.

## PEOPLE WHO HAVEN'T BOUGHT A SOLUTION

Moving on to the last group: What about the people who haven't bought a solution yet? There are two categories within this group. The first group is (actively or passively) looking for a solution. They are aware that they have a problem, they are looking around for a solution, but they just haven't decided on a solution yet. Hopefully, they are talking to your colleagues in sales, which is also the best entry you have to this group. So, set up a meeting with sales to talk about their prospects and suspects. Seek to learn what drives these potential customers. What options are they considering? What factors do they weigh? Obtaining such insights may lead to a different kind of innovation.

The second group without a solution is a group of people who are not aware that they have a problem yet. This is a group for whom your product marketing becomes important. Since they don't realize they have a problem, they need to learn that they do. You can't reach this group by telling them how fantastic your product is. It won't help much to talk about the fancy features it offers, nor will it help to offer them a big discount if they order today. What will help is to explain the symptoms of the problems they might experience. It might help to visualize some of these problems and their effects. Customers tend to recognize these symptoms. Segmenting your market by the problems that your product solves will offer focus to you, your stakeholders, and your teams. It will help you to talk to the right groups of people to learn from them. The insights gathered will drive outside-in innovation, rather than inside-out innovation, and some great, new, and disruptive ideas might emerge.

# THINKING DIFFERENTLY: DRIVING BUSINESS MODEL INNOVATION

Apple is widely regarded as an innovative company. They seem to have the ability to go against what is common in the market, yet desirable to a large audience. In business, success is not guaranteed, and many disruptive ideas die quickly or never lift off. However, placing some bets now and then might lead to big wins and big rewards in comparison to sticking to business as usual. So, might it help to think differently sometimes? What would thinking differently look like for a Product Owner?

## MARKET ANALYSIS AND TRENDS

The last chapter covered how market segmentation can be useful for gathering innovative ideas from potential customers. However, it's not useful for only that purpose. Establishing a clear market segmentation can also be useful when doing market research, or desk research. Consider collecting data and trends about the market, for example. Is the market growing or declining? What are some trends in the market? Where is the market evolving over the next few years? What are some customers or competitors to watch? Such insights may help you to drive the product.

But where should you start? What are good sources for analyzing the market? What are good sources for finding those trends? This depends on the industry you're in. There are various sources to use to learn more about the automotive industry, chip manufacturing, jewelry, software development, and other industries. You or your colleagues in marketing or sales are probably aware of some of those sources.

In general, if you work in the United States, census.gov provides a good starting point for data collection. If you work in the European Union, Eurostat and worldwide Statista are some great public sources of data. For the case study created for the Professional Scrum Product Owner–Advanced training course, we used Pew Research, journalism.org, and Reuters to get some ideas about what is happening in the newspaper industry.

These resources can be overwhelming at first. It may be difficult to use them effectively, and you'll need to learn what to look for. Many factors influence market trends, but as a rule of thumb, Table 16.1 shows some aspects to consider.

**Table 16.1** Market Research and Analysis Aspects to Consider

| Political | Economic | Social | Cultural |
| --- | --- | --- | --- |
| Technological | Legal | Environmental | Demographic |

Market trends may serve as a leading indicator for how demand for your product will develop over time, and where potential opportunities are. A product manager of an A-SMGCS[1] product (a product that allows airports to keep their runways and taxiways open when visibility is low) noticed that it was becoming more difficult to attract new clients. Potential suppliers often influenced sales success by being willing to listen carefully and to define the requirements for the system.

So, the question that emerged was, How could they get there first? Some of the data this product manager analyzed included the number of flight movements per airport and the number of runways and taxiways. Based on the

---

1. Advanced Surface Movement Guidance and Control System.

growth figures, a fair prediction of runway utilization could be created. However, this data didn't offer insights into how often the low visibility problem occurred or whether it would be a worthwhile problem to solve.

The next step was therefore to combine the location data of the airports with historical weather data. This helped to identify which airports would suffer the most from low visibility weather. Then forecasted growth, in-flight movements, and potential extra days open during low visibility weather were added to the mix. Analyzing such data helped this product manager to make an accurate prediction of where to direct their marketing and sales efforts. Of course, it's not a guarantee that you'll win each of those customers for your product, but it helps you find customers who may benefit from your product the most.

## GETTING INSPIRATION FROM OTHER COMPANIES

In 2013, St. Gallen University published the results of a study[2] on the categorization of business models. They identified 55 different ways for businesses to capture value from the market. In essence, the value that every product or service creates for the company can be captured by applying one of these business models. Popularity and application of the various models change across time and industry. Some models were extremely popular in the past, others are extremely popular in the present. Think of a subscription model, for example. (It seems like almost every company does subscriptions nowadays!)

STIHL is a good example. STIHL is a chainsaw and outdoor power equipment manufacturer. The company started a rental service, allowing people to rent equipment rather than own it. The company was heralded as exceptionally innovative, and that's probably true, but its business model is not so different from that of other companies: Xerox rents out photocopiers, Redbox rents out films, and Europcar rents out vehicles.

---

2. Oliver Gassmann, Karolin Frankenberger, and Michaela Csik, "The St. Gallen Business Model Navigator," working paper, University of St. Gallen, 2013, www.thegeniusworks.com/wp-content/uploads/2017/06/St-Gallen-Business-Model-Innovation-Paper.pdf.

Doing the same thing that the market leader in an industry does is not likely the most profitable approach to running a business. Although it varies across industries, it is usually the top three players that capture most of a market's value, and it's a tough fight in the remaining bits. What might be more useful than looking at your biggest competitor is to look at other companies outside your industry. What could you learn from successful company X, which operates in a different industry? It could be useful to ask yourself this question, especially in the following situations:

- In a rapidly expanding market, you could try to follow the market leader. In this case, you are trying to learn from the big competitors. Questions to ask in this case include, What is common in our industry? and How does company X capture value from the market?

  Videoland, for example, is a video streaming service in the Netherlands. The company considered both Netflix's flat fee business model and YouTube's advertising business model, to evolve its own business model, pricing, and content strategy.

- In a more saturated market, with strong incumbents, a different approach could (or should) be applied. Ask yourself the same question as before: What can we learn from X? However, X in this case relates to a company that is not present in your industry. It is not your big competitor. Consider that, while Xerox, Redbox, and Europcar make different kinds of products, their business models are quite similar.

  The idea of looking at totally different businesses and industries is often frowned upon by Product Owners because the industries are so dissimilar. There are, however, a finite number of business models available, and drawing inspiration from other business models may lead to interesting results and innovations.

  An enterprise steel manufacturer produces large rolls of steel that it sells to various industries. Its customers process the materials into semi-finished products for other industries. This steel manufacturer has rarely changed its way of doing business since the company was founded 70 years ago. When it was confronted with different approaches to running the business, its leaders first laughed at the idea that there might be something to gain.

However, they decided to move forward and asked themselves the questions: What if . . .

- . . . the board of McDonald's ran our factory?
- . . . Amazon Web Services created our pricing sheet?

These seemed crazy questions at first. After all, what can a steel manufacturer learn from a fast-food company? Well, for starters, the typical onboarding time for employees at McDonald's is only a couple of hours[3] before they start flipping burgers. This is not because the job is simple but because the company focused on onboarding employees quickly. The onboarding time at the steel manufacturer was quite different, though. Improving its onboarding process, especially for jobs with a high turnover, would improve its business results.

Amazon applies a pay-per-use model for some of its services, which was another source of inspiration for the steel manufacturer. The company's leaders decided to run some experiments with this alternative business model. What they learned is that customers were unhappy with all the waste created by their own processes when punching and cutting the rolls of steel. Customers were willing to pay a higher price if they were charged only for the material they used and not for the waste materials. They also wanted the steel manufacturer to take back the waste created by the customers. This was a win for both parties because the "waste" was a very high-quality resource. The steel manufacturer could turn this waste into rolls of steel with far less effort than required to turn raw materials into rolls of steel.

The most important finding was that the company solved an unidentified and unmet need for its customers. It learned that taking inspiration from other business models could set the company apart in the market.

So, what are these 55 business models? What principles are they based on? And what does it all mean? Rather than copy the entire research paper by St. Gallen, we list a sampling of frequently used business models from well-known companies in Table 16.2. If you want to learn more about all of them, look up "The St. Gallen Business Model Navigator" online (see footnote 2).

---

3. This depends strongly on the role.

**Table 16.2** Business Models for Your Inspiration

| Company | Principle | Explanation |
| --- | --- | --- |
| SAP | Add-on | Core offering is competitively priced, but add-ons and the capability for customers to tailor product to specific needs increase the price |
| Amazon | Affiliation | Support others selling their products in return for a fee-per-sale. Enables customers to reach a larger assortment of potential customers |
| Nintendo | Judo | Offering is the exact opposite of what is common in the industry: it attracts new users and is hard to copy due to inertia |
| eBay | Auction | Sell at highest acceptable price |
| Groupon | Liquidity | Customer pays upfront, minimizing risk and working capital |
| Tchibo | Cross-sell | Additional revenue from added products/services that integrate with the core product but do not compete directly |
| Marillion | Crowdfund | Use up-front, crowdsourced funding to kick-start ideas |
| American Airlines | Loyalty | Retain customers through incentive-based programs |
| Survey Monkey | Digitization | Turn existing products into a digital variant |
| Dollar Shave Club | Direct selling | Skip the middleman and sell directly to customer |
| Starbucks | Experience selling | Value of product is enhanced by the experience that surrounds it. Raising customer experience and prices |
| Netflix | Flat rate | Customer pays one fee for "all-you-can-eat" rather than per-usage rate. Customer does not own the product |
| Skype | Freemium | Basic version that is free drives users to the premium version |
| Toyota | Just in time | Build to specification after order. Affects entire supply chain |

| Company | Principle | Explanation |
|---------|-----------|-------------|
| Google | Customer is product | Provide a free service and make users' data the product |
| ARM | License IP | Develop intellectual property but rely on a third party to produce products with it |
| LEGO | Vendor lock | Initial purchase locks user in an ecosystem that is hard to escape |
| Easy Jet | No frills | Offer the basics to compete at the lowest price |
| RedHat | Open source | Provide the product for free, earn money on consulting and supporting the product |
| Cars2Go | Pay per use | Pay only for what is used; though pricier per usage, attracts those who strongly object to waste |
| Rolls-Royce | Performance-based | Value is captured by the performance or outcome that is created for the customer; sometimes the product remains the property of the supplier |
| Gillette | Cross finance | Basic product is (nearly) free but creates the demand for a constant supply of consumables |
| Xerox | Rent vs. buy | Customer rents the product, reducing price to the renting period but at a higher rate |
| Nokia | Reverse innovation | Simple and inexpensive products targeting emerging mass markets |
| IKEA | Self-service | Co-creation with customer allows lower prices and increases the perceived value of the product |
| Best Buy | Supermarket | A large assortment of low-price goods allows customer freedom of choice and reduces shopping time |
| Quirky | User designed | Allow user to co-create/design the product |
| Foxconn | White label | Allow multiple vendors to brand and sell your product for you, creating economies of scale |

Source: Adapted from Oliver Gassmann, Karolin Frankenberger, and Michaela Csik, "The St. Gallen Business Model Navigator," working paper, University of St. Gallen, 2013, www.thegeniusworks.com/wp-content/uploads/2017/06/St-Gallen-Business-Model-Innovation-Paper.pdf.

# THE IMPACT ON YOUR BUSINESS

Congratulations! We're assuming that you have found a market problem worth solving, you have gauged its size using market analysis, and you have drawn inspiration from other companies. It sounds like you're all set, and it's time for implementation, right? Well, one of the key reasons that Product Owners taking the Experimenter stance are often frustrated in their job is that they didn't account for potential organizational inertia. You may remember the following from your physics class. It describes Newton's first law of motion:

> An object at rest stays at rest, and an object in motion stays in motion with the same speed and the same direction unless acted upon by an unbalanced force.

The property of remaining at rest or in motion is what we know as inertia. This basic law of physics can also be used to describe the behavior of people and organizations.

Inertia exists in all organizations. When being asked why they are doing things or why they are doing things in a certain way, people often respond with a variation of, "We have always done it that way." When alternatives to a small but improvable inefficiency are proposed, the response that follows is typically something like, "It's just how we do things here." The organization and its people have grown attached to these routines and habits. Any external force that pushes it to change can provoke a contrary reaction. This phenomenon is well known, especially by change agents (like a Scrum Master or Agile Coach), and is also described by Newton in his third law of motion:

> For every action, there is an equal and opposite reaction.

This is also known as action-reaction, meaning that the mutual actions of two bodies are always equal and directed in the opposite direction. These two laws of motion also reflect two human tendencies: One, we don't like to change because it is often painful, unpleasant, or costs energy. Two, when we are forced to change, we resist. Now, why is all this useful? Well, with all your acquired insights and observations from customers and the market, you may feel the need or desire to change things around. So, let's look at business model innovation in the next section.

## THE RETURN OF THE BUSINESS MODEL CANVAS

In Chapter 13, "Maximizing Value through Effective Pricing Strategies and Tactics," the Business Model Canvas was briefly introduced to capture the product vision and strategy. It is a tool that facilitates good conversations about a product because it captures all business aspects of the product you envision, but it can also do that for the existing business.

If or when you decide to join a new company, or when you start managing a different product within your company, it is a good practice to create a business model canvas in that situation. It will help you to get a better understanding of the product, the company, the business model, and some key stakeholders or partners, for example. By talking to people about the canvas you created, you'll be able to validate assumptions, test your ideas, learn if you understand the product well, and it may also reveal some differences of opinion.

Another useful endeavor would be to host a business model innovation workshop with stakeholders, in which the Business Model Canvas will prove to be useful. This workshop helps you to identify new ideas and potential changes to the product, for example, by getting inspiration from other companies.

The availability of people and resources is limited. You won't be able to deliver on all ideas. If you want to do work in one area, it means not doing work in another area. Performing work on the ideas gathered from the business model innovation workshop will have an impact on the value proposition for customers. It might impact the value delivered. It might impact how we get the product in their hands (channels or distribution). It might impact our relationship with customers. It could even mean stopping to serve one market segment in favor of another. The key activities we do to create value may change, as may our assets and resources. Alliances and partnerships may shift, as may our cost and revenue streams. Overall, many elements of the

Business Model Canvas may change when considering innovation. Isn't it great that the Business Model Canvas can help you to identify those potential changes, and some potential first experiments to run?

If you want to make big changes, you'll need to overcome big organizational inertia. Although it may feel that way sometimes, organizational inertia is not necessarily a bad thing. It's also a way for the system, the organization, and its people to protect themselves from harm. However, if you want to make some changes, it's probably a good idea to take it slowly. Take small steps. Do small experiments. Let people experience the change. Allow them to see and experience the results. Rather than telling people what to do, show them the way forward. Explain the need to change. Explain what might happen if we do not change. But also, be open to their reaction. After all, so far all you have is an informed assumption. All you have are ideas. Remember that value is only created when something is put in the hands of the customer. So, how do you move forward? Well, it's time for experimentation!

# SELECTING PRODUCT EXPERIMENTS TO RUN

## THE TRUTH CURVE: SELECT THE RIGHT EXPERIMENTS AND TESTS

Language is difficult. We often find people struggling to explain the words *assumption* and *hypothesis* and especially explaining the difference between the two. Some languages simply lack distinct words to indicate the subtle difference between them. In many organizations, these concepts are from outer space. When talking about assumptions, we refer to something we implicitly *assume* to be true. An assumption is a thing that is accepted as true or as certain to happen, without having the proof for it. It can be anything from expected customer behaviors to product performance to the optimal pricing strategy, to the color of the product, its interface, the time people spent using the product, and so forth.

When you start thinking about it, you'll likely find that your product contains many assumptions. Some are easier than others to validate and are based on common sense or general acceptance. Thus, not all assumptions need to be tested. Some assumptions carry little to no risk or offer low value if validated. So, why consider these assumptions? Some assumptions offer high value and have little risk; these are the ones you can just build. Another group contains high value and high-risk assumptions. These assumptions are the ones that should be tested explicitly because they can have a major impact on the product. To validate assumptions, you can formulate a hypothesis.

A hypothesis can be defined as a supposition or proposed explanation made on the basis of limited evidence as a starting point for further investigation. A hypothesis forms a basis for reasoning by stating what it is that we assume. It allows room for discussion on how the assumptions will be tested, how much that testing would likely cost, and how success will be defined. Hypotheses are typically defined in a hypothesis statement, meaning that a hypothesis is explicit and can be communicated and discussed.

What do Google Glass, Apple Newton, Harley-Davidson Perfume, and Ford Edsel have in common? Well, all were built with a lot of assumptions and ultimately failed. So how can we avoid spending a lot of money on building something that nobody wants? Well, the so-called truth curve comes to the rescue! Giff Constable created the truth curve model for the Qcon Software Development Conference, back in 2013. It is a helpful model for making informed (time and/or monetary) investments in product development.

Let's start with an idea because all great products start with an idea, an idea that typically contains a ton of assumptions. Let's see how the truth curve model can help (see Figure 17.1).

The X-axis expresses your product sophistication, or rather, how much time and money you are spending on product development. A variety of experiments, work, minimum viable products (MVPs), and other activities can be conducted to grow the product over time. The closer you are to the left side of the graph, the less effort those activities will cost. For example, conducting an interview or doing observations costs several hours to several days. As you move to the right side of the graph, building Wizard of Oz MVPs or a product that's ready for production, for example, the costs will run into weeks, months, or years. When working on a new product, you'll want to learn quickly. If you aren't learning fast, you may be residing in a fantasy land, and most of the things you do should be considered as assumptions, with a good dose of skepticism.

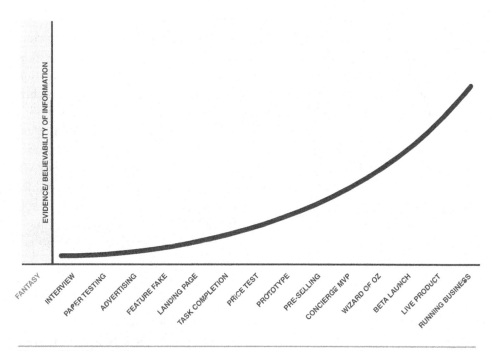

**Figure 17.1** The truth curve

The Y-axis illustrates the amount of evidence that was gathered. The Y-axis represents how much you can believe your learnings, considering that these are probably filtered through your judgment and vision. The only way to know for sure that a product will become a success is by putting it out in the market and measuring relevant product metrics. You still need qualitative research, of course, to understand why things are happening, but the quantitative metrics reflect reality.

To learn and validate fast, you could start with qualitative customer development by running lightweight experiments such as paper prototype tests, landing pages, pre-selling, concierge MVP, or Wizard of Oz tests. We'll explain these later. For now, just remember to start with low-effort experiments.

Different types of experiments also generate different levels of believability. In other words, they produce different levels of evidence about the product. The more *experiential* the test (e.g., observing customer behavior during the experience with the product), the more the results are trusted to be true and representative. Conversely, the earlier (the more to the left) your product resides in the truth curve, the more you will need to filter observations and learnings before drawing conclusions. You may have noticed that some of the early tests on the left side of the graph are not so much focused on how to build the product as on identifying whether a product should be built at all. In other words, the left side focuses on the problem space and problem validation. The right side focuses on the product space and validating product-market fit. Another perspective to consider is that running experiments will help you to test the assumptions behind the 5 Ps that make a viable product. (Remember? The 5 Ps are Problem, Pervasiveness, Positioning, Pay, and Possible.) Once you have validated the 5 Ps through various experiments, you may want to move forward and learn how to build the product and how much technology is needed.

*Perhaps a bit overfocused on the technology, I once told a team: "Just make the site incredibly fast, resilient, and scalable, since the old site is falling apart when we have too many customers." After a couple of Sprints, one of the team members talked about how excited he was about the technology they were using. They had applied a similar architecture as LinkedIn, resulting in a solution that ran in failsafe configuration spread out over three countries and could scale up to millions of users. The product was a web shop that had about 2 million visitors per month; LinkedIn had 1.2 billion.*

*— Chris*

Matthew Godfrey provided a different perspective for the truth curve (see Figure 17.2): he created an alternative scale for the Y-axis. This perspective asks, How much are you willing to bet on the success of your product? Are you willing to bet today's lunch on it? What about a day's pay? Your car? Or house, perhaps? How sure are you? So, the next time you are "gambling" with company money, ask yourself these questions. And start thinking more about placing small bets instead of big ones, because you will lose some of them for sure.

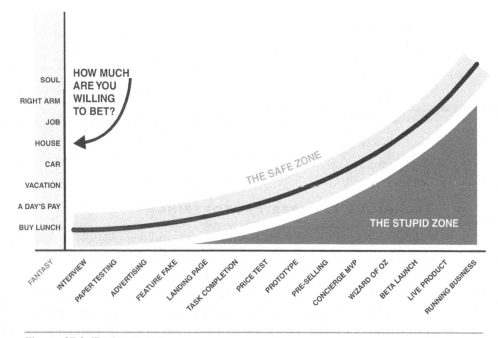

**Figure 17.2** Thinking in bets

## EXPERIMENTATION TECHNIQUES EXPLAINED

There are many great resources on experimentation and evaluation of results. In this book, we explore seven different types of experiments you may want to try. This should help you to know enough about them to make a good start yet leave enough room to dive into them in more depth, using more specialized resources. We find it particularly valuable to have people with strong user experience (UX) skills on your teams. They usually have more knowledge about and experience in experimentation than we as product managers have, and it also allows you to delegate the work related to running experiments to your teams. If you don't have any UX people available in the company, then you probably need to do some of this work as a product person. Without further delay, let's explore the following experimentation techniques in more detail:

1. Paper prototyping

2. Preorder page

3. Explainer videos

4. Landing pages

5. Feature fake

6. Concierge MVP

7. Wizard of Oz

## TECHNIQUE 1: PAPER PROTOTYPING

Paper prototyping allows you to create, use, and test possible designs or solutions quickly and in cost-effective ways. The product or user interface is sketched out using several sheets of paper and a marker, as shown in Figure 17.3. Potential customers can interact with the product by "pressing" the paper representations of buttons, menu items, and so on. Depending on their interactions, they are given the next sheet of paper representing the next step in the process (e.g., next screen in a user interface).

Questions such as, What stands out to you? What would you do on this screen? and What other things would you expect? can reveal assumptions that were made about the product and its design without the need to build a fancy, fully featured version of the product. Paper prototyping is ideal for testing the flow of an application and the interactions with and responses to the product.

**Figure 17.3** Paper prototyping example

## TECHNIQUE 2: PREORDER PAGE

A preorder page, as shown in Figure 17.4, allows people to sign up for a product or service before its official or public launch, allowing companies to gauge interest among potential customers. Using preorder pages, you can test whether customers can find your product by recognizing the problem it aims to solve and whether they are interested enough to order the product before it has even been launched.

In 2019, Tesla presented a new model car and received over 150,000 preorders. Many people paid deposits to get their hands on one of the first cars being produced. This is a great way to test the desirability of a new product. This concept is also widely adopted in the gaming industry. Large companies such as Ubisoft, Electronic Arts, Microsoft, and Sony announce their new products months before launch and allow people to preorder their new games and consoles.

**Figure 17.4** A simple preorder page

## TECHNIQUE 3: EXPLAINER VIDEOS

Explainer videos are an experimentation technique whereby a company explains how a product or service works (see Figure 17.5). The product doesn't have to be fully functioning at the time the video is released. A well-known company that used explainer videos effectively is Dropbox, the file-sharing service that we all know and love. In the early days of Dropbox, it was not always that easy for the company to find customers and investors.

Various ways for sharing files across different computers and with other people already existed when Dropbox was founded. FTP services were popular, for example, although they frequently corrupted your files if you forgot to set the bin flag. Another alternative was Microsoft SharePoint, but it didn't function very well at the time. So, there were some options, and many people had accepted the status quo. File sharing was a complicated product.

Dropbox therefore released on YouTube an explainer video in which company founder Drew Houston explained the product for new users. He showed how easy it was to install and set up the product and to sync files, and people got hooked right away. The Dropbox explainer video showed how magical the Dropbox experience was and how a user could instantaneously make a change on one computer and then see it reflected directly online. Dropbox saw its beta product waiting list grow from 5,000 people to 75,000 people overnight.

**VIDEO TUTORIALS**

**Figure 17.5** Dropbox is a well-known example of a company that applied explainer videos to validate assumptions.

## TECHNIQUE 4: LANDING PAGES

A landing page experiment can be seen as a simple one-pager for your product (idea). The landing page provides an overview of the problem to solve, the product's unique value proposition, perhaps various key features, a call to action, and a conversion mechanism. An example landing page is shown in Figure 17.6.

As discussed earlier, preorder pages are used primarily to sell a product. Landing pages, on the other hand, are often used for testing and validating interest in the market. Landing pages can also be used as preorder pages, but in digital marketing, a landing page is often used as a standalone web page, allowing a company to build a marketing funnel of potential customers. It is often created specifically for a marketing or advertising campaign. A landing page is often the place where a visitor "lands" if they click on a link in an email or if they click on ads on the Internet.

**Figure 17.6** Example landing page

If your product is training, for example, then having a landing page could provide a high-level overview of the training. It could also offer links to additional information around the topic, such as blogs, webinars, videos, and audio podcasts. We used this type of experiment in 2019 when we launched the Professional Scrum Product Owner-Advanced course. It was a simple one-page website containing course information, a brochure, upcoming training dates, and a short video. This allowed us to gauge interest in the market and to find some early adopters for the training product.

## TECHNIQUE 5: FEATURE FAKE

Feature fake experiments, also known as "fake door testing" (see Figure 17.7), offer users the illusion of a feature to test customer interest before the feature is actually developed. Users click on a button or link, but the link leads to a dead end. Clicking on the fake feature is like opening a door and finding just a wall on the other side. The feature fake technique is a simple experiment to test ideas. It is often used in existing products or services.

**Figure 17.7** A feature fake or fake door experiment shows a way, but the way leads nowhere.

The Bank of America, for example, used this technique to test whether customers would use its mobile app to report lost credit cards. The company added a "Report your lost credit card" link in its mobile app. When users clicked the link, they got a pop-up explaining that it wasn't possible yet to report a lost credit card via the app. Instead, they could click on a phone number in the pop-up to reach customer support directly. Fortunately, this fake feature made it easier for customers to contact the bank, and Bank of America was able to capture data to see how often this feature would be used and whether it was worth building the feature out to a fully in-app experience.

Of course, you don't want your product to be full of feature fakes—that would make it very annoying to use. But starting small and testing ideas this way might be very helpful. When you start using feature fakes, make sure to track usage and to capture and analyze the data. And don't send your users on a wild goose chase—provide them a way out (as Bank of America did by including a phone number on the pop-up).

When we developed a new e-commerce platform for a customer, we found that we could not implement all the payment methods at the same time. We needed to make decisions on what to build now and what to build later. We decided to feature-fake the credit card payment option but offered customers some alternative payment options instead. In the platform, we tracked how often various payment methods were clicked and used, so we were able to present actual usage data and missed order basket value during the next Sprint Review. Tracking this data allowed us to measure the interest in alternative payment methods and allowed us to express their value in money when deciding on the next steps.

## TECHNIQUE 6: CONCIERGE MVP

A concierge MVP experiment (see Figure 17.8) involves manually helping your users to accomplish their goals. It's an experimentation technique used as a means of validating whether users need an offering. All the features and functionalities in a concierge MVP are carried out manually. You aren't building the product in this experiment but rather faking it through human interaction and human support.

**Figure 17.8** Sometimes working with a spreadsheet or calculator is sufficient to validate ideas and assumptions

A well-known example of this technique was used in the early days of a company called Food on the Table. This company, founded by Manuel Rosso, delivers a product that specializes in generating a shopping list, which is tailored to an individual's needs and preferences. When the company was founded, Manuel didn't even have a product or website. He just sold his service in person to shoppers for $10 a month. Through these interactions, he created the recipes and grocery lists for his customers while accompanying them around the store.

Notice that all the work done in this example is manual labor. There is no product or automation of work in this experiment. So, a disadvantage of this experiment is obviously that it doesn't scale very well. The product will still need to be built at some point, to make it more scalable, effective, and efficient. However, this is a great experimentation technique to do a lot of learning before building the product. In addition, because the concierge service is a personal service delivered by an individual, the results of the experiment could be biased by the likability of the concierge.

Some big advantages are that you have direct interaction with your (potential) customers and users. Manuel, for example, learned a lot about how his grocery list service could incorporate allergies, diet preferences, and health targets by creating lists and sharing them in person with customers. Another advantage is that you can delay spending a lot of money on building the product until you've done some proper problem, market, and product validation.

## TECHNIQUE 7: WIZARD OF OZ

If you haven't seen the movie *The Wizard of Oz*, this is your spoiler alert!

It turns out that the wizard is an old man who pulls levers behind a curtain, and the big scary green head is just an illusion.

Much like the illusion in the movie, the Wizard of Oz MVP offers the impression that your product or service is fully functioning on the outside. Customers and users won't know or experience that most of the work in the back is done manually, by people. Wizard of Oz experiments help you to learn how to best provide a service, without building most of it.

A classic Wizard of Oz example is found in Zappos (see Figure 17.9). Although it was acquired by Amazon for $1.2 billion in 2009, Zappos started on a very different level. Company founder Nick Swinmurn decided to test his assumption that people would be willing to buy shoes online without trying them on first. To test this idea, he went to various local shoe stores, photographed their shoes, and then advertised them online. Once people ordered a pair of shoes via his website, Swinmurn returned to the store where he photographed the shoes, bought them, and then shipped them to his customers. Customers had no idea, however, that Swinmurn did not have a single pair of shoes in stock or that all orders were processed manually.

**Figure 17.9** Zappos is well known for applying a Wizard of Oz experiment approach.

From the outside, this MVP looked like a fully functional system, but all the tasks that automated systems should have been doing were being completed by a human. There are several advantages to the Wizard of Oz MVP approach. It's much cheaper to mimic a functioning system by paying humans to do the work behind the scenes than to build a fully functioning system. In addition, it is possible to learn more quickly how the system should behave. A disadvantage of this experiment is that it requires humans to do the work behind the scenes. This might be more costly in the short term and isn't very scalable, but it's a great way to validate product and service ideas.

# How to Design
## and Evaluate
## Experiments
## and Tests

Experimentation and validation of ideas and assumptions are important. However, there is a risk of taking it a step too far. In some teams, before you know it, everything has become an experiment. Just running a bunch of experiments doesn't create value. Making everything an experiment might be as bad as just building everything and hoping for the best. So, there are a couple of things to consider before starting an experiment so that you can learn from it.

Eric Ries introduced the term *innovation accounting* to explain that running experiments is not just about doing the work but also about accounting for their results. Product Owners are accountable for maximizing value. Experiments can help you to create value by eliminating risk. So, why wouldn't you define up front what risk it is that you are trying to mitigate, and why wouldn't you keep track of what you have mitigated and learned so far?

## DEFINING HYPOTHESIS

Strategyzer is a company focused on training and consulting, especially in the domains of business modeling, value proposition design, and testing business ideas. It created a handy template to capture the essence of an experiment or test. Although there are other tools, templates, and techniques available, we find the Test Card to be a valuable tool.

Hypotheses like the Strategyzer Test Card (see Figure 18.1) often start with an assumption, something you believe to be true. This belief should cover a certain persona, or target audience, which will display certain behaviors and yield specific results. Note that behaviors can usually be observed, and thus can be measured and counted.

A typical description in step 1 of the Test Card is therefore something like this:

> *We believe that <persona> will <display certain behavior>, to achieve <reason/need>.*

Step 2 in the Test Card describes the experiment to run. Based on your hypothesis and beliefs, you'll want to run a specific experiment. This experiment can be almost anything but think about the different experimentation techniques listed in Chapter 17, "Selecting Product Experiments to Run," for starters. When selecting the right experiment, think back to the truth curve discussed in the same chapter. You'll want to select an experiment that aligns with your current level of evidence. In other words, be careful building minimum viable products (MVPs) if you haven't discovered a problem fit yet, which can be done by talking with or observing customers.

The third step is about measuring the experiment's success. We don't want to run experiments without learning from them. Experiments and tests are used for learning! So, make sure to describe how you'll measure success, by listing one to three actionable metrics.

**Figure 18.1** The Strategyzer Test Card

Step 4 is about setting a target for the metrics as defined in step 3. If you run an experiment that should result in a higher click-through rate, just stating that you want more clicks is not good enough. Do you want ten more clicks? Do you need 10% more clicks? Do you need to double the current click-through rate? What's the goal? Without such criteria, experiments just measure whether something will happen, and because you are releasing an experiment, something always does.

When designing tests and experiments, we recommend you collaboratively do this. Work with your teams and involve stakeholders. Perhaps have everyone first write a Test Card or hypothesis statement by themselves. Then compare them, discuss them, and learn from each other. Are there any interesting differences? Great! Imagine what would have happened if the team had started working on this experiment whilst having different assumptions. Test cards are great conversation starters because they reveal hidden assumptions when being created together. It also makes experiments more tangible because we write some ideas down together. Use them to facilitate a discussion and align stakeholders and Developers.

## CAPTURE LEARNINGS

In the days before Agile, UX, and Lean, we used to do a lot of project management in product management and product development. Project management is still widely used, and for good reasons, in construction projects, for example.

One of the practices used in classic project management is to create a "lessons learned" document. It was a useful exercise to do in the projects we've been on in the past. Thinking about what could be done better next time is a great idea. However, in most companies, this exercise is only done at the end of the project, and, unfortunately, the document often ends up in a binder in a closet, and nobody ever looks at it again once the project is complete.

In Scrum Teams, when Professional Scrum is applied, these learnings are captured more frequently. By using the Sprint Retrospective, Scrum Teams seek learning and continuous improvement at the end of every Sprint. This information is to be implemented in the upcoming Sprints. A good practice we've learned is to take one improvement from the Sprint Retrospective and put it at the top of the Sprint Backlog for the next Sprint.

So, learning can (and should) be made explicit. We have created Strategyzer Learning Cards (see Figure 18.2) for various clients to capture the learnings from the experiments we ran. We added those learnings to our Product Wall to capture all that information in one place. At some point, an entire wall was covered with these Learning Cards. When we wanted to run new experiments, or when we thought we had already tested something, or when we wanted to reconsider the next steps, we would just walk up to the wall and have a look. Visualizing all the tests and learnings is also interesting for users and stakeholders, to show and explain that you're constantly testing, learning, and discovering, to maximize the value of the product.

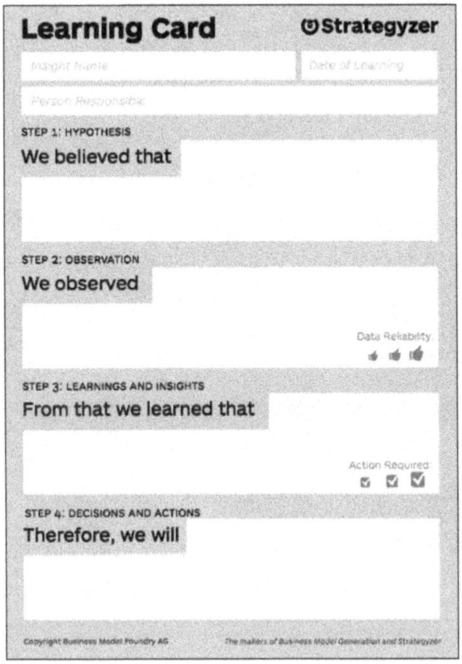


**Figure 18.2** The Strategyzer Learning Card

# APPROACHES FOR SCALING SUCCESSFUL PRODUCTS AND TEAMS

## SCALING APPROACHES FOR PEOPLE AND TEAMS

A pattern we've seen in practice in various organizations is a senior leader saying something along the lines of "So, we have seventy people working on the product. Since we decided to adopt Scrum, we need you to organize them into separate teams," the CEO explained. So many things were interesting about that phrase, but we decided to take a holistic product perspective on this comment from the CEO. "Do you need all seventy people to build that product?" we asked. "Well, I don't know," the CEO responded, "but that's how many people were working on it, and I don't think it will go any faster with fewer people."

In many organizations, scaling is not considered to be an experiment. Many organizations use a copy-and-paste approach when adopting Scrum to increase agility or for other benefits. They see other companies in their industry adopting the "Spotify model," so they do the same. They recognize their existing roles, positions, and structure in the Scaled Agile Framework (SAFe) big picture and think that implementing the SAFe framework (or Spotify model, or another one) will help them to become more agile. They're hoping that this copy-and-paste action works flawlessly, but it often doesn't. In most cases, new and more complex problems are created or amplified. Even if the copy-and-paste worked, scaling often introduces a new set of problems and challenges.

 **What Could Go Wrong?**

Aiko, the IT manager and Noa's direct boss, looked at Noa with great disbelief, shook his head, and tried again. "Look, we need to build and release features faster, so I've contacted this nearshoring company that helped us out in the past. I'm telling you, they can speed up and make more progress."

Noa was unsure how to answer. Sure, getting things done faster would have been quite vocal about the speed at which they had been releasing Product Increments to the market. Most of their experiments had failed, which prevented them from building a product and functionality that nobody needed. However, discovering what customers needed was proving to be quite difficult.

"I don't believe that adding more people will make us go much faster, Aiko," she started.

Aiko shook his head and interrupted: "Look, if I need to print twice the number of magazines, then adding another machine solves the problem. Your teams are releasing software every two weeks now, so if we add two more teams, we can cut that time in half easily."

"But, Aiko, the work we do isn't as simple as printing a magazine," Noa countered. "Imagine that your magazine changed all the time. Imagine that after each batch of magazines was printed, multiple changes had to be made to them. Imagine that the printing press you need has never been built before, and the people you would need to build that press and print the magazines have never worked together before. Surely, adding people will only slow the process down."

Realizing that the metaphor that he used had not helped him, Aiko shook his head. "Next thing you are going to tell me is that we will go faster if we reduce the team size," he snapped at her.

*Well, as a matter of fact, . . ."* Noa thought.

Adding teams to work on a product often leads to diminishing returns. At some point it creates additional dependencies, single points of failure, communication issues, alignment needs, and more overall chaos than it resolves, often making the whole effort spin out of control. A big problem with scaling is that it is not approached as an experiment but rather as something with a given output. The fundamental problem is that scaling *effectively* is a complex challenge. It is context dependent, and it is not something you can copy from someone else. So instead, run some experiments to discover how to scale in your *specific* and *unique* context. When defining such experiments, the same Strategyzer Test and Learning cards we discussed in Chapter 18, "How to Design and Evaluate Experiments and Tests," can be applied. Here are some examples:[1]

- We believe that we can naturally grow the teams by adding people to the existing team. Once they are settled in, which can be measured by the average time to complete a task, we can onboard another new person without a decrease in the delivered value, as measured by <metric>.
- We believe that our senior developers can take two apprentices who will grow within four Sprints to the level that they are confident enough to start their own team. We will assure their ability to design, implement, and roll out feature XYZ to validate this assumption.
- We believe that reducing the team size to three people will allow us to deliver more value in a shorter amount of time, which can be measured by <metric>.
- We believe that having one Product Owner for our digital product, working with all five digital teams, will improve decision speed, dependency management, and value produced per Sprint. To verify this assumption, we will run an experiment for the next two Sprints, in which we reduce the existing five Product Owners to just one Product Owner for all five teams. We will measure <metric> and are right if <condition>.

Note that each of these scaling experiments is described as a test with desired outcomes and measurable results. The results of the experiments can then be inspected and adapted to make data-driven decisions in your specific and unique context.

*There are no such things as best practices in product development. There*

---

1. These examples are based on Jesse Houwing, "Scaling Scrum to the Limit," Scrum.org, October 26, 2018, https://www.scrum.org/resources/blog/scaling-scrum-limit.

*are only practices that are adequate within a certain context.*

—Craig Larman and Bas Vodde[2]

Scaling brings some unique challenges for a Product Owner:

- It is more difficult to maintain close relationships with all Developers as the number of people involved increases.

- Having many teams working on a product may result in increased time spent to understand the unique problems and opportunities that technology offers.

- Clearly expressing Product Backlog items is not a one-person endeavor. It involves interaction, discussion, questions, and answers. Increasing people's understanding about the problem to solve takes time, but time to communicate with everyone becomes scarcer at scale.

- The order of the Product Backlog is based on many elements, such as value, risk, opportunities, timing, dependencies, and others. When multiple teams work from one single Product Backlog, it might become more difficult to keep everybody busy. This seems to be important to many people in practice. However, is keeping everyone busy the point of being a great product person?

- Keeping the vision, the strategy, and the goals to be achieved transparent and well understood for all involved may become more difficult.

So, how to deal with these challenges effectively? Let's first explore a common antipattern used in many organizations, before diving into some alternative solutions.

## TYPICAL ANTIPATTERN FOR SCALING PEOPLE AND TEAMS

Typically, when a product becomes successful, when it takes off, and when we feel the need to add more people to the team(s), a common scaling antipattern is implemented. Remember that you are in a specific and unique

---

2. https://less.works/less/framework/introduction#ExperimentsGuidesRulesPrinciples.

situation, so the following may or may not apply to you. It is however an example you'll likely recognize. A visual representation of the following story is visualized in Figure 19.1.

Imagine you are the only Product Owner, and you own and manage one Product. You also have one Scrum Team to work with and one Product Backlog to manage. Things are great and running smoothly. After some initial successes with the product and working with your team, you've secured additional funding, and now you consider hiring more Developers. Let's say you went for it, and you now have four teams of Developers working on your one product.

You are still the only Product Owner but are getting somewhat overwhelmed. You receive many questions from the Developers. You need to explain a lot about the vision, strategy, goals, and features to build. You meet with stakeholders more frequently and spend more time with the Developers on Product Backlog refinement. At some point, you hear somebody say that "every team needs a Product Owner." You are now under the impression that every Scrum Team needs their own Product Owner, and thus you decide to hire one (less experienced) Product Owner for every team. These Product Owners are now set up between you and the teams.

You thought adding more Product Owners would make life easier for you, but new and additional problems are revealing themselves. It's increasingly difficult for you to spend your time effectively. You find yourself stuck between time with the stakeholders and teaching the new proxy Product Owners about the product, customer problems, the market, and your vision and strategy.

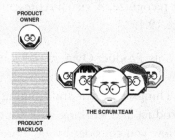

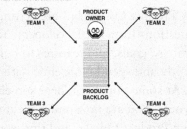

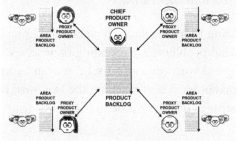

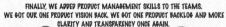

**Figure 19.1** A typical pattern (or antipattern) for scaling.

You also notice that tension is building up in the teams. The proxy Product Owners are getting overwhelmed by the teams, who were used to interacting with you directly, being the Visionary, Customer Representative, Collaborative, and Decision-Maker Product Owner that you were. They report becoming slower, more dependent on others, and having integration issues.

To increase the visibility of the work to be done, each proxy Product Owner has created a team-level Product Backlog for their teams. At the same time, you are now responsible for managing the overall Product Backlog. The result is that you now also need to spend a significant amount of time on coordinating and synchronizing your Product Backlog with the team-level Product Backlogs. In addition, you must integrate the team roadmaps with your product roadmap. The number of mistakes being made is increasing, extra meetings are necessary to communicate and align, but tension keeps growing. "We need more experienced Product Owners," the teams and stakeholders tell you repeatedly.

Sound familiar? Over the last decade, we've been asked to help at dozens of organizations that all ran into this problem or a slight variation of it. Many companies adopt Scrum with the wrong principles in mind. The sentence "Every Scrum Team needs a Product Owner," for example, doesn't mean that every Scrum Team needs their own exclusive Product Owner. Quite the opposite; it's likely that a Product Owner will need multiple teams to work on their product, especially if it's a large and complex product. Many organizations are already complex systems with complex products and complex structures and architectures. Adding more complexity to the mix results in chaos. Adding multiple Product Owners sounds a lot like adding complexity, not reducing it. So, in general, having large products with multiple Product Owners just isn't very helpful.

## A Better Approach for Scaling People and Teams

As we mentioned earlier, your situation is unique—and likely rather complex. There is no magic solution or silver bullet to remedy this situation. This chapter about scaling is part of the Experimenter's stance for a reason—because you'll need to conduct experiments and learn what works best in your unique context. There are some things to consider:

**Simplify—there is only one Product Backlog.** Eliminate individual team backlogs. Having multiple Product Backlogs for one product creates dependencies, a need for alignment, and a need to keep the backlogs in sync. It adds complexity rather than reducing it. In contrast, having only one Product Backlog, ordered by the Product Owner to solve problems and fulfill the needs of customers, leads to more focus on outcomes to be achieved and less focus on outputs to be delivered.

Having one Product Backlog also enhances transparency by making clear the direction of the product and the Product Goal teams are working toward. It puts the teams on common ground, and each team can now ask themselves, "How can we contribute to achieving that goal?"

**Product management activities done by Developers.** Another step to take is to identify the highest-potential proxy Product Owner and make them an apprentice to the Product Owner. Do not label this person as Product Owner or apprentice Product Owner, though. They are not the Product Owner; they are learning from the Product Owner. They are doing product management–related work, so instead of Product Owner, call them a Developer.

Scrum uses the term *Developer* for people who contribute to the creation of the product. This term is somewhat confusing, in our experience, because *Developer* is also used to describe someone who creates software or code—that is, a software engineer. In the context of Scrum, though, the Developer role is not limited to software engineering. A Developer in Scrum can be anyone with any skills that are needed to build, sell, market, or deliver the product. So, consider a Developer in Scrum as a "product developer."

Thus, the apprentices can help the Scrum Team as a Developer. They are a member of the group of (product) Developers yet are not focused on creating software, code, or tests. Instead, they are focused on doing product management work. They might, for example, contribute to the Scrum Team by having regular customer calls, doing competitive and market research, facilitating design or problem-solving workshops, doing data analysis and presentation, or performing any other product management activities.

As in any apprentice model, the apprentices should have a clear learning journey, and they need to pick up specific tasks and responsibilities under the supervision of the Product Owner. One day they may have their own product, but for now, they are a Developer, with a focus on product management and adding product management skills to the Scrum Team.

An important goal of this setup is to create self-sufficient and self-managing teams. When Scrum Teams are operating as mature, high-performing, and self-managing teams, they should be able to take on more broadly defined problems. They should be able to interact with customers and users directly, seek problems to solve, and identify experiments to run.

Think about this question for a moment: *Do I offer the team problems to solve, or do I offer them tasks to complete?* If your answer weighs more toward tasks to complete, it might be dangerous to even consider scaling. Don't add more complexity by scaling in this situation. Build that self-managing team first, then consider scaling if needed.

## APPROACHES TO SCALING THE PRODUCT OR SERVICE

During one of our podcasts, we talked about scaling with a large group of Product Owners and product managers. We showed them three different pictures of roads and traffic, as shown in Figure 19.2. We then asked them which picture made the most sense in relation to scaling, and why. Interestingly, we got some different answers.

**Figure 19.2** Which picture best represents scaling to you?

Some people said that picture A, showing an overcrowded crossroads, made the most sense to them because it shows utter chaos. They experienced scaling as having many teams, many different interests, many different products, and hundreds of people in smaller and larger teams trying to move their own goal forward but jamming others in the process. To them, scaling seemed like a big plate of spaghetti—a mixed up, tangled mess.

Other people felt that picture B was the best analogy. It illustrates a huge intersection of highways and roads, as are common near many US cities. If you haven't experienced them firsthand, you've certainly seen them in movies. These massive intersections consist of six or more lanes of traffic, on-ramps, off-ramps, over- and underpasses, and so forth. They are created to resolve traffic issues, but in many cases, traffic problems still exist. People who saw this picture as a good metaphor for scaling stated that their organization created tons of infrastructure, held meetings and alignment sessions, and added to the workflow new practices to deal with scaling. In other words, the organization created a very complex structure and way of working, making it even more difficult than it had been. It applied a very complex solution to a complex problem.

Picture C illustrates a straight and empty road through a quiet forest. This picture was selected by only a handful of people. But it is the metaphor that makes the most sense to us. Scaling is all about simplicity. Scaling is not about adding layers and complex structures. It's about making things simple, improving the flow of value, and maintaining speed. Therefore, scaling in most cases should be a discussion about descaling rather than upscaling. Don't accept more complexity. Don't fight complexity with complex solutions—find simple ones. It's about getting back to basics, getting back to what is important, optimizing value delivery.

## FOCUS ON THE PRODUCT FIRST, THEN ON PEOPLE AND TEAMS

When people talk about scaling, it's often because they have many people working in the company. They are talking about scaling teams, expanding capacity, and how to organize all those people into teams effectively.

Especially among Agile Coaches and Scrum Masters, scaling seems to be top of mind, which makes sense because this perspective focuses on the human and process side of scaling. How do we grow a motivated team? How do we deal with scarce skills? What becomes the cadence? How do they integrate the work into a single Product Increment?

When managers and company executives talk about scaling, they often point out the importance of alignment. How do we know that everybody is working on the right things? Sure, they are busy, but is it effective? What kind of forecasts can we make? What goals aren't we meeting, and why not? What dependencies need to be managed? What can we promise to customers and the board of directors?

Rarely do we talk about the third perspective on scaling. This is the perspective that we, as product people, should be talking about. This is about scaling the product itself. From this perspective, we aren't talking about organizing people in teams. We aren't talking about aligning work or managing dependencies. We are talking about scaling the product. How can we increase revenues, or impact customers? How can we expand our product into new markets? How can we increase our efficiency without adding complexity or cost? For example, software as a service products tend to scale very well if they are built correctly.

But why don't we talk about product scaling? Maybe it's because we are part of a larger organization, an enterprise organization, perhaps, and it might feel like we need a framework to structure how employees will collaborate. Or maybe it's because we are dealing with a lot of complexity in the processes, tools, products, and other structures in our organization. It seems like we are often trying to solve complex problems by creating complex solutions, and your organization would not be the first one to struggle with problems such as too many dependencies within and across teams, dependencies on knowledge and experience of the Product Managers, . . . or slow decision making, perhaps?

So, when you talk about scaling, make sure to align on the perspective to take. Are you talking about the same kind of scaling? What we found to be quite interesting is that most people come up with scaling frameworks when talking about this topic. But, if scaling the *product* is what we should care about most as product people, then why are we spending *so much time* talking about frameworks such as LeSS, Nexus, and SAFe? Why aren't we talking more about effectively scaling the product?

## EIGHT EFFECTIVE STRATEGIES FOR SCALING A PRODUCT

Let's explore eight strategies that can be used to *scale the product*. Figure 19.3 visualizes the different scaling strategies.

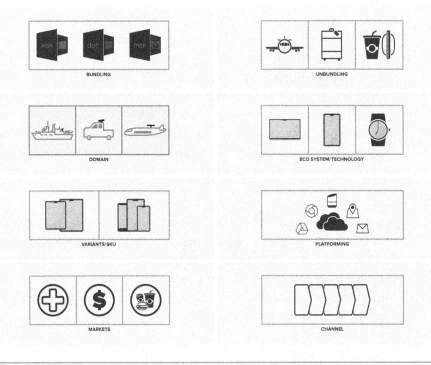

**Figure 19.3** Eight effective strategies to scale a product

The year is 1992, and Microsoft releases the first version of Microsoft Office. Why? It wasn't because customers expressed a need for it. Excel was obliterating the competition (Lotus123), but Word was struggling to compete against WordPerfect. By creating a bundle of products, Microsoft created a product line that didn't require much additional work to set up, but it did offer a unique value proposition for customers. If you were already using Excel, then why not buy Word as well? Microsoft has since repeatedly used this technique, which is called **bundling,** as a way to scale a product. Common examples of products using this scaling principle include Microsoft, Adobe, McDonald's, Burger King, and all-in-one Internet, TV, and telephone providers.

Fast forward 3 years, and airline company Easy Jet does the exact opposite. It takes the luxury commodity of air travel and strips it down to the essentials, leaning out the product in the process. You can still get the additional services and amenities, but they are now "real" products. This way of scaling a product is commonly called **unbundling.** This technique is used by various low-cost airlines, travel and hotel websites, and car manufacturers, for example.

Have you noticed that big black box on the back of the magnificent frigate of the Royal Dutch Navy? That thing is a SMART-L long-range ballistic missile detector. You can put the frigate in a convenient spot and defend a region against the threat of missiles raining down on you if they come from space. Great product, right? Well, it turns out that you can't put a frigate everywhere on earth. There are some spots on this planet where we will find this thing called "land." The Thales Group (creator of such technology) therefore organizes products into **domains.** Mimicking the SMART-L radar, there is also a land-based L-band radar. Thales considers this to be a separate product. By organizing the product in domains, the company can optimize its products for different parameters and variables while sharing the same technology. This helps to simplify a very, very complex product.

The **technology** involved can also be used to scale a product. One can argue that there are advantages to maintaining a single codebase for any platform you are deploying on. But, as Electronic Arts demonstrated with its popular game The Sims, there can be great value in creating unique experiences on different platforms. It might be a way of scaling a product for different target audiences, industries, or customer experiences.

TomTom started with a single product, the iconic navigation "box" on your car's dashboard. Within several years, they made many different **variants,** or **SKUs,** of the device, each targeting a specific niche market. Internally, there were even more variants because some of the products used different hardware and used multiple suppliers. Of course, this created additional complexity in TomTom's product portfolio, but it also created an opportunity for teams to come up with unique solutions.

**Platforming** is an opposite strategy for creating product variants. With the platforming strategy, various product components are integrated into one platform. Examples of such products include Amazon AWS, Google Cloud, and Facebook. These products can be used as a platform within the company or can be sold as a product externally. Product managers cannot ask themselves the following question often enough: *What can we remove from the product?* Building platform products helps to reduce dependencies, allows for easier and more standardized integrations, and offers alternative business opportunities.

A Canadian robot company switched its strategy from industrial robotics to autonomous automated workers by targeting a new **market**. The company used its knowledge, experience, and technology to build warehouse robots. It combined its relatively simple industrial robots with data, artificial intelligence, and machine learning concepts, turning them into smart warehousing "employees" (robots). These robot employees (which never tire) use learning algorithms to predict product-ordering patterns for upcoming weeks. Oh, and they automatically make way for humans, too.

The final way of scaling your product is one we've seen at Picnic. Picnic is a company that has become incredibly successful as a deliver-to-your-doorstep grocery delivery service, because it integrated the entire supply chain and went directly to the consumer. It scales the product in a sense that the risks and margins of the chain are now absorbed in the profit and loss of the product itself. This way of scaling is referred to as a **channel** scaling strategy.

# HOW PRODUCT OWNERS CONTRIBUTE TO PRODUCT SCALING

It may feel like you are just a small cog in a large engine when working in an enterprise company. However, consider the Product Owner to be the bougies, producing the spark in that engine. Having great Product Owners makes a huge difference for the product, for its customer and users, for teams working on the product, and for the organization delivering it. So, engage in these conversations about scaling your product; offer guidance, vision, and direction. Here are some other things you can do to scale effectively:

1. Share your business, customer, user, market, and domain knowledge with the Developers. Help them to increase their knowledge over time.

2. Ensure there is direct communication and feedback between customers, users, and the Scrum Team. Don't be a single point of contact. Bring people together.

3. Ensure that the product vision and strategy are clear to everyone. Share your vision often.

4. Ensure there is a clear, measurable, and motivating Product Goal to work on.

5. Ensure there is a clear, goal-driven roadmap that is known to the stakeholders and teams.

6. Ensure the Product Backlog is clear, ordered, visible, transparent, and accessible to all.

7. Spend the right amount of time with the various stakeholders and Developers.

8. Get a Scrum Master on board who can coach, train, mentor, and facilitate the team, stakeholders, and organization.

9. Do proper Professional Scrum with the support of a great Scrum Master.

# THE EXPERIMENTER IV

## SUMMARY

### KEY LEARNINGS AND INSIGHTS

This concludes Part IV, in which you explored the Experimenter stance. In this part, you learned how great Experimenter Product Owners approach innovation, testing, and experimentation. You explored various approaches to inside-out innovation and to outside-in innovation and learned how each approach provides different results and insights. You also explored how business model innovation, doing market research, and learning from other organizations outside your industry may drive innovation for your product. You explored the truth curve, a model for helping you to select the right kinds of experiments, and you learned how to design them using Test Cards and Learning Cards. Finally, you explored different approaches to scaling and descaling winning products for future growth and how scaling is often incorrectly focused more on people and teams than on scaling the product. In order to create winning products in the marketplace, Product Owners and product managers need to take a curious, learning, and open-minded approach to product management. They need to use data, insights, testing, and experimentation to validate ideas and assumptions. In some cases, your gut-feel will do just fine. However, in most cases, experimentation and validation is the way to go if you want to maximize the value of your product in the marketplace.

## QUICK QUIZ REVIEW

If you took the Quick Quiz at the beginning of Part IV, compare your answers to those in the following table. Now that you have read about the Experimenter stance, would you change any of your answers? Do you agree with the following answers?

| Statement | Agree | Disagree |
|---|:---:|:---:|
| New business models are always emerging as others fall out of fashion, never to be heard of again. | ✓ | |
| Experimentation is the only way to discover if your business model innovation is going to work. | | ✓ |
| Successful scaling of product development is achieved by applying a proven framework such as Nexus or LeSS. | | ✓ |
| A company is either innovative, or it isn't. A Product Owner can use little to no influence to promote innovation. | | ✓ |
| Making decisions around bundling or unbundling products is the responsibility of a Product Owner. | ✓ | |
| Product management responsibilities and tasks should be performed solely by the Product Owner. | | ✓ |
| The team of Developers should include skills such as sales, marketing, business analysis, design, and product management if required for the product. | ✓ | |
| The main question to be answered when it comes to scaling is, How do we organize all our people into teams? | | ✓ |

## WANT TO LEARN MORE?

In this part, you learned about the Experimenter stance. Various topics, tools, techniques, and concepts will help you to strengthen your Experimenter stance.

If you want to improve this stance, consider identifying a couple of experiments that you want to run. Use the truth curve model to select the right kind of experiments, and then design your experiments with a Test Card from Strategyzer or a Growth Experiment Canvas for example.

If you want to learn more about the Experimenter stance, consider reading *Lean Startup: How Today's Entrepreneurs Use Continuous Innovation to Create Radically Successful Businesses* by Eric Ries (First Crown, 2014), *Business Model Navigator: 55+ Models That Will Revolutionise Your Business* by Oliver Gassmann, Karolin Frankenberger, and Michaela Choudury (Pearson, 2020), and *The Nexus Framework for Scaling Scrum: Continuously Delivering an Integrated Product with Multiple Scrum Teams* by Kurt Bittner, Patricia Kong, and David West (Prentice Hall, 2018).

You could also explore the concepts of Lean UX, user research and testing, and user experience design in more detail. They offer excellent resources on different experiments to run.

# THE DECISION MAKER

*Product managers are in charge of whipping up all the other departments and getting them to work together. This is to make sure that the product gets pulled forward by a coordinated team of horses, rather than torn apart by horses running in different directions.*

—Donald S. Passman

## QUICK QUIZ

To connect to Part V, answer each of the following statements by checking the Agree or Disagree column. The answers are shared in the Part V Summary.

| Statement | Agree | Disagree |
|---|---|---|
| Making decisions faster can lead to more success for your product. | | |
| Each decision has two outcomes: the right one and the wrong one. | | |
| Decisions are deterministic in nature; given enough time and expertise, the correct answer can be found. | | |
| Product Owners make no decisions about technology and people. | | |
| Product management is more like a game of poker than like a game of chess. | | |
| Effectively navigating dilemmas is very complex. You need to do a lot of research and analysis to figure out what the best option is. | | |
| Product Owners should take an enterprise-level view when making decisions. | | |
| When evaluating decisions, you should mostly consider the results that were achieved. It's not about luck, it's about results. | | |

# Improving Accountability, Maturity, and Authority

## Introducing: The Decision Maker

One of the many benefits of having a great Product Owner is improved speed and quality of decision making. Especially in complex situations where many things, like requirements, people, and technology, change frequently, the speed of decision making can make a huge difference between success, and always playing catch-up with the competition. It's probably for a good reason that we've witnessed some enterprise organizations launch start-ups as separate companies to compete with their own business. It seems like there is great value to be found in being a small, nimble, and flexible company where decisions can be made much quicker.

Sir Alec Issigonis, a British car designer who worked at the Morris Minor Company from the age of 18 and went on to design the Mini, said, "A camel is a horse designed by a committee." Clearly, Issigonis saw the camel's hump and extra water capacity, its oversized feet, and its increased intelligence as add-ons that a horse simply doesn't need. His comparison suggests that committees regularly fail to recognize when a product or a decision is "good enough." It also suggests that building products with committees is a recipe for developing bad products. Committee or consensus thinking and decisions may lead to helpful insights, productive discussions, and varied perspectives.

However, designs and decisions made by a committee don't always result in an improved product or a great new one. This is a somewhat strange idea because most great products are created through collaboration, so how do you find a balance between welcoming varied input and knowing when you've had enough of it?

In the Toyota Production System[1] and in the Japanese culture, *nemawashi* refers to an informal process of laying the foundation and building a consensus before making decisions. Translated, *nemawashi* means "going around the roots" in the sense of digging around the roots of a tree to prepare it for transplant.

A Product Owner is accountable for maximizing the value of the product. This doesn't mean though that a Product Owner should make all the decisions themselves, nor make all the decisions alone. If you have gone around the roots, you will find that many decisions can be delegated, for example to the (Scrum) teams working on the product. Similarly, you can evaluate your autonomy and authority as a Product Owner, by inspecting what kind of decisions are delegated to you.

So, what are some of the characteristics of great Decision-Maker Product Owners? First, great decision makers listen and then apply a suitable style specific to the situation:

- **Call the shots:** These Product Owners have a strong sense of urgency or simply don't like waiting. They like action and make decisions quickly. They also tend to decide independently of what other people think. They get stuff done.
- **Pace car:** A distinct different variant makes sure that the work gets done but is down in the trenches with the team, making sure they get through the consequences of the decisions they make.
- **Salesman:** Some Product Owners spend significant time convincing people of their idea. Usually, the decision still lies with them, but they make sure people believe it is the right thing to do.

---

1. Much of our current Agile and Scrum thinking has its roots (pun intended) in the principles of the Toyota way of working.

- **We are together:** Scrum is about leveraging the team, hence the phrase "Take it to the team." Good advice, but it slows down the decision-making process to check if everyone is on board. These Product Owners make decisions that are often widely respected and supported.

- **Democratic:** A different variant often results in a majority vote. It's faster, and everyone is involved but it is not about reaching a consensus but finding the most widely supported outcome.

- **Coaching:** These Product Owners ask broad questions: How would we tackle this? If X went wrong, what would we do? They nudge the team into asking the right questions themselves. They usually thrive when the product begins to scale.

Some decisions you make will turn out to be wrong, and some will turn out to be right. There are ways for improving decision-making skills, and there are ways to discover which decisions are and are not worthy of your time. This is sometimes referred to as the *law of triviality*.[2] What was found various times in organizations is that senior managers, even boards of directors, would have long discussions about something relatively unimportant or inexpensive. An often-used example is about where to position the bicycle shed, what it should look like, and how much it may cost. This relatively cheap project is discussed in meeting after meeting, while meantime, the company has a multimillion-dollar (or multibillion-dollar) atomic reactor to build. Quick decisions, without a lot of discussion, are made around the reactor despite that it's a million times more expensive than a bicycle shed. Interestingly, it seems like the more expensive something is, the less time we spend discussing it. A reactor is so vastly expensive and complex that an average person cannot understand it, so one assumes that those who work on it understand it. In contrast, everyone can visualize a cheap, simple bicycle shed, so planning one can result in endless discussions because everyone involved wants to add a touch and show personal contribution. Often, we find Product Owners who aren't focused on the atomic reactor of their product but on the little things that are easier to understand.

---

2. C. Northcote Parkinson, *Parkinson's Law: The Pursuit of Progress,* John Murray, 1958.

*The law of triviality is something I'll never forget, and it resonates with me better as, "the pop-up example." In early 2021, I was training and coaching Product Owners at an online flowers and bouquets company. One of the Product Owners explained how she was having long discussions and arguments with one of her key stakeholders about a new search feature in the software. This key stakeholder wanted to have a pop-up that enabled users to search for flowers and add them to a bouquet.*

*The Scrum Team designed a different kind of search feature, which was simpler and faster to use. The Product Owner and this stakeholder had some long and intense discussions about this small and simple pop-up. In the meantime, though, the stakeholder wanted to delay the release of the software until all features were fully built—something about the old English saying, "penny wise, pound foolish," I guess. Anyway, I'll never forget this pop-up.*

— Robbin

**Making all decisions yourself** is not the best way forward, but neither is delegating all decisions to others. In daily practice, we often find that the maturity of a Scrum Team influences how much is delegated. This works for the decisions that company leaders delegate to Product Owners, and it works for the decisions that Product Owners delegate to their teams. You will find that delegation of responsibility and authority creates time and space so that you can do other work. To advance as a Product Owner, you'll often need to let go of some smaller decisions and responsibilities before you can start working on bigger responsibilities and receive more authority for more impactful decisions.

A technique we've often used to talk about decision making and delegation of decisions is Delegation Poker, as described in *Management 3.0*[3] by Jurgen

---

3. Jurgen Appelo, *Management 3.0: Leading Agile Developers, Developing Agile Leaders,* Addison-Wesley, 2011.

Appelo. This technique works particularly well when you want to discuss which decisions you will make yourself, which decisions you'll make together with the team, and which decisions you will delegate to them. It also works very well between two parties.

As a Product Owner, you often find yourself in a situation with three parties. There are management or company executives above you, there is you, and there is the Scrum Team. Some items are delegated to you, and some you will delegate to others. We therefore adapted the Delegation Poker technique slightly to be more applicable for a Product Owner. Table 20.2 illustrates what we ended up with.

**Table 20.2** Levels of Delegation

| Level 1 | Level 2 | Level 3 | Level 4 | Level 5 | Level 6 | Level 7 |
|---------|---------|---------|---------|---------|---------|---------|
| Is decided without me | Is decided after consulting with me | Is decided by me alone | Is decided by me after consulting with others | Is decided in mutual agreement | Is decided by the team; I am consulted | Is decided by the team; I delegate the decision |

Level 1 decisions are decisions made by other people in the organization without consulting the Product Owner. These decisions are typically made by company leaders and can include decisions about the company vision, company strategy, company values, available product budgets, and compliance standards. When decisions are made in a level 1 way, company leaders *tell* you their decisions.

Level 2 decisions are also made outside of your control. The final call on such decisions is still made by company leaders, but you can now influence their decisions. In this case, company leaders reach out to you, and perhaps other Product Owners, to gauge your opinion and perspective. Level 2 decisions are generally made when the company strategy influences the product strategy, or vice versa. Company leaders will likely *tell* or *sell* you their final decision.

Level 3 decisions are made by you, the Product Owner. These decisions are typically about the order of the top of the Product Backlog, the goal and work to be done in the next Sprint, or the next customer problem to start exploring. Decisions that you make on your own are typically simple or low-risk decisions that require little buy-in. Other decisions might involve which stakeholders to invite to the Sprint Review or how much budget to offer to each stakeholder during a value estimation session. Well, let's not appoint a committee for that! Product Owners speed up the process by making decisions on their own as well.

Sometimes, of course, there are more important and impactful decisions that a Product Owner must make. The Product Owner should have the final say about such items as product vision, product strategy, goals, and roadmap. However, for most of those decisions, they talk to the stakeholders first, learn about their perspectives, and then make the decision. This is what level 4 decisions are about. The Product Owner makes these decisions after consultation with others. It's much like level 2, where company leadership consults the Product Owner before finalizing their decision. But in this case, it's the other way around. These are usually the more complex decisions that carry risk but require little buy-in. Examples are the order of the Product Backlog, the high-level product roadmap, or how to express and measure value for the upcoming Sprints.

Level 5 decisions are made by mutual agreement of a group and require buy-in from others. Hence, you must ensure those others are part of the solution and decision. If you force your own decision on people in situations where buy-in is required, people will just shrug their shoulders when things do not unfold as planned and will likely lay the blame on you. It was *your* decision after all. So, at level 5, make sure decisions are *our* decisions and plans are *our* plans.

When decisions are made at level 6, the decision is delegated to the team, but they keep you in the loop or consult with you before finalizing decisions. Again, this level is much like levels 2 and 4, but now it's between the Product Owner and the Developers. A great way to experiment with leaving level 6 decisions up to the team is to let them handle the refinement of Product Backlog items (PBIs). Perhaps they can decide how to solve a customer problem. Perhaps they can agree on the solution, acceptance criteria, and design. Do you need to be in the loop for every detail?

When you get to level 7, a decision is delegated to the team completely. You trust them to make the right decisions, and you don't want or need to be involved in these decisions. These are often "how" decisions but can also have bigger implications. For example, the decision about what technology to use can have an impact on the costs of the product. Another example could be deciding which software, tools, practices, or development frameworks to use. Perhaps you can agree on a maximum budget and let the team decide whether purchasing tools or licenses is valuable enough to them.

What decisions must always be made on what level? It depends on the organization, the maturity of the Product Owner, the maturity of the Scrum Team, and many other elements. A good starting point is to make the current situation transparent. Create transparency about how decisions are made and who makes them. Then discuss your findings with management and your team. Alternatively, do a Delegation Poker workshop to identify the current and desired delegation experience. Common decisions and examples to be discussed are listed here.

## PRODUCT

For product, these decisions should be made:

- Product vision
- Product strategy
- Business model
- Value proposition
- Go-to-market strategy
- Legal/compliance requirements
- Products to include in the product portfolio
- Whether to add a product or service to the product portfolio
- Whether to remove a product or service from the product portfolio
- Whether to bundle or unbundle products or create product variants

## PRODUCT GOALS AND OBJECTIVES

For product objectives, these decisions should be made:

- Financial product goals and objectives
- Operational product goals and objectives
- Customer-satisfaction-related product goals and objectives

## BUDGET

For budget, these decisions should be made:

- Setting the products' budget
- Setting budgets for innovation, maintenance, fixing issues, operations, etc.
- Whether to spend/invest less than $10,000 of the budget
- Whether to spend/invest $10,000 to $50,000 of the budget
- Whether to spend/invest more than $50,000 of the budget
- Setting the team budget (for social events/team events)

## VALUE

The following decisions should be made regarding value:

- How to define value
- Estimate value
- How to measure value
- Revenue targets
- Cost-saving targets

## MARKETING AND BRANDING

To go to market, these decisions should be made:

- Product or service positioning
- Product or service branding
- Product or service campaigns/advertisements

## PRICING

The following decisions should be made regarding pricing:

- Product pricing strategy
- Product pricing tactics
- Product/service customer price
- Approve (standard) price deviations/exceptions

## TOOLS AND TECHNOLOGY

The following decisions should be made regarding technology used and/or needed:

- Whether to start a new tool/technology selection process
- Technologies used to develop the product
- Whether to purchase tools/technologies costing less than $1,000/month
- Whether to purchase tools/technologies costing more than $1,000/month
- Whether to terminate a tool/technology used

## RELEASE PROCESS

The following decisions should be made regarding the release process:

- How the release process is conducted
- When to release a product (Increment)
- Whether to roll back/withdraw a released product (Increment)

## PEOPLE AND TEAMS

The following decisions should be made regarding the teams involved:

- Start a new team
- Expand a team (in size/number of people)
- Reduce a team (in size/number of people)

- Stop a team
- Required skills
- Hire a new team member
- Fire a team member
- How performance review process is conducted
- Team members' salaries
- Team members' bonuses
- Team bonuses
- Team manifesto/working agreements
- Team meetings and events
- Team members' holidays
- Team-building activities
- Working hours
- Purchasing a team training at less than $500 per person
- Purchasing a team training at more than $500 per person

## PRODUCT BACKLOG MANAGEMENT

For the Product Backlog, the following decisions should be made:

- Size of the Product Backlog
- Add a Product Backlog item to the Product Backlog
- Remove a Product Backlog item from the Product Backlog
- Size/effort estimate of a Product Backlog item
- Value estimate of a Product Backlog item
- How Product Backlog items are written/expressed (e.g., user story, free format, hypothesis statement)
- Order of the Product Backlog

## MANAGING EXTERNAL PARTIES AND VENDORS

For vendors, the following decisions should be made:

- Contract outlines
- Accepting contracts (conform standard terms)
- Accepting contracts (conform nonstandard terms)
- Deciding on service level agreements or experience level agreements
- Hiring temporary staff/team members costing less than $1,000 per day
- Hiring temporary staff/team members costing more than $1,000 per day

That is a huge list of potential decisions, and it is far from complete.

Start with this list, add your ideas, leave others out, and use it to discover how decisions should be made in your company through an open dialogue. What would it take from the organization to delegate more decisions to you? What would it bring in terms of value? What might be the risks? What can you delegate to your team? What behaviors or responsibilities should the team display before you trust them to make more impactful decisions themselves?

The beauty of Delegation Poker is that it turns a binary discussion (I decide, or I delegate) into a scale. The scale leaves much more room for experimentation and facilitates an easier discussion, especially if you want to move only one step on the scale. "I know you make these decisions, but could you consult me?" is a great question to help you gain more authority and grow your influence.

# EVALUATING YOUR PRODUCT DECISIONS

## PRODUCT MANAGEMENT: A GAME OF POKER OR CHESS?

Look at the business- and strategy-related books on your bookshelf. You may find that most of those books around strategy illustrate chess pictures on the cover, which is a cute, if misleading, metaphor for strategy. Not in the sense that chess is a game without strategy—on the contrary, it entails a lot of strategizing. But some aspects of the game do not translate well to the profession of product management.

For starters, the rules and chess pieces allow for only certain specific and limited moves. It's not like knights can start moving diagonally suddenly, whereas we have all seen customers and users behave in ways we didn't expect or report problems and ask for features and solutions we didn't have in mind. The biggest difference between chess and product management, though, is that all the pieces are on the board in a game of chess. There is no hidden information. If you think long and hard, or if you use computers, data, and AI, you can likely calculate and find all potential and possible chess moves.

Therefore, computers can pretty much always beat humans and win the game.[1] Product management is not like that at all. It's much more like a game of poker.

## A QUICK GAME TO TEST YOUR DECISION-MAKING SKILLS

Let's explore decision making via a quick game of rolling the dice. Are you up for it? We will play four games; the rules are listed in Table 21.1. Look at each of the four games and decide whether you will join the game and bet some money or will bail out. There is a fixed investment and fixed return if you make the right decision, so here we go.

**Table 21.1** A Quick Rolling-the-Dice Game to Test Your Decision-Making Skills

| Game 1 | Game 2 |
| --- | --- |
| Pay $10 to join and play the game. | Pay $10 to join and play the game. |
| Get $20 in return if you roll a 1, 2, 3, 4, or 5. | You get $20 in return if you roll a 1. |
| You get nothing if you roll a 6. | You get nothing if you roll a 2, 3, 4, 5, or 6. |

| Game 3 | Game 4 |
| --- | --- |
| Pay $10 to join and play the game. | Pay $10 to join and play the game. |
| Get $20 in return if you roll a 1, 2, 3, 4, or 5. | You get $20 in return if you roll a 1. |
| You get nothing if you roll a 6. | You get nothing if you roll a 2, 3, 4, 5, or 6. |

Are your bets placed in the four games? Then let's inspect your results.

If you think that we made a copy-paste error in the table, we didn't. You may have noticed that games 1 and 3 are the same, and so are games 2 and 4. It's not a mistake. In these four games, most people seem to be willing to bet their $10 in games 1 and 3, but they are reluctant to play games 2 and 4. However, when we run this exercise in a course setting and reveal a game's

---

1. 1997 Deep Blue beats Kasparov, who had run circles around the same computer the year before.

results after betting, people get the hang of it at game 4 and end up placing their bets after all. So, after playing four games, here are the results:

Game 1: won

Game 2: lost

Game 3: lost

Game 4: won

Let's say you played all four games. You won twice and lost twice. So, in which of these games did you make a good decision? And which ones were bad decisions?

**Game 1:** In this game, you would have made a good decision to place your bet. Deciding to join the game led to a good outcome or result, and the decision was a good decision because the odds were strongly in your favor.

**Game 2:** In the second game, it would have been a bad decision to place your bet, and this decision would have led to a bad outcome or result. In this case, the odds were clearly not in your favor, yet you took the bet anyway. You could have expected a bad outcome or result to happen.

**Game 3:** In this game, you made a good decision to place your bet, but you had a bad outcome or result in the end. Although the odds were strongly in your favor once more, you had some bad luck this time and didn't double your investment.

**Game 4:** In this game, you made a bad decision but were lucky to achieve a good outcome or result. Although the odds were not in your favor, you just happened to win this round.

This gaming exercise reveals a pattern across organizations when it comes to decision making. When talking about good or bad decisions that people made in the past, they often identify decisions as "good" ones if the results or outcomes were positive. Similarly, they identify "bad" decisions as decisions with negative results or outcomes. This is often referred to as a *resulting pitfall*. Of course, considering the results and outcomes is important when evaluating decisions. However, the results and outcomes achieved are not always directly related to the quality of the decision itself. As we've seen in the four games, sometimes we get lucky, and sometimes we don't.

## EVALUATING DECISIONS IN AN HONEST AND TRANSPARENT WAY

When you want to evaluate decisions more effectively, it helps to look at decisions from a broader perspective than the results only. As with any skill, to become better at decision making, you need regular practice and evaluation to learn from. You must inspect and learn from your decisions, regardless of the result. To evaluate decisions more effectively and to learn, here are some reflective questions that might help:

- Was the decision made by the right person or the right group of people? Was the decision made alone, or after consulting others?

- What information was available, transparent, and used to make the decision? What information was missing?

- Could more information have been gathered before making the decision? Would that have changed the decision?

- What type of decision was it? Easy? Complicated? Complex? Or chaotic?[2]

- Did the decision require a lot of buy-in or little buy-in from other people?

- What was the process for making the decision? How was it made?

- Was the decision made at the right moment? Was it made fast/slow enough?

- Was it a good decision? Or were you lucky this time?

---

2. The Cynefin framework discusses these different kinds of environments, including several ways of dealing with situations, work, and decisions within those environments. We recommend you explore this model, as it may help you in dealing effectively with work and decisions in various types of environments.

# MAKE BETTER
# DECISIONS: THINKING
# IN BETS

Considering that a lot of our product management work takes place in the complex domain where there are more unknowns and uncertainties than knowns and certainties, chess doesn't feel like a good metaphor for our situation. Instead, poker seems to be a more appropriate metaphor. In a game of poker, there are more cards hidden than revealed on the table. There are more cards in the deck than in your hand. In addition, players are unpredictable. They might place big bets without having a great hand of cards. They might also check or call despite having a great hand of cards. Above all, poker is a game of missing information. There are more unknowns than knowns. So, we need to make good guesses, try to read our opponents, and think in small bets.

Annie Duke is a former professional poker player and author in behavioral decision science. Apart from instructional books on poker, she wrote an interesting book, *Thinking in Bets*.[1] This business-oriented book might help you to find ways to improve your decisions. It offers various practices to improve your decision-making process. Some of these ideas are very applicable for a Product Owner too.

---

1. Annie Duke, *Thinking in Bets: Making Smarter Decisions When You Don't Have All the Facts,* Portfolio, 2018.

## THE BUDDY SYSTEM OR DECISION POD

The buddy system or a decision pod is a commonly used practice among professional poker players, and it is usually very valuable among a group of Product Owners as well. It's a gathering in which people inspect and evaluate decisions that they themselves did not make. The decision pod can be made up of people who work at the same company or of Product Owner friends you made at a training, meetup, or a previous employer, for example. It's useful to include a Scrum Master, company leader, or people from adjacent domains in a decision pod.

Be careful with inviting only like-minded people. Discussing decisions with people who think like you do isn't particularly useful if you want to obtain alternative ideas, opinions, and perspectives. This pitfall is commonly called the *confirmation bias*. Once an idea has settled in our brains, we start seeking evidence that supports that idea. Inviting like-minded people to a decision pod is bound to result in you cherry-picking data, perspectives, and opinions that back up your idea. Instead, invite people who are different from you. Also, be mindful of potential conflicts of interest. You may not want to evaluate decisions with people who are likely to use your openness, honesty, and transparency to stab you in the back.

When holding a decision pod with your buddies, someone should share a recent decision that they want to evaluate or a decision that they are about to make. The person sharing the decision is preferably open, honest, and transparent about all known information. It should be a safe space in which information is discussed openly but confidentially. In other words, what happens during the session stays in the session. When sharing a decision for evaluation, make sure to explain the decision process, people involved, the decision to be made, potential and foreseen outcomes, and so forth.

However, do not share the outcomes or results of the decision, ever. The results should never be shared in a decision pod because those outcomes might bias people toward a certain opinion. This bias is like the resulting pitfall, which you could have stepped into during our rolling-the-dice game.

Focus only on the process, people involved, key decision information, and other relevant information. The outcome of a decision, though, is irrelevant during a decision pod.

## ACCEPTING UNCERTAINTY IN DECISION MAKING

Like poker, product management could be considered as a game of incomplete information. There is a certain level of uncertainty, and we therefore need to test, experiment, verify, release, and learn. In this process, we can be open and transparent about what is known and what is unknown. Being open about what you know and don't know provides boundaries for your reasoning. In addition, it might allow a buddy to point out opportunities and observations such as, "I notice you don't have this and this information. Have you tried getting that from XYZ?"

Think of decisions like placing small bets in a game of poker. Acknowledge that two factors affect the success of your decisions as a Product Owner (as well as life decisions in general): the quality of your decisions and a good dose of luck. It's okay to make some decisions that produce other outcomes than expected. We can't be lucky all the time. However, it is important to learn from those bets that didn't deliver the outcomes you hoped for, right?

Often, this means we must redefine "right" in our organizations. We need to identify and define what makes a decision a good one. Establishing a good process for decision making and delegating decisions to where the most relevant information resides are good practices. If we aren't wrong just because things didn't work out, then we aren't right just because things turned out well.

# Navigating Product, Process, and Team Dilemmas and Decisions

## Making Choices

Product Owners in the field face various kinds of decisions. Some are simpler, as the first example in this chapter shows, and others are more difficult, like the second example. Imagine you are the Product Owner for a product. You must decide which of the following feature sets you are going to build and release. However, you can only do one of them in the next Sprint, so which of the following would you decide to build and release (see Table 23.1)?

**Table 23.1** Making a Decision: Part 1

| Feature Set A | Feature Set B |
|---|---|
| Feature Set A will likely generate around $50,000 of additional revenues. | Feature Set B will likely generate around $20,000 of additional revenues. |
| It will cost around ten days to build and release. | It will cost around nine days to build and release. |

It's rather unlikely that you would build and release feature set B because it adds way less value than feature set A does. Most Product Owners will go for feature set A, although there is not a lot of information available to base this decision on. The difference between nine and ten days of development isn't that much of a risk, and the potential benefits of feature set A are more than twice that of feature set B. It seems like a simple decision and a done deal, right?

Most decisions we make as Product Owners, though, aren't like this first example. In practice, decisions are often more complex and typically look more like what's shown in Table 23.2. Which feature set would you develop in the following case?

**Table 23.2** Making a Decision: Part 2

| Feature Set A | Feature Set B |
| --- | --- |
| Feature Set A will likely generate around $50,000 of additional revenues. | Failing to implement Feature Set B will result in a $25,000 fine and might decrease our reputation. |
| It will cost around ten days to build and release. | It will cost around ten days to build and release. |

Now other factors in addition to revenue increase come into play. If the main objective is to increase revenue in the short term, feature set A seems to be the logical choice. However, it is rather difficult to put a price on image or reputation damage. Many of the Product Owners we have worked with must regularly comply with laws and regulations. Therefore, they usually favor feature set B. In smaller, startup, or scaleup-like companies, we see more people selecting feature set A. They decide to do things differently after having given the damage control mindset some thought. And they frequently advocate for building feature set A first, which already generates revenues to pay off the potential fines. So, your answer in this situation might depend on your unique context, background, and past experiences. There is no clear right or wrong. There is no "best" decision to be made here.

*It takes 20 years to build a reputation and five minutes to ruin it. If you think about that, you'll do things differently.*

—Warren Buffett

# NAVIGATING DILEMMAS

But now, we get to the real interesting decisions. The following types of decisions are called *dilemmas,* and dilemmas—those are the real deal. They are real struggles and painful decisions to make. So, what do you think about this decision (see Table 23.3).

**Table 23.3** Making a Decision: Part 3

| Feature Set A | Feature Set B |
| --- | --- |
| Feature Set A adds all the basic features to our product, which are market standard, and all our competitors already have them. | Feature Set B adds a unique set of features to our product, which no competitor in the market has today. |

What would you do? Would you build feature set A and build all the basic features that your competitors already have? Interesting choice, because now you will be playing catch-up with the competition, potentially for a very long time. Or did you select feature set B? Another interesting choice, allowing you to position your product uniquely. However, how will you get any paying customers if you don't even have the basics in place? Tough situation, and a tough decision to make.

Some decisions can be considered choices. You can choose A or B. Some of those choices are easy, like the first example was. Some choices are more difficult decisions, like the second example was. A choice is a decision that can be made, and afterwards, it may turn out to be a decision to applaud or regret. Perhaps it was an easy decision, perhaps it was a tough one. Perhaps it was a good decision, maybe a bad one. Either way, you can decide to choose A or B, and you can evaluate that decision afterward.

When talking about dilemmas, though, it's not an option to choose A or B. It needs to be a decision to do both, at least to some extent. Think of a dilemma as trying to dodge the bull horns in a bullfight. You want to avoid getting hit by both horns. You don't want to dodge horn A only to get hit by horn B. You want to dodge the bull entirely, not partly. Thus, in a dilemma, you must always acquire the best of A combined with the best of B.

Not resolving both A and B results in potential drama and compromises on both sides. Choosing either A or B results in a short-term win on one of them but a long-term loss on both in the end. In a dilemma, you must tackle both A and B for a long-term, viable solution.

If you plot a diagram of these two options, they are represented by two orthogonal axes, as shown in Figure 23.1. Let's say that the vertical axis means an increasing pursuit of realizing option or value A. When we lean toward only choosing option A, we get ourselves into the single-sided solution in the top-heavy zone. This zone could be referred to as the land of the unicorns. It's the land of hopes and dreams that all will be okay someday.

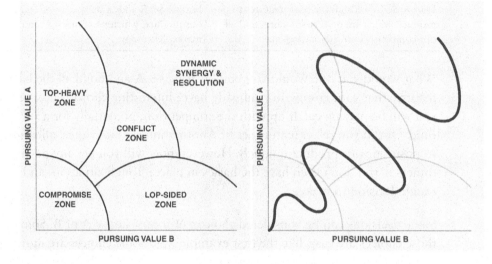

**Figure 23.1** Navigating dilemmas with the dilemma framework. (Adapted from Gerard D. Drenth and Ciarán McGinley, "Some Thoughts on 'Dilemma Thinking," white paper, NormannPartners, 2019.)

The alternative is to pursue the horizontal axis, or option B. When solely focusing on option B, we may end up in the lop-sided zone, or the land of the dinosaurs. Although amazing creatures, most animals from the dinosaur age are extinct. In other words, this is also not a place where we want our product to end up.

The way forward, and the only solution in a dilemma situation, is to work from the compromise zone, through the conflict zone, toward the resolution zone. Dealing with dilemmas is a process of trial and error, experimentation, failures, learnings, inspecting, and adapting. There are no best practices for dealing with dilemmas, because dilemmas are often unique in themselves and in the context of the organization. However, the first step is usually to get our heads out of the sand and acknowledge that we're dealing with a dilemma (in the compromise zone). The next step mainly involves experimentation and balancing work on options A and B (getting through the conflict zone) to get to a proper resolution. Fortunately, we at least have a framework that may help us in dealing with all this complexity, right?[1]

Successful resolution of dilemmas requires flexibility and accommodation on the part of all viewpoints. Dilemmas are never truly solved but must be constantly navigated to maintain the balance.

---

1. In case you are wondering which framework this might be, it's the Scrum framework, of course! Helping people and teams in solving complex problems in complex environments is what Scrum does.

# Improving the Speed and Quality of Decisions

## The Cost of Delaying Decisions

The previous chapter explored various types of decisions that Product Owners make. We explored simple and more complicated decisions as well as dilemmas. At some point, a decision needs to be made, sometimes by the Product Owner, sometimes together with others, and sometimes through delegation. In Chapter 21, "Evaluating Your Product Decisions," we explored how decisions are also influenced by the quality of the decision, the process, the people involved, and the factor of luck. In addition, it seems that the speed of decision making is also important.

Research advisory company The Standish Group has published interesting research about the cost of delayed decision making. One study showed that if decision latency is reduced from 5 hours to 1 hour, time to market increases by approximately 30%. That probably makes sense, right? If we make decisions faster, and if we don't have to wait too long for others to make—or be involved in—the decision, we can speed up the entire process.

On the other hand, it seems contradictory to other effective concepts, such as delayed decision making. Principles such as just-in-time decision making and queue management are valuable in decision making as well. In some cases, it helps to preserve options and make decisions at the latest responsible moment in time. So, some decisions should indeed be delayed to the last responsible moment, but that is no excuse for procrastination or for wanting everybody's opinion before deciding.

## FAST DECISIONS ARE MORE SUCCESSFUL THAN SLOW DECISIONS

Nowadays it is well-known that small projects are typically more successful than large projects. The Standish Group has collected data since 2008 about the success, failures, and challenges in projects, including the impact of project size on project success. It publishes its findings in annual CHAOS reports.

That research has proven that small projects are more successful. This finding makes sense: in a complex domain, making projects smaller, working in short iterations, delivering results, and getting feedback all make it easier to see the bigger picture and to continuously inspect and adapt. The idea of taking small steps and delivering something that is "Done" every Sprint is at the heart of Scrum.

This is also one of the paramount reasons why Scrum works: it is the ultimate slicer of projects! The limitation of the Sprint length forces teams to come up with small "projects" that must deliver something by the end of the Sprint (or sooner).

Figure 24.1 illustrates research data from the CHAOS Report 2018. The graph shows that projects are often more successful if good decision latency occurs in the project. It also shows that projects are much more likely to be challenged or to fail if poor decision latency exists. But what is good latency? Unfortunately, no clear definition of good decision latency is provided. However, you are probably familiar with projects where discussions go on and on and on. By the time the company has made a decision, it gets reversed. We can at least say that taking a long time to make decisions, or changing the high-level direction all the time, is likely to result in poor decision latency.

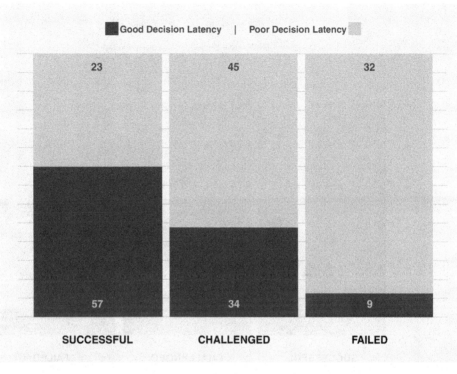

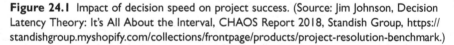

**Figure 24.1** Impact of decision speed on project success. (Source: Jim Johnson, Decision Latency Theory: It's All About the Interval, CHAOS Report 2018, Standish Group, https://standishgroup.myshopify.com/collections/frontpage/products/project-resolution-benchmark.)

Another interesting—yet unsurprising——data point in the report illustrates that highly skilled people and teams deliver successful projects more often than do their less-skilled counterparts (see Figure 24.2). The more skillful teams are at making decisions, the less often their decisions are slowed, reconsidered, or reversed. Having good decision-making skills in the teams enables them to make higher-quality decisions faster, which improves decision latency, decision quality, and overall project success.

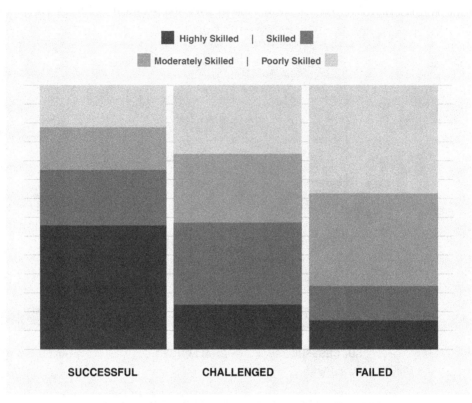

**Figure 24.2** Impact of decision skill on project success. (Source: Jim Johnson, Decision Latency Theory: It's All About the Interval, CHAOS Report 2018, Standish Group, https://standishgroup. myshopify.com/collections/frontpage/products/project-resolution-benchmark.)

So, what's the point of showing this data? Well, looking at the data and projects in daily practice, it seems to be very important to hire highly skilled, self-managing people when doing projects in the complex domain. It's important that projects are staffed by people who can make good decisions and are able and willing to make those decisions (quickly enough). The CHAOS Report 2018 also introduced the "five cards of a winning hand for project success," which includes some interesting statements:

**First card:** The project needs to be small.

**Second card:** The Product Owner or sponsor must be highly skilled.

**Third card:** The process must be Agile.

**Fourth card:** The Agile team must be highly skilled in both the Agile process and the technology.

**Fifth card:** The organization must be highly skilled at emotional maturity.

## SPECIAL SNOWFLAKE SYNDROME

*These are some interesting data points, guys,* you might think, *but we are a unique company. We are special. We do some complex and advanced stuff. Things just work a little bit differently in our organization.* Whether your company is a bank, an insurer, a car manufacturer, a hardware company, a software company, or anything else, there is usually a good reason to delay decisions. However, it happens only rarely that the cost of these delayed decisions is calculated and included in the decision to be made. Imagine building a hardware product. Decisions are usually delayed when building hardware products because of the costs for producing electronics for fast-moving consumer goods, for example.

*California Management Review* published a study[1] of 391 teams that designed custom integrated circuits. This study shows that frequent and early releases resulted in increased errors, but because they used low-cost prototyping technologies, their time and total effort required were significantly less than when trying to get their design right the first time. By delaying decisions, you are potentially delaying the discovery of critical problems and challenges.

It is similar to the batch-size problem in Kanban: think of it as buying a supply of vegetables. If you buy a four-month supply on a single trip, your transaction cost is low, but most of the vegetables will spoil, increasing your holding cost. If you buy a one-day supply, your spoilage will be low, but your transaction costs will be high. Intuitively, you try to strike a balance between the two, driven mostly by picky eaters in your household who seem to change their habits on a whim.

---

1. Stefan Thomke and Donald Reinertsen, "Agile Product Development: Managing Development Flexibility in Uncertain Environments," *California Management Review* 41, no. 1 (1998), 8, https://doi.org/10.2307/41165973.

## WHY YOU SHOULD PROBABLY MAKE DECISIONS FAST(ER)

In addition to increasing development costs, delayed decisions delay your time to market. Getting to market more quickly gives you significant advantages:

- **Increased sales and profit margins:** The earlier the product reaches the market, the longer the life span of that product.
- **Larger market share:** A quick introduction allows more time to build market share before the product becomes a commodity.
- **Greater market responsiveness:** You can react more quickly to competitors' moves or market changes.
- **Lower operating capital:** Think of product development as an investment; faster time to market frees up financial and operating resources for other value-adding activities.

Data and research done by Supply and Demand Chain Executive (sdcexec. com) shows that a fast-moving consumer product that launches 9 months after a competitor typically yields only 50% of the anticipated revenues. Therefore, you would have to create something to leapfrog the competition, which is an expensive catch-up race that you could have avoided.

## HOW TO SPEED UP YOUR DECISION MAKING

Here are a couple of steps you may consider to shorten decision-making time:

- **Simplify:** Use short iterations, focus on a single goal, and define the benefit you want to achieve and how to measure it. Clear goals remove the need for many hour-to-hour decisions on your end.
- **Collaborate and inspire:** Make sure your teams know what they are doing and why. Leverage their collective intellect to let go of the things that the Product Owner has to decide.
- **Constantly order your Product Backlog:** Make sure it reflects the most important problems that need to be solved and that you are testing a working increment with real users. Evidence speeds up decision making and creates a shared understanding.

- **Let it go:** Take a page from Elsa in *Frozen* and think about what you need to do yourself and what others can do. Delegate explicitly (e.g., "I expect you to take these kinds of decisions").

## EMPOWERED PRODUCT OWNERS

*Delegate to others? I must get buy-in on every decision myself!* Well, that is a bad place to be. We already know that empowerment directly influences success, but now you know why. See Figure 24.3, which illustrates that projects are more successful when Product Owners are empowered to make decisions.

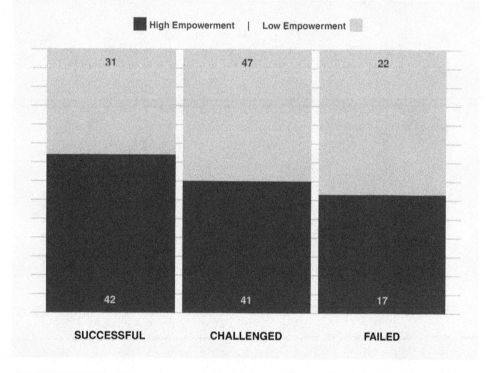

**Figure 24.3** Impact of an empowered Product Owner/sponsor on project success. (Source: Jim Johnson, Decision Latency Theory: It's All About the Interval, CHAOS Report 2018, Standish Group, https://standishgroup.myshopify.com/collections/frontpage/products/project-resolution-benchmark.)

# THE DECISION MAKER

# SUMMARY

## KEY LEARNINGS AND INSIGHTS

This concludes Part V, in which you explored the Decision Maker stance. In this Part, you learned about the skills, traits, practices, and tools that great Decision Maker Product Owners frequently use. You explored how to delegate more decisions to other people, using Delegation Poker. You also explored an example set of typical product-related decisions to make, how to reflect on your own decision-making, and where to delegate more or take more ownership. You learned about better ways to evaluate decisions, avoiding the common pitfalls and confirmation bias, and how to think more like a professional poker player at times by placing small bets instead of big investments. This part also explored the differences between decisions that you may or may not regret, and you explored how to navigate dilemmas that don't offer a select-A-or-B choice. Finally, you learned why improving the speed of decision making is critical to product success, therewith improving not only time to market but also the quality of decisions. In order to create winning products in the marketplace, it is vital that product-related decisions are made by the right people, at the right time, using the right information. In other words, Product Owners need to develop themselves into strong decision makers.

## QUICK QUIZ REVIEW

If you took the Quick Quiz at the beginning of Part V, compare your answers to those in the following table. Now that you have read about the Decision Maker stance, would you change any of your answers? Do you agree with the following answers?

| Statement | Agree | Disagree |
|---|---|---|
| Making decisions faster can lead to more success for your product. | ✓ | |
| Each decision has two outcomes: the right one and the wrong one. | | ✓ |
| Decisions are deterministic in nature; given enough time and expertise, the correct answer can be found. | | ✓ |
| Product Owners make no decisions about technology and people. | | ✓ |
| Product management is more like a game of poker than like a game of chess. | ✓ | |
| Effectively navigating dilemmas is very complex. You need to do a lot of research and analysis to figure out what the best option is. | | ✓ |
| Product Owners should take an enterprise-level view when making decisions. | ✓ | |
| When evaluating decisions, you should mostly consider the results that were achieved. It's not about luck, it's about results. | | ✓ |

# WANT TO LEARN MORE?

In this part, you learned about the Decision Maker stance. Various topics, tools, techniques, and concepts will help you to strengthen this stance.

If you want to improve your Decision Maker stance, consider exploring Daniel Goleman's six styles of leadership[1] and Delegation Poker as described in Jurgen Appelo's book *Management 3.0: Leading Agile Developers, Developing Agile Leaders* (Addison-Wesley, 2011). Also, learn more about Liberating Structures,[2] which is useful for large group decision-making facilitation.

In addition, you can consider reading *Thinking in Bets: Making Smarter Decisions When You Don't Have All the Facts* by Annie Duke (Portfolio/Penguin, 2019), *Escaping the Build Trap: How Effective Product Management Creates Real Value* by Melissa Perri (O'Reilly, 2018), and *Extreme Ownership* by Jocko Willink and Leif Babin (St. Martin's Press, 2017).

---

1. For example, https://medium.com/the-value-maximizers/making-better-decisions-as-product-owner-a8cefec1271f.
2. https://www.liberatingstructures.com.

# THE COLLABORATOR

*The Internet is a reliable system composed of loosely connected and imper-fect parts that works because nobody is in control.*

— *Wired*

## QUICK QUIZ

To connect to Part VI, answer each of the following statements by checking the Agree or Disagree column. The answers are shared in the Part VI Summary.

| Statement | Agree | Disagree |
|---|---|---|
| There is no such thing as an Agile contract. | | |
| If a contract starts out as fixed price, fixed scope, fixed time, there is no way to change it. | | |
| Governance "just is," and we must deal with it. It's not up for discussion. | | |
| All governance is defined and decided upon outside the reach of Scrum Teams. | | |
| Contracts can be described in ways that promote Agile behavior and agility. | | |
| Finance stakeholders are not interested in emerging or changing backlogs. They want a fixed plan that doesn't change for the next four quarters. | | |
| One way to look at the budget is through the perspectives of market and product strategy. | | |

# How Agile Governance Affects Product Owners

## Introduction to the Collaborator

Obviously, Scrum is all about collaboration in the Scrum Team between the Product Owner, Scrum Master, and Developers as well as between the Scrum Team and stakeholders, users, and customers. The Scrum framework provides the events, artifacts, and Product Owner accountabilities to optimize collaboration in order to deliver done, usable, and valuable work at each Sprint. The ability to collaborate with other people effectively is a core skill for any Product Owner.

So far, we've discussed various tools, techniques, practices, concepts, and tips around effective product management. Although it wasn't explicitly mentioned earlier, most of the contents from previous parts require plenty of collaboration. You can collaborate on the vision, strategy, goals, personas, market analysis, experiments, and so forth. What is so special about the Collaborator stance?

### I Spy with My Little Eye

"What do you mean you can't authorize that?" said Noa. She was clearly agitated, and Sandra was not sure how to handle that—she wasn't very good with emotions.

"I'm sorry, but it just isn't in the budget," she started. "We can't go and hire agencies to do the design if it is not in the budget." She explained. Noa blinked twice, "Surely you understand that the budget was set last year? Before we understood what we needed to do to make this product a success?"

Sandra nodded. That was true, yet there was very little she could do about it. The budget for this year was approved by the accountant and was signed off on by the CFO. The budget cycle was difficult enough as it was, and she was not going to go through that again.

"Look, I know we have policies, and I understand that we need to come up with a plan, but there must also be a way to make this work," Noa said. "What if the printing press burned out? Surely, we wouldn't wait a year to buy a new one. Is the budget really set in stone by our accountants?"

"Well, there is—," Sandra started, and at the same time she felt her stomach turn. She really didn't like change.

For starters, here are some positive outcomes and benefits that we have observed when Product Owners take the Collaborator stance:

- **Improved flexibility of the organization:** When collaboration improves, so does the organization's ability to handle change. Strong teamwork and collaboration make it easier to pivot when the customer needs change or when disruptive technologies or competitors enter the marketplace.

- **More engaged employees:** "Unfortunately, only 33% of employees in the US are engaged," says Nick Sanchez, chief people officer at Namely.[1] This is a big risk for many organizations; however, it seems that one of the best ways to get workers more engaged is to improve teamwork.

- **More productive meetings:** Meeting efficiency and effectiveness increase when people and teams are collaborating effectively. With proactive teamwork enriching the corporate culture, workers need fewer meetings as they

---

1. Kat Boogard, "Employee Engagement Strategies That Work," Wrike Inc., October 15, 2021, https://www.wrike.com/blog/5-strategies-employee-engagement/#Why-employee-engagement-matters.

accomplish their tasks and use tools to document work progress or delegate work yet to be done. And when meetings must be held, there is more proactive information sharing, more engagement, and more support for each other's efforts.

- **Accelerated business velocity:** With a collaborative culture, you gain the ability to bring products to the market faster. Teamwork and communication speed up the entire process and make it easier to produce anything. The entire organization's ability to create value accelerates as a result.

- **Innovative ideas:** Sure, collaboration is never easy. It generates as much friction as it does productive output. But surely there is a silver lining behind all that friction between conflicting personalities and work styles, right? Right! It generates dynamic, innovative ideas. And without those new and vibrant ideas, your organization dies a mediocre death.

- **Better alignment with stakeholders:** When you talk about collaboration, it's a good idea to especially focus on external collaboration with your customers, partners, and vendors—the stakeholders whom your product directly affects. If you can leverage their feedback into your product development process, then there will be better alignment between the customers' actual needs and your product's features. Win-win.

- **Increased profitability:** And then, of course, there's the bottom line. Collaboration improves it because after recruiting all the superstar geniuses and building a culture worthy of their skills, they get to work generating the innovative ideas that will propel you forward and bring home the bacon. Everyone is happy!

Although there may be many other benefits, regularly taking a Collaborator stance as a Product Owner should lead to improved team performance, more effective collaboration, happier and more engaged Developers, and increased customer and stakeholder satisfaction.

So, collaboration is important and valuable. Collaborating with other people is also something that many Product Owners in practice do automatically. It's part of the job, and it's necessary. There are, however, elements such as governance and compliance that may greatly impact the ability to collaborate. In addition, we sometimes need to work with external parties for which contracts are created. Or we might be contracted by another party ourselves. And of course, product finances and budgeting influence collaboration as well.

Here is what great Collaborators do:

- **Great collaborators are open and transparent:** Telling stakeholders and teams the truth is part of being open and transparent, of course, but it tends to happen after someone has asked a question. Being open and transparent goes beyond answering questions honestly to proactively and openly sharing information that may or may not be relevant to the stakeholders and Developers. Transparency builds trust because people will never feel as though the Product Owner is keeping something from them.

- **They say what they do, and they do what they say:** Nobody likes to work with people who drop the ball, even if it just happens on occasion. Beware: dropping the ball isn't the same as making a mistake. In complex environments, people make mistakes, and that's part of the complex work that we typically do. Strong Collaborators, though, can judge how long it will take them to get something done and then manage their schedule to deliver on time. People can count on them to do what they say they will do, and consequently, people love working with these great Collaborators.

- **They allow for a little give and take:** Collaboration should benefit everyone—not just Product Owners but the teams, the individuals on the teams, and the stakeholders. A question great Collaborators ask themselves is, *What am I contributing to this relationship and how am I supporting the greater good?* Stakeholders and teams are more likely to help Product Owners who are willing to collaborate with them when they need help as well.

- **They listen to understand, not to respond:** Great Collaborators know that people like to be heard and to know that their ideas and thoughts are being taken into consideration. Listening to each other and exchanging ideas and opinions is a key element of collaboration. Product Owners who want to be effective Collaborators must listen—*truly* listen—to all parties and be prepared to make changes based on their input and feedback when it makes sense to do so.

- **They are open to other options, and they are willing to compromise:** Collaborators understand that life isn't about always being right or winning every battle. Good Collaborators choose their battles. They know that just because they prefer option A over option B, it doesn't mean that they should always fight for option A.

- **Collaborators are kind to those they collaborate with:** Product Owners carry a lot of weight on their shoulders. Between the endless work to be done and the many deadlines to deliver on, the pressure can wreak havoc on moods and manners. However, great Collaborators know that work can get done without making enemies along the way. People work harder, smarter, and faster when they like the people they work with. To maximize the value of their product, Collaborator Product Owners are kind to those they want—and need—to collaborate with.

- **They understand that they need to step up:** Great Collaborators understand that collaboration is a two-way interaction. When collaborating with others, they don't settle for doing the bare minimum, and occasionally go above and beyond in unexpected ways. They gain a lot of goodwill and buy-in because people know they will step up to the plate when necessary, which makes collaborating with them a lot easier.

In this part, we focus on increasing your knowledge and understanding about various elements that influence your collaborative abilities, such as governance, contracting, and finances and budgeting. The first topic? Let's talk about governance.

## INTRODUCING AGILE GOVERNANCE

Every organization, small, medium, large, or enterprise, needs a form of governance. What is governance? What does governance relate to? There are many different definitions, types, and elements of governance. There is corporate governance, for example, as well as project governance, portfolio management governance, financial governance, and so on. You may find that the definition of governance varies greatly among organizations.

Although most Product Owners don't get too excited about governance, it will help you in your work to have at least some understanding about it. In addition, because there are so many different perspectives on governance, it will likely prove to be helpful to reach a consensus in your organization about what governance means. It may help you to reflect and argue some of the rules, policies, and agreements made in the company.

## DEFINITION OF CORPORATE GOVERNANCE

We often use the following definition of governance:

> *(Corporate) governance is the collection of mechanisms, processes, and relations by which corporations are controlled and operated. Governance structures and principles identify the distribution of rights and responsibilities among different participants in the corporation and include the rules and procedures for making decisions in corporate affairs.*

From this definition, you can discern two main divisions of governance: there are the processes, agreements, rules, mechanisms, and structures that exist *inside the organization*, and there are processes, agreements, rules, mechanisms, and structures that exist *outside the organization*. These are often created by companies, governments, and regulators if something goes wrong or when they are afraid that something might go wrong. Governance is, in that sense, a way of managing risks, problems, and potential escalations. If a customer service employee is a bit too generous with cashbacks upon hearing problems from customers, the company might create a process that requires approval before cashbacks are given.

Alternatively, governance could be seen as a way of providing opportunities. Consider, for example, that some countries have created laws about free and accessible education for all citizens. Or consider that companies create career pathways for employees to offer them growth opportunities, personal development, and financial benefits progression.

A pattern and form of governance often seen in Scrum Teams is that the Developers want the Product Owner to always formally sign off on every functionality that was developed in the Sprint so that they never run into surprises during a Sprint Review. Such policies and agreements seem necessary at the time they are created. Their purpose, after all, is to prevent mistakes being made in the future. It all makes sense . . . until it doesn't. In order to improve organizational agility, implementing these kinds of sign-offs will slow product teams down, rather than speed them up.

*This is a story about an elderly woman whose husband had recently died. Due to the loss of her husband, who always took care of finances, this lady needed to visit a local bank office to verify her identity. She couldn't drive a car, she wasn't very mobile, and public transport was difficult for her to use. Hence, it was rather difficult for her to get to her local branch. When a customer care employee contacted this customer to schedule an appointment for verification of her identity, the lady explained her situation.*

*In the past, customer care employees had to ask management for permission to arrange special accommodations for their customers. However, the bank decided to experiment with giving their customer care employees full responsibility and authority to help customers to the best of their ability. People buy cars and houses, get loans, and raise children, so surely they are responsible enough to make $100 decisions, the bank's leaders figured. So, customer care employees could now decide to arrange compensation, send flowers, send a card, or, as in this case, arrange a taxi. And they did.*

*The lady was brought to the bank by taxi, and she was taken back home afterward. In the meantime, the customer care employee had sent a sympathy card to the lady's home to express condolences and wish her all the best in the difficult times ahead. The lady was so happy about the service provided and the postcard she received that she sent a card back to the customer care employee to thank them for their compassion and outstanding service.*

*Think about that for a moment. How often do employees at your company get a thank-you note from customers who are thrilled about your services? How often do you create customers and fans for life just by arranging a taxi and sending a card? Well, the customer support employees at this bank got loads of cards when management decided to delegate and let it go. The bank's net promoter score went up like crazy. Oh, and by the way, this "letting go" by management and delegating decisions to the team didn't increase overall expenses—it reduced them!*

*— Robbin*

In many organizations, we add rules, processes, structures, and governance when things go wrong. We keep adding more rules, but we hardly ever remove them when things go right. This type of governance is under our control—we can change the rules—and in many cases, we should seriously consider doing so, if we want to enable and improve organizational agility.

Okay, so what about external governance? External governance is created outside the organization. It's defined by governments, associations, regulators, instances, or other governing bodies. External governance is often found in the form of laws, by-laws, rules, and regulations. You can find external governance all around you: in the laws of your country, the local rules in traffic, the by-laws of your sports club, or the rules applied in your favorite sports game.

Various companies in the maritime safety industry joined forces with their clientele in the International Association of Lighthouse Authorities (IALA). Together, they set international rules and standards to regulate safety, set standards for data exchange, and defined what "good performance" looks like. A small company from the Netherlands learned that if you play together, you can influence the outcome. For example, at the Open Inter VTS Exchange Format website,[2] you can find not only a picture of the main players in the domain but also a picture of a very young version of one of the authors of this book as they agree on an exchange format that Vessel Traffic Safety systems must adhere to.

---

2. http://openivef.org.

Similar examples can be found everywhere. Euro Control sets the standard for air traffic, for example. The Fraunhofer-Gesellschaft in Germany came up with the mp3 standard. The European Union creates laws, rules, and regulations across Europe. The European Central Bank and Authority Financial Markets influence a lot of things that happen within the walls of a bank, and the list goes on.

As a Product Owner, you will likely need to deal with such external governance effectively and seek to influence that governance so that you can deliver value for the people who matter most of all, your customers.

## ORGANIZATIONAL GOVERNANCE ENTAILS MANY ELEMENTS

Governance is a broad topic. It can be connected to many different elements. The rules, processes, and agreements made in your organization about topics such as risk management, documentation, technology, architecture, security, privacy, and so forth, are all part of the organization's governance. Most of this governance is defined internally and can therefore be changed. Some of it might be external governance and more difficult to change.

Figure 25.1 shows various elements that are likely part of your organizational governance. Although not all elements might be applicable, most probably are if you are working in a small or mid-sized company or large corporation. This list of governance elements is far from complete, but listing everything that has to do with governance would result in dozens of pages, and you're not likely to read that as a Product Owner.

During our Professional Scrum Product Owner-Advanced courses, we often run this governance chapter as a series of exercises. One of the exercises includes organizing all these governance elements into groups: internal vs. external governance, and as a second step, connecting them to the Product Owner versus Scrum Master versus Developers versus outside the Scrum Team, as shown in Figure 25.2.

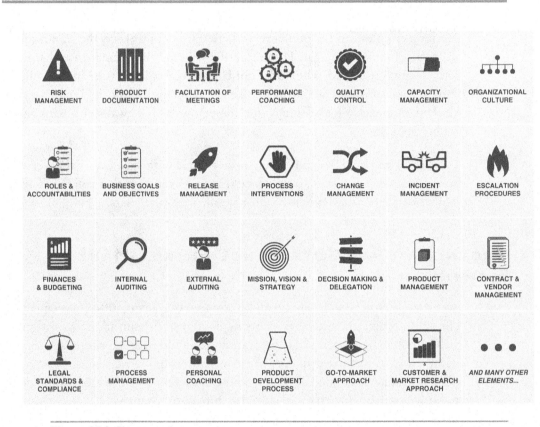

**Figure 25.1** Elements of governance

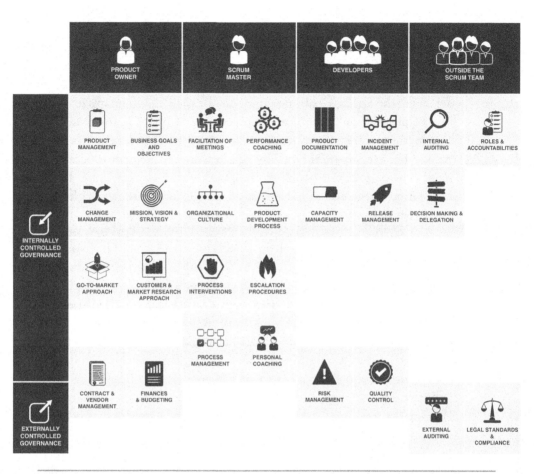

**Figure 25.2** Exercise from the Professional Scrum Product Owner-Advanced training

During this exercise, people start discussing what the governance elements mean. For example, risk management, finance and budgeting, and change management are often linked to multiple roles, typically including the Product Owner. The takeaway is that the point of this exercise is to discuss what these elements mean. Let's explore two examples.

Risk management can be connected to the Product Owner. It's the Product Owner's responsibility to identify strengths, weaknesses, threats, and opportunities for the product as well as to order the Product Backlog and to consider value and risk in that ordering. The Product Owner also assesses risks in the market, product, and industry to handle in the product. Risk management can also be related to risks in technology or in the solution space. Identifying and assessing potential security, stability, and performance risks can be taken care of by the Developers. Then there are risks related to the process, culture, people, and way of working. Risks that might prevent the Scrum Team from achieving the Sprint Goal (impediments) or risks that jeopardize the application of professional Scrum can be taken care of by the Scrum Master. And of course, there is the perspective of risk management in large corporations, like banks. These companies typically have a risk management function or department. These groups of people do risk management all day long. It's their job to identify, assess, communicate, and manage corporate-level risks, such as those that may affect the bank's license to operate.

Let's inspect a second example: product documentation. How you handle product documentation may be completely up to your team and the company. Some (typically smaller startup-like) companies don't have any governance about documentation at all. Other organizations set standards for documentation such as technical, user, architectural, in-code, marketing, sales, operational, and more. With product documentation—that is, documentation about the product's unique value proposition, customer problems to solve, and key features—the Product Owner likely plays a role. With technical or architectural documentation, the Developers likely take responsibility. Documentation about the way of working, culture, and values is likely worked on by a Scrum Master. And there may be many other forms of documentation used outside the Scrum Team. In some cases, you need to comply with industry standards. For example, pharmaceutical companies need to always include prescribed use with their medicines. Other companies need to be able to track changes in documents, processes, or systems.

You'll notice in these examples that governance elements can be explained in many ways. There is (at least some) room to define your governance and your ideas. And that's the thing about governance: for the most part, it is whatever you and your company define it to be and describes who is accountable and authorized to make decisions and how it needs to be handled. So, if governance is mostly defined by us, then we can also change it!

# EFFECTIVELY DEALING WITH GOVERNANCE

To change existing governance or install new governance, you first need to define what governance or its elements mean in your context. You may have discovered that most of the processes, rules, and regulations are internal governance, but some might be outside your circle of control or influence. This is usually the case with legislation of industry standards.

Over the past 20 years, we've heard many people say things like, "That's just how it works here" or "We've always done it that way." Although that might be true, and although things have indeed been done in a certain way for potentially a very long time, it doesn't always mean that it must stay that way. Most of the governance defined in organizations is still internal governance. So, if you run into issues that block you from being an effective Collaborator, try to change it. Of course, not every battle is worth fighting. But, if you truly believe that you could be more effective at maximizing value if the governance were changed, then you probably should make the effort.

With most governance elements being internally defined, a Collaborator Product Owner could enlist the help of the Scrum Master and Developers to change the governance. Although it is often not the case when you have just started your Scrum adoption, trusting a Product Owner to handle the product vision, strategy, roadmap, decision making, and product finances should make sense. Taking ownership of return on investment and longer-term product success leads to faster decision making and more ownership, so a Product Owner should likely step in. Similarly, process improvements and process management are great elements to be tackled by a Scrum Master. Personal coaching is a profession. Perhaps not all Scrum Masters make outstanding personal coaches, but the great ones do. Define what this governance element means, and then see who should take ownership of it. Many things can be handled by the Developers, especially when they have grown beyond code writers and have become product Developers with the skills to develop all aspects of the product. Self-management of the team happens within boundaries; governance can make these boundaries transparent and allow the teams to grow.

Some things might also be outside of your control. You might contribute to elements such as organizational culture and internal auditing, for example, without actually owning them. Perhaps you don't even need to influence or know about some of the example elements listed in this chapter, but having some awareness of them is useful. Although there is a lot of work to be done by a Product Owner already, there are two governance elements that don't get enough attention in most organizations: budgeting and contracting. These elements are important for a Product Owner to consider, so we offer you some additional guidance and inspiration on these topics in the next chapters.

# Product Budgeting Done in an Agile Way

"Sorry, our budgeting process is not yet very flexible or Agile; you will just have to make those numbers that we forecasted last year." Have you ever heard something similar in your company? Have you ever been in that situation where the budgets, forecasts, targets, or plans were set in stone and couldn't be changed? When a product fails to meet its budget, target, or forecast, it could be failing because the Product Owner

- Produced a bad plan.
- Produced a good plan but failed to execute it.
- Produced a bad plan and failed to execute it.

There may be many other reasons for not making the targets, of course. External factors such as market changes, changes in customer needs, an international crisis, and changing environments can all influence plans and budgets. Perhaps the plan, budget, or forecast was the best that could possibly be made given the information available at the time. A changing environment can be hard to deal with effectively (though we can also understand the situation of the company and its leaders). Perhaps investments were made that were based on those budget forecasts and plans. Perhaps the organization needed some plans and forecasts on which to base hiring, marketing expenses, procurement of tooling, or changes in infrastructure. Regardless of all other factors, the company must be able to pay employee wages and operate as a sustainable business. So, forecasting budgets and targets, and alignment on financial aspects, is a crucial part of professional product management.

Some Product Owners focus too much on all the uncertainties. We have often heard Product Owners say things like, "We don't know when the product will be shipped, because we are Agile," or "We can't make a budget forecast because we can't control when customers will sign the deal." Although such comments sound fair in Agile minds, the point of being Agile is to not stop planning. So, an important question to answer is, How can we bridge the traditional world of long-term plans with the Agile world? What forms of budgeting and forecasting can we apply that allow finance and control to be compliant while also allowing for agility and a changing environment?

## THREE HORIZONS

In most large or enterprise organizations, people are used to setting yearly budgets. Most of these budgets are set in a yearly cadence. Typically, near the end of the current year, the forecasts get fixed for the next year. For certain parts of the organization, this makes a lot of sense. If the company expects to remain in the same office building for the next year, then those office costs (potentially including inflation) can be forecasted and are likely to stay the same throughout the year. When it comes to people's wages, it's a bit more difficult, because some people might leave, others might join, and some might move into new positions with higher salaries. Although an educated forecast can be made, the budget cannot be set in stone because HR changes can impact it, sometimes significantly.

Then there are forecasts for the products and services. These are the most difficult budgets to forecast because a company doesn't know for sure how many new customers will join, how many existing ones will leave, how many additional revenues can be extracted with new products, and so forth. Once again, an educated guess can be made on the basis of past performance, market growth, current market share, sales goals, and other inputs, but those budgets can't be predicted with 100 percent certainty.

One of the problems with providing a budget is that companies tend to provide a fixed budget for teams or projects, without clarifying the return period of that investment. This can lead to favoring short-term development over strategic long-term development. That is not necessarily a bad thing. In the complex domain, it is hard to get a long-term goal right. Therefore, the short-term goals that we set should drive toward validation of that long-term goal and not simply follow opportunities when they arise.

In *The Alchemy of Growth,*[1] Mehrdad Baghai, Stephen Coley, and David White introduced the three horizons framework. This framework provides a structure for companies to assess their potential growth opportunities without neglecting present performance. The three horizons framework is based on research into how companies sustain growth over time. Although the three horizons framework was initially designed for assessing growth potential, it can also be used effectively to classify budget forecasts with different return on investment (ROI) periods. Thinking in these horizons can help to avoid starvation of long-term developments while maintaining maneuverability for shorter-term goals.

The three horizons can be connected to your budgeting strategy as follows:

- Horizon 1: Business as usual. The first horizon relates to the company's or product's current business. Investments made into this horizon are done to fuel the business as usual. The purpose of budget spent on this horizon is to keep the product in a state where it continues to operate, perform well, and add value for current customers and users. Products and services in this category are usually the current cash cows of the organization and provide the greatest profits and cash flow.
- Horizon 2: Sustaining innovation. As was discussed in Part IV, "The Experimenter," sustaining innovation is achieved by building on top of the existing products and services. Investing on horizon 2 might be needed to convince competitor customers to switch to your product. Investments on horizon 2 could also include a technology upgrade or overhaul to maintain

---

1. Mehrdad Baghai, Stephen Coley, and David White, *The Alchemy of Growth: Practical Insights for Building the Enduring Enterprise,* Perseus Books, 1999.

revenue/cost ratio. Initiatives that are funded on horizon 2 are typically the larger items in the Product Backlog.

- Horizon 3: Disruptive innovation. Horizon 3 investments are big, ambitious, future ideas for growth. This type of innovation is all about taking a new approach or moving into a new field. Changing the business model or creating a whole new product for a new market, for example, are typical horizon 3 initiatives. Achieving an ROI for these initiatives usually takes time, because they are the big bets to place and potential cash cows of the future.

When deciding how to spend your product budget, it is helpful to connect the budget to these horizons, as it will help you to balance short-term, midterm, and long-term investments. The pitfall for many Product Owners is to focus too much on one of these horizons, for example, spending most of the budget on horizon 1 or horizon 3. Using these horizons and applying inspect and adapt over time helps to balance budget spending with the different needs of the product, company, and your (potential) customers.

## BUDGETING IS LIKE PRODUCT BACKLOG MANAGEMENT

One of the issues we frequently face is that the finance and control department needs a budget or financial forecast for a year or even six quarters ahead. This might be required due to regulations, but in many cases, there is an option to change the forecast after it has been made. If long-term financial forecasting and budgeting is needed in your company, then it's best to comply and forecast one year or six quarters ahead.

However, instead of fixing the budget, use it as the forecast. That is, inspect and adapt the budget, per quarter, at clear and predictable intervals throughout the year. Doing this will allow the finance department to be compliant with regulations and compliance standards and will allow you to spend the budget more flexibly. In that sense, think of budgeting like managing the Product Backlog:

- **The goals for the upcoming Sprints are clear.** The Product Backlog items to be delivered can be roughly identified (although they are not set in stone).

They can be connected to maintenance and improvements (horizon 1), significant product changes (horizon 2), or experiments and strategic goals (horizon 3).

- **The goals, objectives, and high-level ideas for the next quarter are coarser-grained.** You may have some bigger goals and objectives, some big ideas or themes, and some bigger features to build. These goals, ideas, and features could again be connected to horizon 1, 2, or 3 investments. The potential costs and benefits for these bigger ideas can be only roughly estimated—for example, using a generous budget range of $100,000 to $150,000.

- **The forecast for the remaining quarters mostly contains big bets, themes, goals, and/or large future ideas.** These quarters contain a couple of ideas that seem currently valuable. Although you may have more ideas than you can accommodate, select only a few of them as potential options. You want to prevent creating a long list of features that people will expect to be delivered. So, keep them on a high abstraction level (e.g., "We will work on artificial intelligence, Internet of Things, cloud, natural language processing, and/or API management. We don't know which of these areas will be selected to work on, or which one will go first, but we will need at least some of them in order to be competitive").

Make sure you communicate the uncertainty that exists at each level. Being reliable in the short-term forecast will help you to build credit for the longer-term high-level plan. You may be wondering how to decide how much budget to invest in each horizon. The only honest answer we can offer is one that any consultant would offer: We don't know—it depends. You'll surely figure it out in collaboration with your customers, stakeholders, and Scrum Team.

You could consider the product life cycle, its current value and unrealized value, the company strategy, or the needs and desires of your customers, but in general, two aspects influence the rate of innovation that determines the effective use of the budget:

- **Customer adoption:** People did not buy washing machines as quickly as they bought refrigerators[2] even though the appliances were introduced at the same time and were powered by the same electric engine technology. The market will only absorb changes or new products at a certain pace. Sometimes you need to invest in horizon 1 or 2 just to make sure the market can absorb your product. For example, Google Fiber brings the power of search (and advertising) to those who lack the infrastructure to do so.

- **Technology S-curve:** The S-curve suggests that as technology reaches its mature stage, it becomes increasingly vulnerable to substitute technologies. That is, all technology will be surpassed at some point. As you get closer to this point, you will need to invest more in horizon 2 or 3 technologies.

> *The original TomTom Personal Navigation Device (PND) ran on the Microsoft Mobile Operating system, the following generation was powered by Linux, then after a couple of years, we replaced Linux with Android. It lowered development costs and gave the customer the perception of a fresh new product. The problem to solve never changed. It was still about finding your way the easy way. Those are horizon 2 investments, sustaining the current product. Mobile Apps for navigation were an example of horizon 3 investments because, at the time, their performance and experience were lower than what the PND could deliver. That changed drastically, very fast.*
>
> — Chris

How customers and/or users experience the "performance" of a product changes over time, as illustrated in Figure 26.1. Performance, in this case, can relate to the speed and quality of the product, but you can also relate it to customer satisfaction, or the product's ability to solve customer problems effectively.

---

2. Fun fact: People bought refrigerators at almost twice the rate as washing machines. Customers first needed to change their plumbing, which contributed to the slow adoption. Sometimes companies must focus on the infrastructure to make sure their flagship product can really take off.

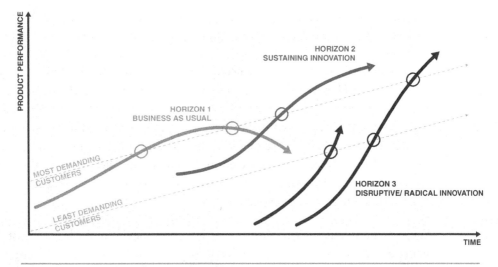

**Figure 26.1** The innovator's dilemma, based on the work of Dr. Clayton Christensen

What you'll notice in the image is that product performance will decrease over time with most if not all products. Think of your first phone or laptop, for example. Fresh out of the box, it was the best thing ever, but it was also already obsolete, and over time, your perception of good performance changed. So will your customers'. Perhaps your product will still be "good enough" for less demanding users, but others will seek a replacement. At some point, not even your least demanding customers will be satisfied with the product.

To prevent that situation from happening, we invest on horizon 2, with product updates, new technologies, new features, and so forth. Investing on horizon 2 helps us to keep the product alive for the near future. It contributes to sustaining the product life cycle over a longer time.

The horizon 3 lines reflect the disruptive or radical innovations that we invest in. You'll notice that some of these investments don't generate enough benefits or performance, as reflected by the first horizon 3 line that stops rather quickly. This effect often creates *corporate antibodies,* an effect where the organization uses the most demanding customers as a yardstick to measure any innovation. Much like the antibodies in our bloodstream seek out and destroy what they perceive as threats, corporate antibodies seek out and block radical ideas by underfunding, ridiculing, or outright sabotage.

If horizon 3 initiatives are to succeed, they need to be shielded from the "normal" process. They require a yardstick that is different from the most demanding customers, or they will simply not survive the budget allocation. Disruptive and radical innovations have a high failure rate. Often, they fail to reach a substantial market segment, solve a problem big enough that customers are willing to pay, or generate enough benefits for the company to keep investing money. However, if they do reach that point of success, their impact is often much bigger than expected.

A good example is the car industry, which continues to make large investments in combustion engines—marvelous pieces of technology that are past their technological peak (horizons 1 and 2). Electric engines are a horizon 3 innovation. They are not yet suitable to replace combustion engines everywhere, but they are getting there rapidly, and when they do, they will overtake the market. Similar effects can be seen in mobile phones, mobile operating systems, process automation software, airlines—basically everywhere.

When you are deciding on the budget for horizon 3, you can look at what new entrants are targeting in your market. For example, we worked with a large software company that creates a product for school administration and noticed that entrants created many small products (virtual blackboards, roster sharing, homework management, etc.) that were somewhat related but never as complete as their flagship products. These were typical horizon 2 features, but rather than trying to keep up with all competitors, they created a platform for them to run on.

## A STRATEGY AND MARKET PERSPECTIVE ON BUDGETING

The final perspective we'd like to share with you allocates the budget from a product strategy and target market perspective. When investing budget in your product, you can do so for many reasons, as we've discussed. Another perspective to take is to allocate a budget based on your target markets.

These target markets, or target audiences, can be split into four main groups: customers, competitor customers, prospect customers, and new market segments. Table 26.1 illustrates how budgeting can be approached from the perspective of strategy and target market. Each category will be explained in more detail following Table 26.1.

**Table 26.1** A Product Budgeting Strategy Canvas

| New Business Strategy | % | % | % | % |
|---|---|---|---|---|
| New Product | % | % | % | % |
| Enhance Product | % | % | % | % |
| New Technology | % | % | % | % |
| | Existing Customers | Competitor Customers | Prospect Customers | New Markets |

Let's explore how a budget allocation to these markets could influence your product:

- **Allocating budget to serve your customers:** Your current customers are people who already have a solution for their problem—your product. You should have access to this group of existing customers and should be able to identify additional needs and problems to solve. When allocating a budget for serving current customers in a better way, we often notice that those companies follow a customer intimacy strategy and favor long customer relationships. For your product, this would mean spending money on keeping customers satisfied, cross-selling and upselling products and services, and reducing churn rate, for example. Good examples are Airbus and Boeing.

- **Allocating budget to attract competitor customers:** Competitor customers also have a solution for their problems. However, it's not your solution. Convincing competitor customers to switch to your product has everything to do with switching costs. When allocating a budget for attracting competitor customers to your organization, we often notice that they focus on ease of switching, free trials, sign-up bonuses, loads of marketing and commercials, and active salespeople. Therefore, you can find a "switch from Android app" in the iOS App Store and a "switch from iOS" app in the Google Play store. Both parties invested in easy switching.

- **Allocating budget to attract prospective customers:** Prospect customers are people who do not yet have a solution for their problem. They might be aware of having a problem and are orienting themselves, or they aren't aware of any problem at all. If you want to spend budget on this target audience, most of the budget will be spent on customer orientation, comparison of products, product branding, company branding, and the buying process for customers. Companies like Booking.com and Amazon make it as easy as possible to buy.

- **Allocating budget to enter new market segments:** Another target audience could be considered as entering a new market or serving a whole new target audience. Targeting new yet similar problems allows you to enter new markets. The company SAAB, for example, delivers maritime safety systems for ports and harbors. This was a saturated market in which most customers already had a solution for their problems. Once SAAB discovered that the protection systems of remotely operated oil rigs solved a very similar problem, they decided to enter this new market.

The second dimension to explore is product strategy. This ties back to the three horizons framework. We have split horizon 3 into two parts: creating a new product and creating a new business strategy. Horizon 2 can be split into sustaining the technology and sustaining the functionality of the product. Allocation of the budget to the strategy could be evaluated according to:

- **Maintaining the status quo:** Maintaining the status quo relates to horizon 1. This category reflects all the small changes, improvements, bug fixes, and maintenance that are done on the product.

- **New technology:** Adding a new technology or replacing existing technology with a new one relates to horizon 2. By adding a new front-end technology to a software product, a whole new experience can be created for customers and users. For example, we have replaced Silverlight front ends with HTML5 + JavaScript front ends. Doing so didn't change much of the functionality but allowed us to operate on modern devices across platforms.

- **Product enhancements:** Enhancing the product with new features, adding new feature areas, and/or solving new customer problems and needs within the same product is also related to horizon 2. These product enhancements sustain the value of the product by keeping it interesting for customers and users.

- **New product:** Developing and launching new products is related to horizon 3. Launching new products is a big bet. Although we do a lot of work as product people to maximize our chances of success, some products will succeed and others will fail. Introducing a new product might be interesting for your current customers, but it might also attract competitor customers, prospect customers, and/or new markets. In the past, we have developed several additional products that complement our core product. These new products made it interesting for current customers to stay and for competitor and prospect customers to switch to our company.

- **New business strategy:** The last product strategy perspective is to launch a new business strategy, which relates to horizon 3. Launching a new business strategy—for example, moving from a flat-fee subscription to a pay-per-use payment model—could offer interesting new opportunities for your product. In the case of World News, adding a proposition for B2B news, in addition to or as a replacement for the B2C news, could be an interesting new business strategy to explore.

Creating a simple budget strategy table in Excel or PowerPoint, for example, may help you to identify where to invest your budget (see Table 26.1). We recommend you discuss your ideas and options with customers and stakeholders. Create transparency on how you want to spend the budget, and why. Discuss other perspectives and align on the vision and strategy for your product and how your budgeting strategy will influence the steps to take. What would happen in your organization if you, for example, asked your stakeholders to identify where they think we should be spending the budget?

Chances are that management would say it should be in new business strategies for new markets. Now ask the same question to the customer-facing teams, like customer support, account management, or operations. They will likely say to invest in current products, tools, and solutions for current customers. It is up to the Product Owner to bridge these two perspectives and align them. Doing so also helps you to create transparency about where budget will not be spent.

### A Great Deal

"And that is how you make a great deal," Kemal concluded his presentation. Dave was looking happy because the numbers sure looked impressive.

"What about lessons learned from our previous rebranding project?" Sandra began.

"All taken care of," said Kemal. "As you can see, the agency is responsible for all changes and delays. We agreed on a fixed price, so there is no way they can take advantage of us."

"Do we have reason to assume that they want to take advantage of us?" Noa asked.

"I should hope not. Why else would we do business with them?" Dave responded.

"Forgive me if I am asking the obvious; I am new here," she continued. "Based on the agreement, it feels like we assume that they want to take advantage of us." Several people blinked with their eyes. "It seems like a strange assumption to start with. They appear to be carrying all the risk."

Sandra nodded. "I raised that concern too, there is a chance that this project will bankrupt them if the risks we have identified materialize completely."

Dave looked less happy now. "We can't afford that kind of problem in the middle of our rebranding project. That would be penny wise but pound foolish."

Kemal's resistance proved to be futile after that. "Perhaps a good deal is not always just expressed in money," Shanice told Noa.

*Indeed,* Noa thought. *Perhaps it is more about mutual trust than about money.* She wondered what things they should and should not trust a supplier with. How "fixed" should a contract really be? How much room should they and their vendors have for maneuvering within a contract?

# CREATING CONTRACTS THAT ENABLE GREAT PRODUCT OWNERSHIP AND TEAMWORK

Perhaps you've asked yourself whether the concept of contracting is compatible with an Agile way of working. Perhaps you wonder why you should care about contracts at all. Well, you should be concerned with contracts if you are a Product Owner. It turns out that entrepreneurial Product Owners need to do something with contracts more often than they would like. It doesn't happen often that a Product Owner creates a contract, and it's unlikely for a Product Owner to manage the contract details. However, it happens regularly that Product Owners influence the contracts for the following reasons:

- They develop and deliver products (or projects) for customers, based on a contract.
- They deliver a product or service to a third party and need to conform to a service level agreement, experience level agreement, or another form of a contract.
- They acquire components for their products or services from a third party.

- Their product is pretty much a contract, and/or their product is a set of clauses, rules, and agreements. For example, think about product managers who manage insurance products. They usually define and/or manage the insurance product policies. They have an important role in defining the contractual boundaries.

As a Product Owner or product manager, it's unlikely that you spend most of your time on contract management or contract creation. Creating and managing contracts is usually the responsibility of legal and/or procurement departments. They are the experts, after all.

Your Scrum Team also contains experts, usually experts in user experience (UX), coding, architecture, security, testing, design, and so forth. These experts could also be experts in sales, marketing, business, or operations. Much like the experts in your Scrum Team need some guidance from their Product Owner about vision, strategy, and goals, the legal team needs guidance as well. It would make sense for you to be involved because, as a Product Owner, you can influence how a vendor contract will be set up. For that reason, we believe that you should have some foundational knowledge about contracting. You don't need to be an expert, but being able to collaborate effectively with legal folks is very beneficial.

## WHAT IS A CONTRACT?

A contract is a legal document that states and explains a formal agreement between two different entities, which may be individuals, groups of people, or organizations. Contracts often exist because two parties engage in a collaborative effort. Whether this is a customer-vendor relationship, a partnership, or otherwise, it is a joint effort. When individuals, organizations, or other parties join efforts and start collaborating, a dependency on each other is created, and all parties want to record and document their commitments. The contracts are created to make agreements, for example, about the scope of work, mutual efforts, payment conditions, and other concerns. Contracts help you to uncover implicit assumptions and are designed to identify and manage risks. Ultimately, contracts are just a solution to manage risks for the parties involved.

Traditionally speaking, many contracts used in product development promote a sequential development cycle. Many of those contracts include exploration, definition, scope determination, product development, testing, delivery, and maintenance. In other words, many contracts used in the past promote a more traditional waterfall way of working. In construction projects, this might work well, but in most complex projects, risks will increase with that approach, as will the chances of failing. So, what would help to make contracts more Agile?

Unfortunately, there is no such thing as an "Agile contract." There is no one way to create an Agile contract because so many different types of contracts are used. There are, however, contract clauses or topics that allow for flexibility, or agility if you will. Rather than focusing on sequential delivery, focus on iterative delivery. Early termination is not a breach of contract—it's the desired situation (assuming we have delivered value). How we collaborate, create transparency, and obtain feedback can be included in a contract to enable us to apply empiricism (and be more Agile) more effectively.

A contract typically describes elements like those shown in Table 27.1.

**Table 27.1** The Various Elements of a Contract

| | |
|---|---|
| How we manage risk | The warranty |
| How we collaborate | The liability |
| What we make transparent | The intellectual property |
| How early termination works | The payment model |
| What the scope is | Timelines, deadlines, delivery dates |
| How we will deliver the work | The contractually agreed budget |

Take a moment to review the items listed in the left column. These items relate to collaboration between both parties. They cover how both parties work together, and a framework like the Scrum framework could be used as a basis for that part. Scrum is all about optimizing value, minimizing risk, and solving complex problems through effective collaboration—so, why not use Scrum as a foundation?

The elements listed in the right column aren't necessarily topics for which the Scrum framework can be of much help. You could argue that Scrum offers Sprints with a maximum length of one month, so that could be used for the timelines. The budget could relate to personnel costs on the Scrum Team. You can probably use the Scrum Values to guide some of the decisions. But Scrum helps less on the right side than on the left side.

The following excerpt is from "Agile Contracts Primer" by Tom Arbogast, Craig Larman, and Bas Vodde. Arbogast is a lawyer, and getting a lawyer's perspective on contracting is very useful when we talk about contracts. We can recommend you read this article to learn more about contracting, as this book offers only an introduction to the topic. We found the following to be the most important for you to read:

> *Legal professionals are wired differently. This rewiring starts from the moment the student enters law school. The concepts of* **Professional Responsibility** *and* **Advocacy** *become ingrained into a lawyer's way of thinking. Legal professionals are trained to act, under a* **legal duty,** *to advance their client's interests and protect them against all pitfalls, seen or unseen. How do you define a client's interests? A client would probably simply say the successful delivery of the project. A legal professional will say she is* **successful if she** *protects her client to the greatest degree possible against exposure and risk, while at the same time advancing the end goal of the contract/project.*
>
> . . .
>
> *The third value of the Agile Manifesto is customer collaboration over contract negotiation. Naturally, when first reading this, a contract lawyer will take note, react, and perhaps think, "That's nice, but I am here to ensure that my client is properly* **protected.** *She can think anything she wants, but I bet she wouldn't say she values collaboration over contract negotiation when everything goes south, and a lawsuit is filed." The lawyer must consider the 'unthinkable' in contractual relationships and provide a framework—expressed in the language of the contract—for dealing with unpleasant outcomes. Lawyers are educated in, and all-too experienced in, dealing with what happens when relationships deteriorate and trust fractures.*

# WHO TAKES THE RISK?

Contracts are used as a way of managing, limiting, and mitigating risks, especially the risk of not getting what you want (or agreed on), allowing either party to terminate the contract. To manage these risks, three main types of contracts are frequently used, shown in Figure 27.1.

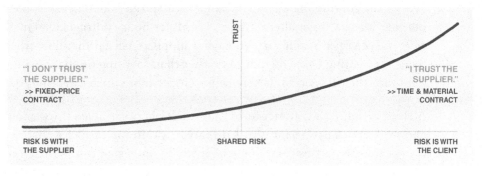

**Figure 27.1** Who takes the risk?

The first variant is a **fixed-price contract** (which typically also includes a fixed time and fixed scope). When using this contract in a customer-supplier relationship, the supplier carries all the risk. If the customer changes their mind, if setbacks occur during product development, if problems arise in the technology, or otherwise, the vendor carries that risk. In practice, that means that vendors will most likely add a (potentially huge) risk factor to their price. If you are working with many subcontractors, each being wary of risk, you may end up paying a very high price. Because it is unlikely that the risk would materialize in *all* subcontracted parties, you may opt to take more risk yourself.

This brings us to the second variant, which is a **time-and-material** (T&M) contract. This type of contract is often selected when there is a lot of trust between the customer and vendor. Customers are trusting the supplier to perform their best, given that any uncertainty in the forecast now becomes a risk for the customer. This is often the case when the product or service is a commodity or if the mutual relationship warrants this level of trust.

T&M contracts may offer an additional challenge when you apply professional Scrum with your teams. They are often set up to be paid per hour or per day. If you want to apply Scrum and collaborate effectively as a Scrum Team (perhaps consisting of people from multiple suppliers), getting paid per hour or per day might encourage ineffective behaviors in the team. In addition, hours spent on continuous improvement and knowledge sharing may seem, in the eyes of the contracting party, less valuable than the hours focused on creating output. So, as a slight alternative to T&M per hour contracts, you might consider a T&M per Sprint variant. Paying suppliers per Sprint allows them to focus on creating Done increments rather than focusing on maximizing hours (and thus their revenues). It may help to focus more on getting things done.

A third variant is a contract form that resides between fixed price and time and material. This variant is called **shared risk.** In the case of a shared risk contract, both parties carry some of the risk, often tied to rewards. Typical for these contracts is that they shift the focus from big-bang payments to a more progressive payment scheme.

## Two-Stage Contracts

A different way to control risk is to use a two-stage contract. Contracts can have two (or even more) stages. Using multiple stages in a contract helps to mitigate risks or delay taking risks when getting involved in large new endeavors, such as the start of new product development.

The funny thing about creating plans, forecasts, and contracts is that the start of a project is usually not the best time to create a plan, forecast, or contract. At the start of a new project, we know the least about it, and risks are typically bigger than at the end. Ideally, then, we would want to create a contract at the end of the project, because at that point we know exactly what the project required. That's a silly thought, of course, but what if we could take smaller steps or create smaller contract stages, or phases? Wouldn't that be more effective for managing those risks?

Figure 27.2 represents the **cone of uncertainty.** It illustrates that our estimates at the beginning of a project could be off by a factor of 4 because of all the unknowns and uncertainties. In most cases, we (as the customer) want our suppliers to carry the risk of underestimating the complexity and effort required for a project. However, if we want our supplier to carry all the risks, we would likely be paying much more "risk money" than needed. An alternative approach for a fixed price is to use a two-stage contract.

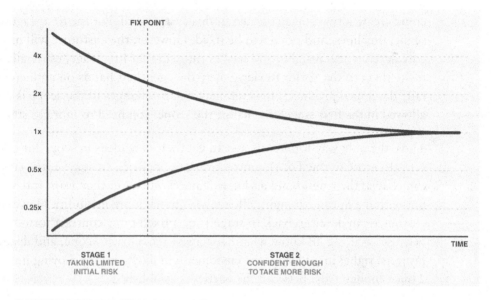

**Figure 27.2** When are we certain? (Source: Serge Beaumont, Agile Contracting, XP Days presentation.)

In the first stage, or phase, of this contract, we should focus on creating a first product increment to reduce risk. We could also develop a product vision and strategy, identify some product goals, create an initial Product Backlog or roadmap, and do a bunch of experiments to mitigate technical risk (can we build it?), business risk (do customers want it?), and social risk (can this team work together and build something valuable?).

At some point (the fix point in Figure 27.2), the customer will have gained enough confidence that this new product or initiative might succeed and deliver enough value to run a sustainable business. The customer can then decide to keep funding the project, but the reduced risk makes other contract forms less problematic. In other words, the collaborating parties could now switch to a T&M contract form, for example, where the customer pays per Sprint and takes on some more risk.

The two-stage contract can also be used the other way around. Imagine a customer that is not very Agile, and they want you to take on all the risks. You could create a two-stage contract in this case as well. For the first stage, the scope, timelines, and price will be fixed. However, the customer will undoubtedly develop new insights and wishes through that first stage, especially if you invite them to the Sprint Review where they get their hands on an incrementally developed product. However, making any changes to the scope is not allowed in the first stage! To change the scope, you need to move to stage 2.

Thus, the only way for a customer to get their new ideas in scope for the project is to move to the T&M contract variant (stage 2). In stage 2, the customer can change their mind and add new features whenever they want (preferably not within a Sprint, though), allowing for much more flexibility. However, the customer can never go back to stage 1, or a fixed price contract form, because, well, we all know what happens to fixed price, scope, and deadline projects, right? In addition, the customer will likely opt for moving into stage 2 once enough trust between the parties is established.

## JOE'S BUCKET

The **Joe's bucket** contract is an alternative to the two-stage contract, as shown in Figure 27.3. In this contract form, the contract describes an expected scope, or objective to achieve, for which a budget is allocated. It also contains two "buckets" that can be used to deal with surprises and unforeseen problems. Each party manages its budget for unforeseen work. The client manages the buffer budget for scope changes. The supplier usually manages the buffer budget for underestimations of work and unforeseen tasks and activities.

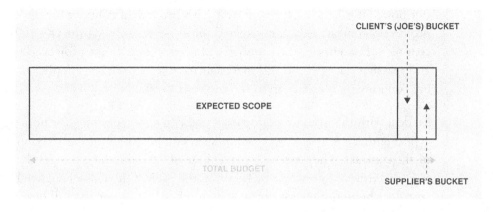

**Figure 27.3** Joe's bucket

If the buckets are not used during the engagement, they constitute additional profit for both parties. The bigger advantage, though, is that you won't need to renegotiate the scope and price every time something turns out differently than expected.

Although you may not have heard it called Joe's bucket, this contracting form is used a lot, and you are probably familiar with the concept. It's much like reserving some money when you're renovating your house. It's a bit of extra cash, reserved for unforeseen events, work, or problems.

## MONEY FOR NOTHING

The Product Owner's accountability is to maximize the value of the product. One way of maximizing value is to stop investing in a product when it is "good enough." Whenever that might be is up to the Product Owner to decide, and it has a lot to do with the law of diminishing returns. This law states that at some point, putting in the same or more effort does not yield an equal result. In other words, there comes a point where we are investing more money than we are getting value in return. That situation is something that you want to avoid as a Product Owner.

But how? How can we stop a project when we have a contract for the whole project? A contract is usually created for doing the whole project—100 percent of it. In addition, the supplier will need to find a new project to work on and reassign their people and materials to other work. The supplier is probably counting on revenues from the project to come in.

To deal with this situation effectively, you can apply a **money for nothing** concept (Figure 27.4) whereby the supplier is compensated for early termination of the contract. They receive a percentage of the remaining budget that, due to early termination, won't be spent on the project. It is also beneficial for the customer because they save money by not needing to pay the full budget that was allocated for the last part of the project. Basically, the customer saves a part of the budget, and the supplier gets *money for nothing*. But wait, wasn't there another line to that song?

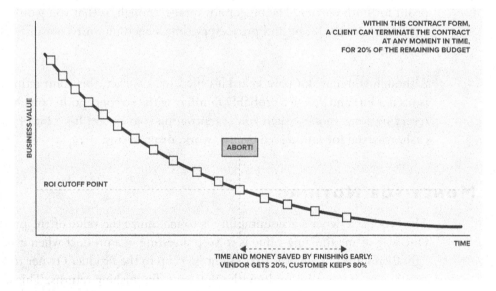

**Figure 27.4** Money for nothing

## CHANGE FOR FREE

A fixed price, scope, and time contract can pose a problem for both the customer and supplier, as new insights, wishes, and needs usually emerge during the development of a product. To allow the customer to change their mind, ask for new features, change the order of work, and thus change the scope, the **change for free** concept can be useful (see Figure 27.5). We believe this concept is a must for any project developed in an Agile way.

Change for free fixes the total capacity of the development work but allows parties to swap elements of equal size. Customers can add new ideas to the scope for the next iteration or Sprint if something else of equal size is traded. In that sense, it is exactly like the flexibility we have from Sprint to Sprint. It's like the Developers pulling items in the Sprint during Sprint Planning.

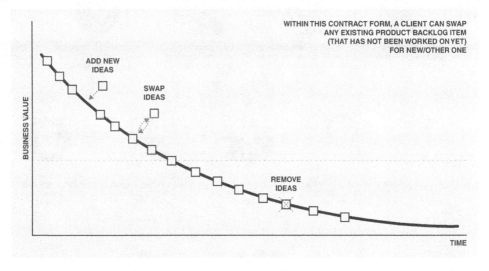

**Figure 27.5** Change for free

# ELEMENTS OF AN AGILE CONTRACT

You have seen several contract variants, techniques, and principles that might help you to embrace change and agility in better ways. Besides the different contract forms, you can also include articles—or clauses—that describe how to collaborate in an Agile way. Figure 27.6 reflects various elements to consider in contracts that can help you to make a contract more supportive of an Agile way of working.

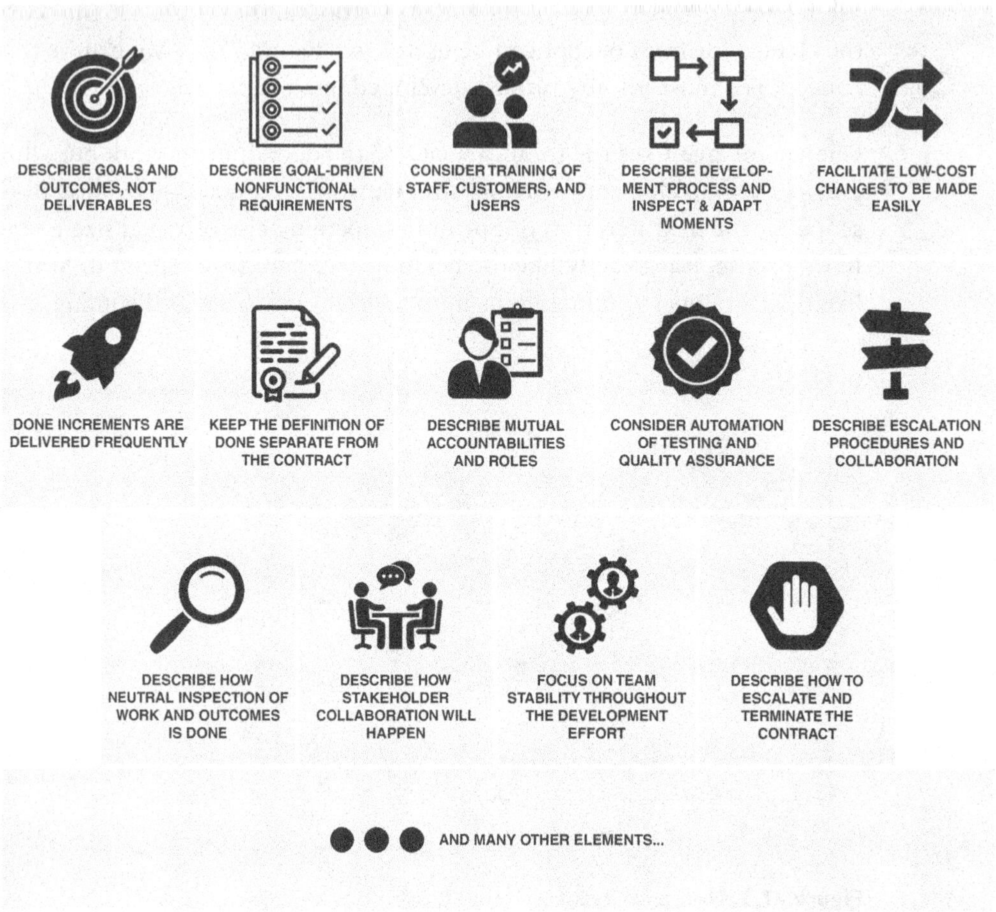

DESCRIBE GOALS AND OUTCOMES, NOT DELIVERABLES | DESCRIBE GOAL-DRIVEN NONFUNCTIONAL REQUIREMENTS | CONSIDER TRAINING OF STAFF, CUSTOMERS, AND USERS | DESCRIBE DEVELOP-MENT PROCESS AND INSPECT & ADAPT MOMENTS | FACILITATE LOW-COST CHANGES TO BE MADE EASILY

DONE INCREMENTS ARE DELIVERED FREQUENTLY | KEEP THE DEFINITION OF DONE SEPARATE FROM THE CONTRACT | DESCRIBE MUTUAL ACCOUNTABILITIES AND ROLES | CONSIDER AUTOMATION OF TESTING AND QUALITY ASSURANCE | DESCRIBE ESCALATION PROCEDURES AND COLLABORATION

DESCRIBE HOW NEUTRAL INSPECTION OF WORK AND OUTCOMES IS DONE | DESCRIBE HOW STAKEHOLDER COLLABORATION WILL HAPPEN | FOCUS ON TEAM STABILITY THROUGHOUT THE DEVELOPMENT EFFORT | DESCRIBE HOW TO ESCALATE AND TERMINATE THE CONTRACT

 AND MANY OTHER ELEMENTS...

**Figure 27.6** Elements of an Agile contract

The figure doesn't describe actual contract articles or clauses, of course. You should describe the articles you would like to see in the contract. Your legal department can then help you to translate your needs into contractual terms and conditions that will hold up in court (although the whole point of collaborating closely in an Agile way is obviously to never need to go to court).

If you want to get a head start or look at some examples, there are various books and articles available about Agile contracting, such as *Agile Contracts: Creating and Managing Successful Projects with Scrum*.[1] You will also find an example, some ideas to consider, and some inspiration in the following excerpt:[2]

> *a) Customer and Supplier define acceptance of the Deliverable as follows:*
>
> > *Deliverable passes all-new automated and manual acceptance tests that were defined before the most recent iteration.*
> >
> > *Deliverable passes all prior automated and manual acceptance tests, verifying that no regression has occurred.*
> >
> > *Deliverable conforms to the "definition of done" that was defined before the iteration.*
>
> *b) Acceptance tests are incrementally defined together by Customer and Supplier members ("Acceptance Group"), including candidate users of the Deliverable, each iteration. The Acceptance Group reviews acceptance at the end of each iteration, starting at Sprint Review.*
>
> *c) Customer will have a period of half the business days of one iteration ("Evaluation Period," "Half Iteration") after provision to it of the final Deliverable to verify that the Deliverable or part thereof is not deficient.*
>
> *d) If Customer notifies Supplier in writing prior to the expiration of the relevant Evaluation Period that the Deliverable or part thereof is deficient in any material respect (a "Non-conformity"), Supplier will correct such Non-*

1. Andreas Opelt, Boris Gloger, Wolfgang Pfarl, and Ralf Mittermayr, *Agile Contracts: Creating and Managing Successful Projects with Scrum*, Wiley, 2013.
2. Tom Arbogast, Craig Larman, and Bas Vodde, *Agile Contracts Primer*, 2012, http://www.agilecontracts. org/agile_contracts_primer.pdf. The primer is derived from Craig Larmon and Bas Vodde, *Practices for Scaling Lean & Agile Development: Large, Multisite, & Offshore Product Development with Large-Scale Scrum*, Addison-Wesley, 2010.

*conformity as soon as reasonably practical but no longer than the length of one iteration, whereupon Customer will receive an additional Half Iteration period ("Verification Period") commencing upon its receipt of the corrected Deliverables or part thereof to verify that the specific Non-conformity has been corrected.*

*e) Customer will provide Supplier with such assistance as may reasonably be required to verify the existence of and correct a reported Non-conformity.*

# THE COLLABORATOR

# VI

## SUMMARY

## KEY LEARNINGS AND INSIGHTS

This concludes Part VI, in which you explored the Collaborator stance. In this part, you explored how governance often has a significant impact on a Product Owner's or product manager's ability to collaborate effectively with other people and other parties. You learned that governance entails many different elements, ranging from documentation to release management, from quality control to budgeting, and from incident management to contracting. Governance is simply about many different elements that prescribe how things are done and controlled in your organization. From understanding governance, you explored how budgeting can be done in other, more Agile ways, allowing Product Owners and product managers to be more effective collaborators. Then, you explored practices and concepts to improve how contracting is done differently in Agile organizations, allowing for more flexibility, agility, value-focus, and collaboration between parties.

Ultimately, winning products are not (just) created by Product Owners or product managers. Winning products are created by winning teams, by people who are motivated and focused on a shared vision/goal, are open and transparent with each other, and are working together as one coherent unit. Hence, to create winning products in the marketplace, Product Owners and product managers need to develop themselves into strong collaborators. But collaboration is not limited to just the product team they work with. They need to be effective at collaborating with customers, users, many different stakeholders, and external parties as well. Understanding and applying the Agile governance practices we explored in this part might just help you to take a next step as an effective Collaborator.

## Quick Quiz Review

If you took the Quick Quiz at the beginning of Part VI, compare your answers to those in the following table. Now that you have read about the Collaborator stance, would you change any of your answers? Do you agree with the following answers?

| Statement | Agree | Disagree |
|---|---|---|
| There is no such thing as an Agile contract. | ✓ | |
| If a contract starts out as fixed price, fixed scope, fixed time, there is no way to change it. | | ✓ |
| Governance "just is," and we must deal with it. It's not up for discussion. | | ✓ |
| All governance is defined and decided upon outside the reach of Scrum Teams. | | ✓ |
| Contracts can be described in ways that promote Agile behavior and agility. | ✓ | |
| Finance stakeholders are not interested in emerging or changing backlogs. They want a fixed plan that doesn't change for the next four quarters. | | ✓ |
| One way to look at the budget is through the perspectives of market and product strategy. | ✓ | |

## Want to Learn More?

In this part, you learned about the Collaborator stance. Diverse topics, tools, techniques, and concepts will help you to strengthen this stance. If you want to improve your Collaborator stance, consider doing the following interesting exercise:

**Step 1:** Imagine that you are a spy at your own company for a day. Your mission for this day is to sabotage as much as you possibly can. Try to sabotage the product, the stakeholders, your teams, and so on. You get some bonus points for any actions you take that cannot be traced back to you. List all these sabotaging actions on (digital) sticky notes.

**Step 2:** Now group all the actions you identified into two groups. Group 1 consists of all the sabotage actions that you perform in your own practice, thus in real life. Chances are that you display some of these bad behaviors, although it might be unintentionally. Group 2 are all the actions that you do not take in real life.

**Step 3:** Identify a couple of *smart* actions that you want to take to stop some of these bad patterns and start being more effective.

In addition, you can learn more about the Collaborator stance by catching up with the following materials: *The Professional Product Owner: Leveraging Scrum as a Competitive Advantage* by Don McGreal and Ralph Jocham (Addison-Wesley, 2018), *Agile Contracts: Creating and Managing Successful Projects with Scrum* by Andreas Opelt, Boris Gloger, Wolfgang Pfarl, and Ralf Mittermayr (Wiley, 2013), and *Beyond Budgeting: How Managers Can Break Free from the Annual Performance Trap* by Jeremy Hope and Robin Fraser (Harvard Business School Press, 2003).

# THE INFLUENCER VII

*A "no" uttered from the deepest conviction is better than a "yes" merely uttered to please, or worse, to avoid trouble.*

— Mahatma Gandhi

## QUICK QUIZ

To connect to Part VII, answer each of the following statements by checking the Agree or Disagree column. The answers are shared in the Part VII Summary.

| Statement | Agree | Disagree |
| --- | --- | --- |
| Stakeholder management is one of the core responsibilities of Product Owners. However, not all stakeholders are equal or need equal attention and influence. | | |
| Many techniques, such as stakeholder mapping and stakeholder radar, and models such as DISC and MBTI, can help Product Owners to manage stakeholders more effectively. | | |
| Negotiation is all about achieving consensus. It's often a situation of give and take. | | |
| In stakeholder management and communication, the most important thing to optimize is the message that you share with stakeholders. | | |
| Negotiation and diplomacy are about getting into the mindset of your partner and aligning their reality with yours. Active listening is key to both. | | |
| During negotiations with stakeholders—for example, about a feature—you want to get to a yes and agreement from stakeholders as soon as possible. | | |
| To be an effective value maximizer, a Product Owner should be versatile by applying various stances in various situations to collaborate with various types of stakeholders (e.g., practice situational leadership). | | |

# STAKEHOLDER MANAGEMENT IN COMPLEX ENVIRONMENTS

## 28

## INTRODUCING: THE INFLUENCER

In the first iterations of creating and naming the Product Owner stances, we weren't sure about the Influencer. We originally called this stance the Politician. We felt that *Influencer* might be linked more to being an online influencer, as in social media platforms. The Product Owner as an influencer, however, is somebody who influences people inside and outside the company to move the product or service in the right direction. When doing so, they often run into company politics, which is why we thought *Politician* was appropriate for this stance. Feedback taught us that people felt offended to be called a politician. Most product people told us that they did not want to take part in corporate politics. Clearly, *politician* held negative connotations for many people. We consequently focused more on the ability to influence others, and that's when we found the right stance: the Influencer.

*Influence is like the Force; it has a light but also a dark side, and those who wield it are easily seduced.*

— Chris

Not all (Product Owner) Influencers are the same. Here are some positive outcomes and benefits that we have observed when Product Owners take the Influencer stance:

- Great Influencers can build a united force, having a positive impact on organizational effectiveness. Inspired by a strong vision, Influencers manage to achieve buy-in among people and bring them together. Influencers build up energy and make change happen. They inspire others and align them to work toward a shared goal.

- They gain better alignment and buy-in among stakeholders, customers, users, and teams around a shared vision, strategy, and approach. Their teams and stakeholders try to have a positive contribution and actively support the product to become successful.

- Having a great Influencer results in fewer arguments, delays of decisions, political games, power struggles, and other forms of negative and wasted energy that slow down the development process.

There are trade-offs to be made when influencing other people. Some Influencers use *rational* approaches to influencing people. These Influencers focus on the facts, figures, and data, and they use logic and reasoning to persuade their stakeholders. They may legitimize choices, exchange, and barter or simply state their beliefs. This way of influencing people may work well. It does require a good foundation in the *relationship* you have with others, though. A good relationship and mutual trust should often be in place already. Socializing, appealing to that relationship, consulting others, and even alliance-building can help the influencer to make the arguments stick.

Some Influencer Product Owners take a different approach. They appeal to *values* that may be their own or the company's values. They might be the Scrum Values or other belief systems in the organization, or they may be the beliefs of the person being influenced. For example, one of the core values at our company is Quality Without Compromise. This means that we always focus on good quality products and services. If this is one of your company's values, then you can argue with any stakeholder against some of the strongest rational arguments simply because quality shouldn't be compromised. If people were to compromise on quality, they would be conflicting with the core values of the company. In a way, the Product Owner is a role model. The Product Owner can influence people by exhibiting values and behaviors such as openness, focus, commitment, courage, and respect.

Of course, there is also a way to influence people through *emotions*. Although it may not seem like a wise strategy up front, we've seen some cases where it helped to be *functionally angry*. It sometimes helps to get feedback from a critical stakeholder, who is angry or disappointed for a good reason. It may sometimes help you, as a Product Owner, to be angry or disappointed and to voice those feelings—of course, while remaining respectful to others.

What great Influencers do:

- **Be honest. Always.** What some great Product Owners and product managers do so well is to always be open, honest, and transparent. Being honest can sometimes be difficult because it makes people vulnerable. It reveals who they are and discloses their mistakes, which allows others to criticize or reject them openly. However, being honest develops character and builds credibility and trust, which are the foundation to evoke confidence and respect from others.

- **They are compassionate.** Compassion is the quality of understanding the suffering of others and wanting to do something about it. While many see compassion as a weakness, true compassion is a characteristic that converts knowledge to wisdom. Great leaders use compassion to discover the needs of those they lead and then to determine the next steps to take.

- **They are flexible and great listeners.** Flexibility is about understanding the give-and-take aspects of politics. It's about understanding the various interests in the company. And it's about the ability to find common ground. Great Influencers listen carefully to the interests, goals, and objectives of all parties. They not only hear all arguments, they also try to learn from the various viewpoints what it will take on behalf of all parties involved to reach a consensus. These skills allow Influencers to recognize setbacks and criticism, to learn from them, and then to move on.

- **Share the credit, take the blame.** Good leaders take a little more than their share of the blame and a little less than their share of the credit. This is how Arnold H. Glasow described a core quality of great leaders. Great Product Owners give the credit to their teams and stakeholders for building a great product. They take the blame when it fails. In the end, it's all about taking responsibility.

- **They are great network builders.** Great influencers move beyond the awareness of the stakeholder playing field and create specific strategies to proactively seek help from stakeholders and rally them to their cause. For example, rather than relying only on Sprint Review to craft a path forward, they massage critical stakeholders and avoid surprises.

- **They can bend reality.** Great Influencers seem to bend the perception of reality. For example, if a stakeholder disagrees with the direction of the product, the Influencer can get the stakeholder to argue in favor of the Influencer's own case by asking, "What might go wrong if we don't do this?" Or if the stakeholder is hesitant to align with the Product Owner's strategy, the Influencer Product Owner might ask, "What additional benefits would we receive from this strategy?"

- **They are familiar with the word *no!*** Perhaps the defining quality of a great influencer is their ability to say no. Handling the resistance that comes from not getting your way and without getting your ego bruised is what makes great Influencers shine.

Other techniques that influence people—which we encourage you *never* to use—are manipulation, intimidation, avoidance, and threats. When we see these techniques used by a character in, say, a good thriller movie, we immediately recognize the character as a villain. In real life, such tactics have the same effect. They are antithetic to great product ownership.

In the remainder of this chapter, we explore various techniques for identifying stakeholders, how to create a stakeholder management strategy, different types of stakeholders, and how to say no to them effectively.

Let's start at the start: What is a stakeholder anyway?

## DEFINITION OF STAKEHOLDER

Every Product Owner and product manager must deal with stakeholders, which means also doing stakeholder management. After all, Product Owners are making a product with and for other people. As a Product Owner, you will need to deal with different types of stakeholders, both inside and outside your organization. But what are stakeholders? Who are your stakeholders? How should you deal with them? This is what we uncover in this chapter.

There are many different definitions of *stakeholder,* and a lot of overlap exists between those definitions. Let's start with a simple one. If you define *stakeholder* from a Professional Scrum perspective, it's simple: everybody outside the Scrum Team is (potentially) a stakeholder.

This definition is so simple from a Professional Scrum perspective because the Scrum framework describes only three accountabilities, or roles if you will: Product Owner, Scrum Master, and Developers. No other roles or accountabilities are defined, basically meaning that each individual will be part of the Scrum Team or else they will be a stakeholder—and thus outside the Scrum Team. To emphasize that the Scrum Team is in this together, Professional Scrum theory doesn't describe the stakeholder as a separate accountability or role. What we often find in practice though, is that Product Owners consider their Scrum Team as a stakeholder. To us, this doesn't make much sense, because you're one Scrum Team, together. It may feel like there is work to be done in building trust in the Scrum Team, surely. However, you shouldn't need a stakeholder map and communication strategy for your own Scrum Team. Rather than managing and strategizing in the Scrum Team, focus on building trust through collaboration. Focus on building a great product, together.

There are also other and more comprehensive definitions of *stakeholder.* An alternative definition of the term stakeholder is found in Schuurman and Vermaak's *Master the Art of No:*[1]

---

1. Robbin Schuurman and Willem Vermaak, *Master the Art of No: Effective Stakeholder Management for Product Owners and Product Managers,* independently published, 2020.

*Stakeholders are individuals, groups of individuals, corporations, or authorities who have a direct or indirect interest (a stake) in the organization, its products, and/or services. Stakeholders can be internal or external to the organization.*

These definitions imply that as a Product Owner, you must deal with a wide variety of stakeholders. From development to marketing, from finance to supply chain, from legal to operations, from sales to management, many people may have a stake in your product or service. Some of those stakeholders are easily identified. For example, think of (potential) customers and users. These stakeholders have a clear interest in your product or service (after all, these are the people who will purchase and/or use it). Other easily identified stakeholders may be some of your colleagues or the managers of other departments. Managers may have an interest in your product or service from a sales, cost, marketing, development, or management perspective. Colleagues may be involved in the creation, delivery, marketing, or servicing of the product.

Besides the obvious stakeholders, there are usually groups of stakeholders who are easily overlooked because they are difficult to identify. These are groups of stakeholders who seem to have no obvious interest, or only little interest, in your product or service. Examples of such stakeholders might include government agencies, social organizations, or the press and media. Of course, their interest depends greatly on your context. Another example might include a manager from another business unit or department, who seems to have no obvious interest in your product yet has an opinion about it and shows up from nowhere. Another group of stakeholders comprises people who, for no apparent reason, identify themselves as stakeholders, sometimes without your knowledge. These "surprise" stakeholders could present a risky, or at least uncomfortable, situation for you to handle. To avoid being surprised by an unforeseen group of stakeholders, think carefully about the many and various possible (special) stakeholders and stakeholder groups.

Keep a close eye on your surroundings. Regularly inspect your stakeholder field, look around and try to identify new stakeholders and stakeholder groups. Make sure to look for stakeholders both inside and outside your organization—those with a lot of interest, a little interest, direct and indirect interest, and even unlikely but possible interest.

## Stakeholder Classification/Categorization

Identifying and categorizing stakeholders may be challenging at times. There are the obvious stakeholders, of course. But not all are that easily identified. In Chapter 29, "Tools for Stakeholder Classification and Grouping," we explore different techniques for stakeholder identification and grouping, but an initial way of categorizing stakeholders is by considering these four groups: users, influencers, providers, and governance stakeholders.

- **User:** The people who buy and/or use your product to solve their problems, challenges, or fulfill their needs. These people either have a direct stake or an indirect stake in the product. Especially with B2C products, this group may be very large.

  Note that one individual may be a user, a buyer, or both, as discussed in Part II, "The Customer Representative." Users and buyers often have different needs and desires.

- **Provider:** The people who help you to create the product or service or who help you to get it in the hands of the user. Without providers, the product does not exist, but there might be more than one way to deliver the product. Providers may be external suppliers, vendors, or partners, and they may include internal teams, other departments, and your Scrum Team of course (although that last one is not a stakeholder, right?).

- **Governance:** We talked about governance in Part VI, "The Collaborator." Governance stakeholders usually do not help you to deliver value directly, but they can block you from delivering value or may delay the process of delivering value. These stakeholders often have an indirect interest in the product because they won't be creating it or using it. They typically want to ensure that the product is compliant to standards, such as legal, security, or architecture requirements.

- **Influencers:** Not to be confused with the Influencer stance of the Product Owner, influencer stakeholders are the people who want to influence the product or service. Their influence doesn't directly contribute to the creation, development, delivery, or distribution of the product. Influencers might include people like the board of directors and management, accountants, the government, politicians, and competitors.

Identifying stakeholders is not too challenging for most Product Owners. The important ones that they collaborate with frequently are rather easy to list. However, we often find Product Owners who forget about relevant stakeholders who are not part of the daily business. Table 28.1 lists 31 types of stakeholders for your inspiration. It highlights the different types of stakeholders, including what kinds of benefits they might provide for your organization.

**Table 28.1** 31 Types of Stakeholders

| Stakeholder Type | Interests/Benefits to the Organization | Stakeholder Type | Interests/Benefits to the Organization |
| --- | --- | --- | --- |
| Customers (and users) | Revenues, product usage | Suppliers | Raw materials, products, services |
| Noncustomers | Future revenues, product usage | Interest organizations | Influence |
| Employees | Time, knowledge, labor | Public organizations | Appreciation, public support |
| Former employees | Social support | Scientists | Confirmation, new insights, new knowledge |
| Shareholders | Funding | Creative minds | Innovation |
| Works council | Internal support base | Advisors/consultants | Specialist knowledge, benchmarks |
| Clients council | External support base | Supervisory instances | Quality control identification, validation |
| Supervisory board/ board of directors | Supervision | Labor unions | Representation |

| Stakeholder Type | Interests/Benefits to the Organization | Stakeholder Type | Interests/Benefits to the Organization |
|---|---|---|---|
| Government | Regulation, infrastructure | Nongovernment organizations | Public support |
| Partners | Network | Social media users (e.g., bloggers) | Feel with the spirit of the times, positive attention |
| Politicians | Public support | Universities | Research, supply of new talent |
| Management (including C-suite roles) | Leadership | Analysts | Financial valuation |
| Competitors | Challenge | Accountants | Approval of figures, transparency |
| Press | Positive attention, based on facts | Distribution partners | Reach, distribution network |
| New talent | Future | Scientific association | Scientific identification/validation |
| Designers | Visual identity, appropriate design | | |

 ### The Ear of the CFO

"Urgh." Noa felt miserable when she left the boardroom at World News. It felt like the board had become increasingly proficient at shooting down her initiatives. She struggled with the gated process and getting approvals for investments, but she also understood that the amount of money she was asking for was significant.

As she made her way back to the team space, she noticed that some people were still working on the prototype for the new app. It was great to see that the team believed in the North Star they had put forth and that they were still working on it was the best expression of that commitment.

"And?" The eyes of the team members looked hopefully in her direction.

She remained silent for a moment, as she had little news to share with the team. "Well, I don't know guys," Noa replied, "I don't think we made the progress today that I was hoping for. Let me think about today overnight, and I'll talk to you all in the morning."

Seiko, the Scrum Master, walked her to the bicycle shed. "I understood that our CFO was not quite convinced yet," he began.

"You can say that again," Noa replied. "I'm not giving up, but I am not speaking his language."

Seiko paused. "Have you tried talking to Sandra? Tell her that I sent you," he said as he jumped on his bike. "And remember, tomorrow is a brand-new day."

The next day, Noa went to see Sandra. She was happy to see Noa, and before Noa knew it, they were pouring over spreadsheets, models, and ROI calculations. World News had its specific way of working, and Noa was happy that she was to be brought up to speed given help in understanding the numbers.

Three weeks later was the next budget meeting. As she walked toward the projector, she could not help but overhear the CFO say to Sandra, "Noa again. Let's see what gibberish she made of the numbers this time."

To Noa's surprise, she heard Sandra come to her defense: "There is nothing wrong with those numbers. We made these calculations together."

Taken by surprise, the CFO leaned back. "Well, well, let's see if we can get this approved then."

Noa flipped on the projector and started her presentation.

## INFORMATION AND INSIGHTS TO GATHER ON STAKEHOLDERS

If you want to engage with and manage stakeholders effectively, it's important to know who they are. For example, it is helpful to know more about your stakeholders than just their names, departments, and jobs. Get to know the *person* behind the *stakeholder:* their interests, motivations, goals, and personality. Before creating your stakeholder management strategy, spend some time discovering what drives them. There are many factors to consider and/or research, but here are some questions that might be worthwhile exploring:

- What goals are important to the stakeholder? What are their personal goals? What are their business objectives? How do those objectives align with your product vision, strategy, and goals?
- What motivates the stakeholder to get out of bed in the morning? What do they seek to contribute to the company, its people, and your product or service?
- What does the stakeholder fear most? Asking them about their fears is often a great way to discover their motivators.
- What interest does your stakeholder have in your product, service, work, or team? Are they supportive or against your initiative? What are their needs?
- What kind of influence do they have? Is their influence high or low? What level of organizational power do they have?
- What type of person is this stakeholder? What's their personality? What is their preferred style of communication?
- Who are some important influencers to this stakeholder? To whom does the person listen? What are the interests and goals of the stakeholders behind this stakeholder? How do those people, goals, and interests influence the stakeholder?

Personal goals, business goals, and needs are strong motivators that can define your stakeholders' behaviors. Their personal goals and objectives may or may not align with their business objectives, and they may or may not be open and transparent about them. However, spending some time on building a relationship and learning about their goals will likely prove to be valuable time spent. It is also important to know who has the respect and "ear" of an important stakeholder—this person may be able to engage with the stakeholder on your behalf. Not having to influence and engage with all the stakeholders directly can be a great time-saver, but nevertheless, you should be prepared to do so.

## THE INFLUENCE OF THE STAKEHOLDER

Once you have identified your stakeholders and perhaps learned more about their goals, objectives, and character, you will want to get a clear idea of how to engage with them. Start by identifying the amount of power or influence and the interest each of the stakeholders may have.

Stakeholders will have many different wishes, requirements, and issues that can vary considerably and that frequently conflict with each other. A valuable wish from one stakeholder may not provide any value for another stakeholder. Having a good understanding of your different types of stakeholders and how to engage with them is therefore key to effective stakeholder management. The balance between the power and interest of a stakeholder determines whether you need to actively collaborate with them or can take a more distant or indirect approach.

You can divide influence into formal influence and informal influence. There are stakeholders, based on their formal, hierarchical position, who have and can use their influence. Think of stakeholders as being at a management or board of directors' level. In many organizations, Product Owners must listen to and deal with stakeholders who can use this form of influence. In addition to the formal leaders, some people can influence informal leadership. They have gained a certain status or reputation among colleagues that gives them clout in the organization. This is an informal influence. You probably know someone who does not have a management position yet gets a lot of things done in the organization. You also want to have a clear picture of these informal influence stakeholders. Examples include human resources departments and executives' administrative assistants. They don't have a lot of formal power over you, but they do influence management's agenda to a great extent.

### THE INTEREST OF A STAKEHOLDER

Stakeholder interest doesn't mean stakeholders are attentive to, curious about, or actively involved with your product. It means what *stake* your stakeholders have in your product. It's more about the benefits they seek to gain through the product or service. Different stakeholders have different (amounts of) stake in the product or service, and therefore different types of interest groups can be defined:

- Stakeholders who have a positive interest in the product and want the product to be a success might be, for example, customers or users. They often positively benefit from the product. You can expect them to have a high amount of interest.

- Some stakeholders have a negative interest in the product; these stakeholders do not want the product to be successful. An example of this group could be a department that becomes obsolete or that relinquishes responsibilities and work when the product or service is delivered. Imagine the product will automate certain processes, making a complete department redundant.

- Some stakeholders have an interest in your team members but not so much interest in the product. Think of the functional manager of your Scrum Team members or your manager, if applicable.

- Another group of stakeholders is those who have a personal interest or departmental interest but who are not so interested in the product itself. An example is an operations manager who wants to keep their metrics in the green and prevent additional work, costs, or pressure on their department or teams.

- And there are of course the stakeholders in whom you as a Product Owner have an interest. They do not necessarily benefit from or get affected by your product, but they could be a part of the value production chain. Think of suppliers, partners, government agencies, or social agencies.

Understanding the different interests, goals, objectives, and targets of your stakeholders helps you to build a better relationship with them. It also helps you to manage them more effectively. This makes it easier for you to bring the right message to the right stakeholder from the right perspective. This becomes extra relevant when piecing out your stakeholder communication strategy.

## DISCOVERING A STAKEHOLDER'S INTEREST AND INFLUENCE

*Alright, that's nice and all,* you may think, *but how do I know what level of interest and what level of influence my stakeholders (should) have?* That's a great question! The honest answer is . . . you don't. It's hard to "know" the exact interest and influence of a stakeholder, especially at the start of a new product development or product discovery effort. However, you will probably learn about their true motivations, interests, and powers quite soon.

You should be asking a ton of questions. The questions listed under "Information and Insights to Gather on Stakeholders" provide a good starting point. Focus on developing relationships with the stakeholders—that's usually the best way to learn more. Seek to better understand them and their objectives.

You could also talk to other people in the organization, people who know and understand the stakeholders well. Perhaps some people who have been in the company for a long time or perhaps the peers, manager, or direct reports of the stakeholder you want to understand can offer insights. Just talk. Listen. Observe. And you'll learn about your stakeholders soon enough.

# TOOLS FOR STAKEHOLDER CLASSIFICATION AND GROUPING

This chapter covers helpful tools and techniques for effective stakeholder engagement and stakeholder management. In essence, stakeholder management is a relationship game. If you build strong connections and relationships with your stakeholders, you will find that collaborating with them becomes easier both when things are running smoothly and during challenging times. Although problems are rarely solved by the adoption of tools and techniques, those discussed in this chapter may help you to acquire insights, create transparency, and design your stakeholder management strategy and tactics.

Tools and techniques, however, do not improve your stakeholder management directly. That's where you come in. Improving stakeholder engagement can be done with some tools, techniques, and strategy to some extent, but above all, it's people business. Being aware of your stakeholder field may allow you to enlist the help of other people (in your team), who have a different communication style or relationship with a particular stakeholder. It's not like you must engage with every stakeholder on your own, nor do you need to get along with everybody. You can seek the help of others.

So, as a first step, let's create some transparency about your stakeholder field. If you have already identified some of your stakeholders, it's now time to make that information transparent. Various tools and techniques can be used for that. Some tools that are probably familiar to you are the stakeholder map and stakeholder radar, which are both discussed in this chapter.

## THE STAKEHOLDER MAP

Stakeholders with a lot of influence can set the tone for the development of your product, regardless of whether the influence is formal or informal. As a Product Owner, it will help you to gain insight into the influence and interest of your stakeholders. By plotting your stakeholders in a stakeholder map (see Figure 29.1), you get an overview of your stakeholder field. With that insight, you can then decide how to deal with the various stakeholders and carve out your communication strategy.

The stakeholder map helps you to classify stakeholders into one of the following groups:

- Stakeholders with little interest and little influence
- Stakeholders with little interest and a lot of influence
- Stakeholders with a lot of interest and little influence
- Stakeholders with a lot of interest and a lot of influence

### STAKEHOLDERS WITH LOW INTEREST AND LOW INFLUENCE

The group of stakeholders with low interest and low influence are those on whom you want to spend the least of your time as a Product Owner. This group of people has low interest in your product and/or gains little to no benefit from your product's success. In addition, they have low influence over you, your team, and/or your product or service. The stakeholder management strategy for this group of stakeholders is therefore to **monitor**.

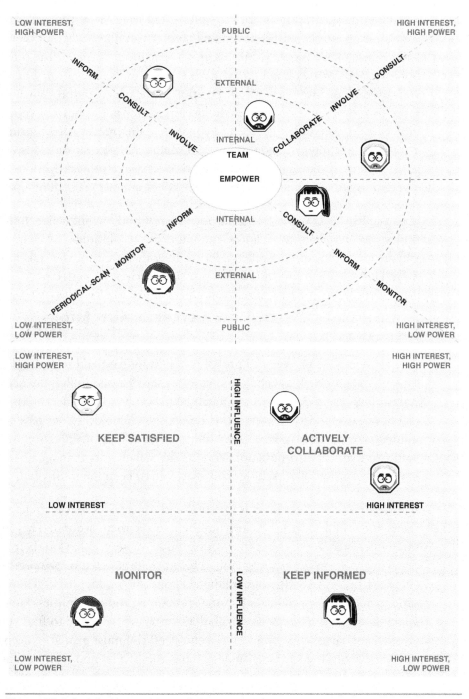

**Figure 29.1** Stakeholder mapping techniques

The monitoring strategy is not the same as ignoring them, though! You do want to keep an eye on this group and regularly evaluate whether there have been any changes. People from this group may move to one of the other stakeholder groups. For example, they may get more influence over or interest in your product due to a new job or position in the organization. When they move to another area of the stakeholder map, they might become more important to you and will need to be managed differently. Also consider how a stakeholder's interest and involvement might change over time, for example, when you're getting closer to a new market release, a project deadline or milestone, or when an audit (e.g., security, risk, compliance) is coming up.

Because this stakeholder group has low interest and low influence, limit the time spent on this group. Choose communication solutions and channels that you are already using for stakeholders in the other areas of the stakeholder map. This saves you time and helps you stay efficient and effective.

## STAKEHOLDERS WITH LOW INTEREST AND HIGH INFLUENCE

As a Product Owner, you will probably also want to spend relatively little time on the group of stakeholders with low interest and high influence. This stakeholder group does not have much interest in your product, not in a positive or negative sense. However, this group of stakeholders does have a lot of influence. With this influence, they may also have a lot of influence over you, your team, and your product or service. The stakeholder management strategy for this group of stakeholders is therefore to **keep them satisfied.**

If this group of stakeholders is satisfied with the results that are relevant to them, you will usually not hear from them or see them around. They are often interested in the effect that your product or service has on their own department, team, or business unit. They may be affected by the product to some extent, yet they do not care much about the product itself. They have little interest in the product's features, functions, and capabilities. However, when things go wrong, these stakeholders often know where to find you. To effectively manage this group of stakeholders, you must primarily keep them informed about the key performance indicators (KPIs) and metrics that are relevant to them. Therefore, do not tell these stakeholders how great your product is or what new features you have made; rather, tell them what positive effect your product has on the metrics that are important to them. In other words, offer the chief financial officer insight into the development of costs, the total cost of ownership, and return on investment for the product; offer the chief marketing officer insight into the success of the marketing campaigns and increase in organizational brand awareness; and offer the chief operating officer insight into how your new developments improve efficiency and reduce the number of manual actions and/or disruptions on operations.

Many Product Owners experience this keep-satisfied stakeholder group as a difficult one to engage with. And to be fair, it is not always easy! To manage this group effectively, it is helpful to have some political skills to navigate your interactions with them. You should realize that this group of people can also help you to be more effective as a Product Owner and to increase your authority. If you keep these people satisfied, you create space for yourself to be more entrepreneurial. This does not mean that you must do everything they ask you to do. If you did that, you probably wouldn't deliver the most value for customers, users, and the organization. What it does mean is that you must build a strong relationship with them. Put yourself in their shoes. Understand their motives. Get to know their interests. Understand what they want and need to achieve and what their goals are. Try to understand what they are held accountable for. With these insights, you can inform, help, manage, and influence them more effectively.

## STAKEHOLDERS WITH HIGH INTEREST AND LOW INFLUENCE

Sometimes referred to as "friends of the show," stakeholders with high interest and low influence could also hold an opposing attitude. Regardless of their interest in what happens, they have relatively low influence to intervene or to change things.

You want to keep these stakeholders informed of new developments, and you want them to be sufficiently involved in the development of the product. This quadrant regularly has users, delegations of users, and customers.

This group cares that your product is successful, of high quality, and is usable and valuable, but they generally cannot make important decisions, interfere with your plans, or change things around. Consequently, they typically rely on formal processes, procedures, and/or meetings, such as escalations or complaints, to change things around to their benefit. The stakeholder management strategy for this group is to **inform (proactively)**.

You want to keep these stakeholders well informed of any new developments, and you want them to be sufficiently involved in the development and delivery of the product or service. It is typically in this group where Product Owners plot their product's users, user delegations, or user committees, as well as customers or customer panels.

What usually works well for this stakeholder group is to inform them *regularly*. In addition to communicating through newsletters, blogs, and videos, you can involve (some of) these stakeholders in Sprint Reviews, additional product demos, user tests, training, and brainstorming sessions. Regardless of the tools and channels you use, ensure that you communicate with this group proactively and schedule recurring appointments. By scheduling the interaction periodically, you ensure that the interaction and feedback take place at times that suit you and your team, thus preventing a group of stakeholders with little influence from determining your agenda.

## STAKEHOLDERS WITH HIGH INTEREST AND HIGH INFLUENCE

The last group of stakeholders, the ones who have a lot of interest and a lot of influence, are of course the most important group of stakeholders to you as a Product Owner. These stakeholders not only have a lot of interest in the success of the product but also have a lot of influence to help you to be successful. The stakeholder management strategy for this group of stakeholders is to **actively collaborate**.

Keep these stakeholders very well informed. You need to actively involve them and ensure that they know what is going on, at least on a strategic level, but also including some tactics. Give them a voice regarding your product's future direction, solicit their help in deciding on the next steps, and include them in strategic decision making. For example, you actively collaborate with these stakeholders on the product vision, product strategy, product roadmap, and ordering of the Product Backlog. Together with these stakeholders, you determine what is important and what is not. Together with these people, you decide how to maximize value, how to deal with risks, and what goals and delivery dates (or deadlines) to set.

Building strong relationships with these stakeholders is crucial to your success and to theirs. It is important to gain their trust and support. This group has a lot of hierarchical influence within the organization. And with this formal influence, they can help you to be the entrepreneur you want to be. Try to turn them into your ambassadors. Building strong relationships will prove to be very valuable, especially when you encounter setbacks, difficult stakeholders, conflicting interests, or stormy weather. Do you want to be able to effectively say no to most of your stakeholders? Do you want your decisions to be supported? Do you want to be backed up by influential stakeholders? Then make sure these stakeholders are your ambassadors!

Because this group is your most important stakeholder group, you will spend most of your time engaging with them. Therefore, you should be certain of whom you put in this area of the stakeholder map. A common mistake by Product Owners is to put too many stakeholders in this area. The more key stakeholders you have, the busier you will be. It is not impossible or unthinkable that you have many stakeholders with a lot of interest and a lot of influence. If that is the case in your situation, then force yourself to make a top three to five selections. Ask a Scrum Master or Agile Coach to help you in this selection. Also, validate the stakeholder map with those key stakeholders and see what they think about it. Start to work intensively together with these three to five key stakeholders on your product vision and strategy. Involve the other stakeholders with high interest and high influence in other areas, such as defining the roadmap or Product Backlog.

Regarding customers, consumers, and the product's users, it goes without saying that this group is a key group of stakeholders. Ultimately, you are building a product to solve a problem or fulfill a need for them. So where would you plot your customers and users in the stakeholder map? As we described in the high interest, low influence section earlier, we often plot our customers, consumers, and users in that area. This might seem strange, as they are some of the key beneficiaries of the product.

However, imagine that your product has 50,000 customers or users. In such cases, it is likely impossible to engage with all of them individually. What often happens is that you will approach customers and users as your key stakeholders, but through the means of the high interest, low influence stakeholder management strategy. There are solutions such as interviews, test sessions, focus groups that allow for more interaction, which is often done through a small selection of your customers and users.

There are also situations (often in a B2B context) where a few customers are in the high interest, high influence area. This is often the case for companies who have one big client and a bunch of smaller ones. We've seen this situation quite often; the big client has a lot of influence, and all the little ones need to adapt. In this scenario, the big client would be plotted in the actively collaborate part of the stakeholder map.

As you move forward on your journey to become an entrepreneurial Product Owner, you will discover you have some weaknesses. There are some things you may not know yet. Perhaps you know too little about marketing, sales, pricing, or technology to drive your product forward across all areas. If that's the case, then keep this in mind: Utilize others for the weaknesses that you have. To do so, ensure that you start to plot stakeholders who can support your weakness in the actively collaborate part of your stakeholder map.

Figure 29.2 captures the different strategies. As an alternative to the stakeholder map as a square, you could visualize the stakeholder map as a circle, connecting the different stakeholder types to the stakeholder management strategies. By applying the right strategy to the right group of stakeholders, you should become more effective at stakeholder management and potentially grow your authority as a Product Owner or product manager.

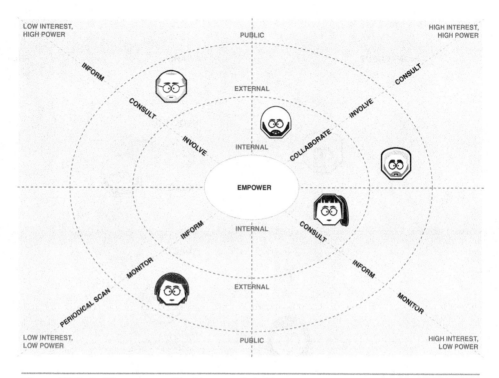

**Figure 29.2** A different way of looking at stakeholders

## THE STAKEHOLDER RADAR

There are various alternative techniques to the stakeholder map when it comes to stakeholder identification and categorization. One of those alternatives is the stakeholder radar. Whereas the stakeholder map focuses mostly on power/influence and interest, the stakeholder radar is more concerned with a stakeholder's **engagement** or **involvement** and **attitude** (see Figure 29.3).

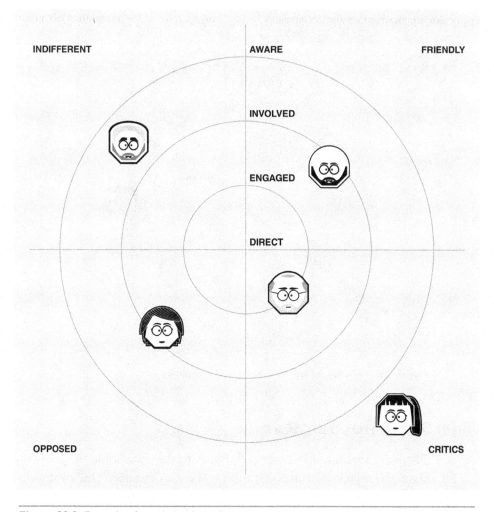

**Figure 29.3** Example of a stakeholder radar

## Involvement or Engagement

The stakeholder radar, as shown in Figure 29.3, consists of four rings that reflect the level of engagement or involvement that the stakeholder has. Some stakeholders may be only slightly **aware** of your product or service. Like the low interest, low influence quadrant in the stakeholder map, you mainly want to keep an eye on these stakeholders in case they move to another circle. Large groups of "aware" stakeholders can also be of interest to you, as they might represent a form of critical mass.

Other stakeholders may be somewhat more **involved** with the product or service, perhaps because they supply you with people, time, funding, or materials. For a typical business-to-consumer (B2C) product, you may find user presentations in this circle. Supply chain or distribution, marketing, sales, and operations are typically found here, but for a completely new product, they should probably be more engaged.

Some people are **engaged** in the product. They may take an active role, for example, by joining demos or Sprint Reviews. Perhaps they help you in the process. Perhaps they offer knowledge, feedback, or time. They are slightly less influential than those in the center ring. Think of sponsors, power users, and departments that depend on or are affected by your product.

Finally, in the center ring of the stakeholder radar, you will find the people who help you to define and set the **direction** for the product or service. Respect for your decisions comes from close collaboration with these stakeholders, not from having been appointed Product Owner. You must be aware of their attitude toward the product.

> For Product Owners to succeed, the entire organization must respect their decisions.
>
> —Scrum Guide 2020

## ATTITUDE

The stakeholder radar offers a second perspective on your stakeholders: their attitude toward the product, yourself, or your team. Their attitude is represented by the four quadrants in the stakeholder radar. These quadrants are more subjective than the four quadrants in the stakeholder map, so it may be useful to gauge some opinions among your team members and/or the stakeholders to learn about their attitudes.

There is always a group of people who don't care too much about your product, which is the **indifferent** group. Hopefully, the people in this group are not in a position where they can influence the direction of the product, which could be very harmful. In most cases, these are people from other teams or other departments who don't have a clear interest or stake in your product. You might find that some of these people are part of your team. These could be team members who have low motivation at that time. Taking the Visionary or Collaborator stance might help to light a spark for them. Doing the complex work that we often do, it helps a lot to have a focused team with a shared mission.

The next attitude is described as **friendly.** These people are your allies, your friendlies, your fans perhaps. You probably know who those fans or friends of the product are within your stakeholder group. These are the people who are supportive of your product, and you probably spent significant time on people in this segment. But do you focus on the people who are involved in the work? Directing the product's future? Or only slightly aware of the product existing?

Then there is the group of **critics.** This group consists of people who haven't made up their minds yet. They are still unsure whether to be in favor of your product or against it. They are significantly different from the group who are indifferent, though! The indifferent group doesn't care. This group, however, does care, but they don't yet know *how* to care. For the time being, they are therefore critical toward new ideas, goals, and work to be done in general. What will probably stand out about the folks in this group is that they often pose difficult questions, and they find facts and figures for you to analyze and respond to. When this group is in the outer rings (aware or somewhat involved), they might not express their feelings and doubts openly. As they become more active (engaged or directing), they will either openly express their disagreement or ask you some difficult questions in front of the whole stakeholder group. The closer they are to the center of the radar, the more paramount it is that you do an intervention to turn them into fans. Alternatively, you might deflect their potentially negative influence on the group by pairing them with a stakeholder who is supportive of your ideas. Here are a couple of additional tips for more effective collaboration with critics:

- Check whether the criticism is valid (e.g., a fair point), inaccurate, or a twisting of the truth.

- Learn about your critics: Who are they? What are their motivations and objectives? What are they doing? Is there any common ground between you?

- Take the conversation offline. Most issues are too complex for a public discussion.

- Meet your critics in person, regularly if you can. Keep the dialogue going.

- Answer their criticisms. Anticipate and be ready to answer their future criticisms too.

- Answer more calmly than your critics (rarely a challenge in my experience), but do not hesitate to affirm your points, views, and positive results as loudly as they do.

- As quickly as possible, get proactive on the issues they are raising. That might involve proactive PR work, roundtables, consultations, reports, events, even social media posts.

The last group of people is the **opposed** group. Although many of us dream about politics-free organizations and companies that are one big happy family with a shared passion and goal, practice is often different. We as Product Owners know better, right? There is always a group of unhappy people in an organization. This could be unhappiness with your product, service, resources, goals, or otherwise. Perhaps your product took away resources and people from their product. Perhaps your product changes the way they work. Perhaps people might, or fear they might, lose their jobs because of your product. Interacting, collaborating, or engaging with this opposed group may not always be fun and exciting. But you need to build good relationships with your opponents too. What is bothering them? What can you do to mitigate the pain they are experiencing? Who or what influences them? Here are some tips for better collaboration with opposed stakeholders:

- **Don't ignore them or their problem.** Their issue isn't going away by itself. It's crucial to understand the opposition and address it. Otherwise, the opposition will intensify and become more difficult to deal with. If you need help, then ask friendlies for support. Keep the dialogue open, so you can learn as much as possible to resolve their concerns.

- **Focus on business benefits and risks.** Opposition often comes from misunderstandings and fear of change. Communicate the benefits of your work. Treat concerns as risks and collaborate with the opposed stakeholders on mitigation strategies. Include friendlies, opposed, and critical stakeholders in such efforts. Ensure that reports and updates provide detail to inform both supporters and opponents. Again, lacking transparency, information, and understanding often causes opponents to become opponents in the first place.

- **Leverage supportive stakeholders.** The benefits you provide to some stakeholders can create concerns for others. Ensure your sponsors are aware of any concerns so they can help counter roadblocks created by opposed stakeholders.

- **Seek opportunities to support your concerned stakeholder.** Understanding your stakeholder's concerns can surface ideas for future projects that will provide benefits. Helping them build a business case for a follow-on project will help you preserve your relationship and further advance your business. It also demonstrates your ability to see the big picture in your business environment.

*Keep your friends close and your enemies closer.*

—Sun Tzu

The stakeholder radar may function as a replacement of the stakeholder map or as an addition to it. Considering people's level of engagement and their attitude toward you or your product may help to design an effective stakeholder management strategy. Once you have applied your stakeholder management strategy for some time, inspect and adapt the stakeholder map and stakeholder radar. Have you seen any evidence of stakeholders changing their mindset? What other strategies, tactics, and interventions can you experiment with? Can you use the help and support of your (friendly) stakeholders to work with the other (critics and opposed) stakeholders more effectively? Finally, don't be afraid to ask people about their ideas, opinions, and perspectives. Imagine how disarming it would be if we could simply ask a stakeholder, "It feels like you are not very supportive of our product. What can I do to change that?"

## ALTERNATIVE STAKEHOLDER IDENTIFICATION AND GROUPING TECHNIQUES

The stakeholder map and stakeholder radar are just two ways to create transparency and insights into your stakeholder field. There are many alternatives for stakeholder identification and grouping. Some of these tools may be useful for you; others won't be. Some of these tools can be applied to your context straight out of the box; others may require some customization. Abraham Maslow has an interesting perspective on tools: "I suppose it is tempting, if the only tool you have is a hammer, to treat everything as if it were a nail."

In summary, design a stakeholder management identification, categorization, and communication framework that works well for you. However, just randomly doing stuff on an ad hoc basis is probably not the best way forward. The following ideas for altering the stakeholder map have worked well for us in the past:

- **Influence vs. dynamism:** How often does a stakeholder change their mind? What would happen if a very influential stakeholder did this all the time? Mapping stakeholders based on their influence and dynamism has been quite useful in environments where traditional lean practices and new product development need to work together. An example is a retail supply chain company (optimized for efficiency) that starts to develop an omnichannel proposition (optimized for responding to change).

- **Influence, legitimacy, and urgency:** Some stakeholders exert power to influence decisions and direction but have no urgency to do so. Others may have urgency but no legitimacy. This way of grouping stakeholders could be visualized in a Venn diagram to define which stakeholders you should listen to more than to others. It can help you even to generate transparency about why you might say no to others.

- **The informal org chart:** You can create an informal org chart by plotting the stakeholders in circles on a sheet of paper. The size of each circle indicates the influence of the stakeholder. The lines between you and the stakeholder as well as among the stakeholders represent your relationship with them (strong, indirect, none) and their relationships with each other. Finally, colors can indicate the state of that relationship (think about the attitudes from the stakeholder radar). This chart is helpful to find indirect paths to stakeholders that could be valuable to collaborate with or influence.

Don't get hung up on one solution. Try some of these tools in practice, make some changes, experiment, and see what works best for you.

# APPLYING STAKEHOLDER MANAGEMENT STRATEGIES AND TACTICS IN PRACTICE

## CREATING A COMMUNICATION STRATEGY

Because time is limited, you will want to do your stakeholder management activities effectively. Not all your stakeholders deserve an equal amount of your time. Some stakeholders are very important, whereas others generally cost you time without delivering valuable insights in return. A practice that may help you to engage with your stakeholders effectively is to design a communication strategy for each stakeholder and stakeholder group. This communication strategy is an easy-to-access, simple overview of how you plan to deal with your various stakeholder groups. It typically contains elements such as stakeholder name, function, information needs, personal goals to achieve, message to send, information to send, communication channels, personality type, and your objective to achieve. Designing an effective communication strategy helps you to spend time efficiently and engage effectively with stakeholders. It also helps to create transparency for your Scrum Teams around how you want to engage with your various stakeholders.

What was valuable to us in the past was to do some analysis around the personality types of our stakeholders. This helped us to better understand our various stakeholders and their personalities, goals, values, and communication styles and preferences. By understanding your stakeholders better, you'll be able to tailor your communication style to match their preferred communication style. To identify your stakeholder's communication preferences, first, get your stakeholder map. Go through the map and list the names of your stakeholders. Then consider using a model or framework that helps you to identify different personalities (e.g., the DISC [Dominance, Influence, Steadiness, and Conscientiousness] model, MBTI [Myers-Briggs Type Indicator], or any other framework you prefer). Use the insights from such models to identify the personality types and communication preferences for your stakeholders. This way, you can create a tailored communication strategy (see Table 30.1 for an example). Remember to spend most of your time on your key stakeholders and be explicit about which stakeholders you are not going to spend time on.

When designing a communication strategy, consider the following:

- **Who** is the stakeholder? The audience and role greatly influence the approach. A C suite manager will require a different communication than an end user of the product or service.

- **What** do they need, and **why** do they need it? This question can be approached from the perspective of "What are they asking for?" or "What are their deeper motives and needs? Why do they need the information?" A security officer may ask for audit trails but is looking for reassurance that we don't release products that will lead to reputation damage. Covering their needs is more important than the actual report.

- What kind of **personality** does this stakeholder have? What are some actions or words they appreciate hearing? What are some dos and don'ts for this stakeholder?

- What is the **message** you want to communicate? What is the message that you will share with them? Also, consider their communication style. Do you want to be direct, cooperative, strict? This is the message content and the formatting.

- **How** will you communicate with them? You can communicate with people through different channels or means. It is not uncommon to deliver the same information in written format to some stakeholders and verbally to others. Reports, updates, data tables, or dashboards can be useful forms of communication. Don't launch PowerPoint for everything. Sometimes, just talking to people might be most useful.

- **When** will you deliver this information? Most information is delivered periodically. You may find it helpful to manage your schedule and define set times for stakeholder communication. It may also be helpful to automate some of your communication work and to identify people who may be of assistance in stakeholder communication.

- What is the **desired effect** of communicating? This is a combination of what you want to get out of the communication and the person's place on the stakeholder map. The desired effect is that this stakeholder remains in their current "influence, interest" (e.g., high influence, low interest) zone on the map. The desired effect greatly influences the channel that you can use.

- Who will be **responsible** for delivering the message? The Product Owner usually remains accountable for stakeholder management, but that doesn't mean you have to do everything yourself. Use help and support from your team members to see if you can automate some communication. Try to simplify your work.

**Table 30.1** Example Stakeholder Management Strategy

| Who (Person and Role) | What (Information Needs) | How (Channels/ Means) | Message (Contents) | When | Desired Effect | Responsible |
|---|---|---|---|---|---|---|
| Dave (CEO) | Financial KPIs, opportunities and risks | Face-to-face meetings and reports | Up-to-date numbers, deviations to the budget, and risks | Monthly | Keep satisfied | Product Owner |

| Who (Person and Role) | What (Information Needs) | How (Channels/ Means) | Message (Contents) | When | Desired Effect | Responsible |
|---|---|---|---|---|---|---|
| Sandra (compliance officer) | Reassurance, confirmation, facts, and figures | Monthly updates and reports | Overview of risks, compliance issues, and audit results | Monthly | Minimum effort | Team |
| Shanice (circulation manager) | Power—knowing more of what goes on than anybody else | Personal mail to her about developments before the announcement | Facts and figures, new features, new initiatives | Weekly | Keep informed | Team |
| Kemal (COO) | How can we get a podium? How can we improve sales? | Face-to-face meetings, co-creation, and offering a stage | Co-create the product vision, strategy, and roadmap | Biweekly | Manage closely | Product Owner |

# TIPS FOR IMPROVING YOUR STAKEHOLDER MANAGEMENT IN PRACTICE

We have seen that stakeholders come in many different forms. Stakeholders can be identified and grouped in different ways, using different techniques. We have also discussed how to design a stakeholder management strategy—or communication strategy—to start engaging with your stakeholders in a structured way. We would like to share with you some tips around the topic of stakeholder management, which hopefully prevent you from the mistakes we and others have made in the past. Here we go.

## TIP 1: START SAYING NO TO YOUR STAKEHOLDERS MORE OFTEN

Maximizing the value of a product involves making tons of choices. Research has proven repeatedly that it's better to do a couple of things well than to do a lot of things halfway. This is a hard job! It's a job in which you can't satisfy everyone. Imagine a product you use yourself almost every day. Is this a product with tons of features? Or is it a relatively simple product that does a couple of things well?

As a Product Owner, you need to make conscious decisions, including what *not* to do and what features *not* to build. So, start saying no to stakeholders more often. There are many ways of saying no, which you will again find in *Master the Art of No*.[1] We have drawn some inspiration from this book, to follow in the next chapter. Alternatively, you could use a more subtle approach, such as, "I am not saying no, but here are my conditions for a yes," or "If you can help me by identifying and describing the added value of this feature in a business case, I might be able to help you."

## TIP 2: TREAT DIFFERENT STAKEHOLDERS DIFFERENTLY

Product Owners and product managers are usually very busy people. They've got tons of work to do, such as refinement sessions, Sprint Reviews, writing Product Backlog items, and of course, working with those stakeholders who eat up so much of their time. If you are one of these Product Owners experiencing this busyness, then this tip may be one for you: Stop treating all your stakeholders equally. In other words, treat different stakeholders differently.

We should always respect the people who influence, collaborate, and contribute to our product. Being respectful is important, always. After all, we collaboratively try to solve our customers' problems. However, being respectful is not the same as treating people equally. As a Product Owner, knowing which stakeholders have a high or low interest in the product, which have a lot of power, and which do not is important to keep in mind.

Not all stakeholders are equally important. Some stakeholders are your "partners in crime," others are merely interested or aware. Be explicit about who your important and not-so-important stakeholders are. You can spend your time only once, so spend it wisely on the most important contributors, collaborators, and influencers of your product.

---

1. Robbin Schuurman and Willem Vermaak, *Master the Art of No: Effective Stakeholder Management for Product Owners and Product Managers,* independently published, 2020.

## TIP 3: MANAGE THE SYSTEM, NOT THE PEOPLE

Another way to improve your efficiency and effectiveness as a Product Owner is to stop managing stakeholders individually. One-on-ones and meeting for coffee are great and informal ways to build relationships and increase your influence, but they also eat up a lot of time. Instead, try to manage stakeholders via groups or updates that can be reused.

For example, invite groups of users to regular demo sessions (not to be confused with the Sprint Review). During these demo sessions, you (or the team) can show all the new product features to a large group of people, sometimes even including some user or system training. A different group of people (e.g., the most important stakeholders) can be invited to the Sprint Reviews to be part of the strategic-tactical session. There you can collaborate on the next steps to maximize the product's value. In refinement meetings, for example, invite users, customers, and other people to work out some new features, brainstorm on ideas, and do market validation. In short, there is time to be saved if you organize stakeholder engagement effectively by putting them together in the same room.

## TIP 4: DON'T FORGET THE CUSTOMER

With all stakeholders asking for your time, it's easy to forget about the customer. Often, we are reluctant for customers to see the first iterations of our product and feel we need to add more capabilities before showing it to them to get some early feedback. This fear of showing things that aren't complete assumes that we only get one chance to make a good first impression. However, that does not apply in complex product development. By developing a product iteratively and incrementally, we get the opportunity to create multiple "first" impressions rather quickly. Being focused on shipping early and often, to get customer feedback, doesn't mean that we'll be cutting corners, acting recklessly, or proceeding without a clear goal. It may be embarrassing at times to launch something incomplete. But that's not a bad thing if you're moving fast, learning fast, and improving your product, with the support and feedback from customers. Don't be afraid of your customers. Involve them, get feedback, treat them as valuable stakeholders.

## Tip 5: Increase Your Authority by Acting Like an Owner

Many organizations that have implemented the Scrum framework struggle with the principle of decentralized control. As a result, many Product Owners and product managers lack the authority to make decisions on their own. They are instead expected to act as a scribe, proxy, or business representative. Consequently, many Product Owners complain that they don't have any power to make decisions, or that they hardly have any freedom to do what they think is right for the product. But guess what? There is something you can do about it.

Many of these scribe, proxy, and business representative Product Owners have adopted a pattern of continuously asking permission or consent from stakeholders—permission to develop a new feature, permission to spend some time on resolving bugs, permission to spend time on reducing technical debt. There is nothing wrong with including or involving your stakeholders, but if you want to become an entrepreneurial Product Owner, you must stop acting as a scribe and start acting as an owner!

Many of the tools, techniques, and concepts in this book will help you move in the right direction. Another way to increase your authority is to state your actions as intentions—for example, "I intend to pursue this goal for the next quarter." This improves the way you present yourself to the stakeholders, the way you present your product, and the way you act.

You can increase your authority by acting as the owner of the Product, taking responsibility, developing a plan (your plan), and showing that you love and care about the product and your team. To put it differently, if you don't develop a plan of your own, you will become part of someone else's plan.

## Tip 6: Know Thy Stakeholders' Interests by Heart

Knowing your stakeholders' interests by heart makes it easier to keep them updated and saves you time when talking to them. For a lot of Product Owners, though, knowing their stakeholders' interests by heart isn't top of mind. You must speak the language of the stakeholder, and this is a lot easier if you know their interests well. For example, if one of your stakeholders is responsible for the operations department, they probably won't be interested in hearing about all the cool and fancy new product features. They might, on the other hand, be interested in the impact of these new features on the straight-through processing (STP) numbers, the expected impact on the net promoter score (NPS), or the expected process-efficiency gains.

## TIP 7: INVOLVE YOUR SCRUM MASTER

Managing stakeholders effectively may be rather challenging and complex from time to time, especially with the more difficult stakeholders. Although you are responsible for stakeholder management, this doesn't mean you have to do it all on your own. A Scrum Master can support you when you are getting a lot of questions about the development process, the way of working, why you're using Scrum, and so forth.

Stakeholders (especially senior management) are often used to having control, which is important for them because they are often responsible for running a business—or at least part of it. Being in control is important also in an Agile environment. The way we achieve control, however, is quite different in Agile environments. We often use other practices, tools, and techniques than we were used to. For example, steering committees are often not needed in Agile environments. But you can't just remove them without replacing this control mechanism with something else. So, let your Scrum Master support you and your stakeholders so that, together, you can find new or other ways of remaining in control while increasing Agility.

## TIP 8: DON'T BE THE CARRIER PIGEON BETWEEN THE SCRUM TEAM AND THE STAKEHOLDERS

Many Product Owners act like a carrier pigeon, a proxy, a gateway, and thus a bottleneck between the Developers and the stakeholders. Many organizations have established a way of working that prohibits the Developers from talking to stakeholders, customers, and users. Instead, communication flows into the team via the Product Owner. This approach is highly ineffective and inefficient. It is often introduced to "shield the team from the stakeholders" or to "ensure that we don't add extra work to the Sprint" or because we believe that "Developers are incapable of talking to customers."

Great Product Owners, though, don't share these ideas. They ensure direct communication between stakeholders, customers, users, and Developers takes place. They encourage Developers to embrace and adopt customer feedback. They ensure that Developers learn to understand customers and users better through collaboration. Clear agreements between all parties involved may help. Ensure that people know the product vision, product goal, and next steps. A lot of self-management and delegated decision making can happen if goals are to be achieved and boundaries are clear. Finally, what is the worst thing that can happen? Perhaps they screw up one Sprint. So what? There are plenty more Sprints to follow.

Also, consider how transparency of information is key. Information radiators such as product walls, Scrum boards, Kanban boards, portfolio walls, or obeya rooms are very helpful tools for communication. If done correctly, these tools help you, the team, and the stakeholders with knowledge and information sharing. So, don't hide stuff in SharePoint. Put it on a wall instead, out in the open for everyone to see.

# How to Influence Stakeholders on All Levels

## Being a Lyrebird

A scale is a great tool for keeping track of your weight, but you still need to put in the work if you want to change the readout. The same thing is true when it comes to communication. Being a great communicator is a trait of a great Influencer, and it is something we can practice.

Although our core focus is to build great products that our customers and users will love, the actual work we do is mostly "people" business. To collaborate with different kinds of people, and influence them effectively, we need great communication skills.

### Penguins, Eagles, Peacocks, and Owls

It is two weeks after the CFO has signed off on Noa's business case for change, and all the important decision makers have gathered in the boardroom.

"This will be so cool! The folks at Apple and Tesla will marvel at our innovative solution!" said Kemal. Noa seriously questioned whether he would be right about that, but it was great to see how passionately he was presenting their latest idea to transform the newspaper business. Noa found herself sitting on the tip of her chair, hung on Kemal's every word throughout the presentation. She forced herself to sit back and observe the rest of the audience. Dave seemed annoyed. *This is taking up too much of his time,*" Noa thought. She was counting down the minutes before he would stop Kemal's one-man show and just decide to approve or reject the solution.

Before Dave could interrupt, Shanice did. "Sorry to interrupt," she said. "You know I love supporting this initiative, but it does feel like a huge change. Are we qualified to make this decision here? It will affect everybody in the company, and I would like to hear from the rest of the staff on how they feel about this."

*Typical Shanice,* Noa thought, *always taking good care of our people, but unfortunately slowing down the whole process.*

"That's a great suggestion, Shanice. Can you help us to organize a representative group?" Kemal deflected.

Before Shanice could respond, Sandra intervened. "Look, we have a process in place for this kind of a project. Can we please adhere to it? Thank you."

Noa closed her eyes with a sigh, and it felt like all the squabbling turned into the chirping of birds. Dave was like a big eagle, looking for the big picture, then swooping in for decisive action. Shanice was like a penguin looking after the herd and making sure that nobody was left out. Sandra favored the facts and figures, like a wise owl. Kemal was showing off his feathers, much like a peacock. *I wonder what kind of bird I am?"* Noa thought, and she settled on a lyrebird.[1]

In this chapter, you'll read about different levels of communicating and about communicating with different types of people. In addition to the basics covered here, we advise you to look at some dedicated communication resources to learn more.

---

1. Lyrebirds can imitate almost any sound, and they have been recorded mimicking sounds like mill whistles, chainsaws, car engines and alarms, fire alarms, rifle shots, camera shutters, dogs barking, crying babies, music, mobile phone ringtones, and even human voices.

## THE PROCESS OF COMMUNICATION

When we communicate with other people, we often focus on the message that we are trying to convey. There are many ways to structure a message to make it interesting, cohesive, logical, and concise. In the Visionary stance, for example, you learned about the 3×3 storytelling framework as a tool to help you format your message when communicating your vision. Of course, there are many ways to structure that message to be cohesive, logical, and concise. However, composing and formatting a message often isn't the biggest problem for a Product Owner. Communicating effectively is more than just formatting and sharing a message, so let's explore the process and the four layers of communication.

Communication between people sounds quite simple: a message is sent by a sender to one or more receivers. Although this exchange of messages from one person to another is what communication is essentially about, doing so effectively seems to be more complex.

Ineffective communication can result from many different causes. Surely it has something to do with the sender, the message, and the receiver, but there is more to it. Some common challenges hinder effective communication in organizations:

- Cultural differences
- Attitudes, emotions, and a lack of motivation
- Listening skills
- Written communication quality

- Language problems and jargon
- Hierarchy
- Badly expressed message/information
- Distrust, mistrust, and fear
- Application of inappropriate channels and tools of communication

There may be many other causes for ineffective communication, but how can we solve them? First, it is important to understand that communication consists of different components and actors: senders and receivers as well as messages and channels. A simplified model of communication is visualized in Figure 31.1.

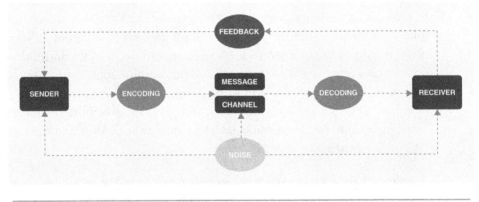

**Figure 31.1** A simplified model of communication

When the sender communicates the message to the receiver, some additional elements need to be considered. First, the message will be communicated via a channel, such as verbally in one-on-one communication, via e-mail, via a report, or in a memo, for example. Selecting the right channel, medium, or tool for communicating a message is very important. For example, if you need to communicate that a goal won't be achieved, a deadline will be missed, or a feature will not be delivered, then prefer face-to-face or at least real-time verbal communication. If you want to update people about good progress, then you could prefer an email, report, or other written update. Consider what the most effective channel would be for communicating certain messages because some channels suffer more from "noise" than others. An important email might easily get lost in crammed inboxes. Yet another quick-update meeting in a packed schedule won't help people to remember the message. Therefore, the channel is an important element of the stakeholder communication strategy that we discussed in Chapter 30, "Applying Stakeholder Management Strategies and Tactics in Practice."

Before the message can be shared via the channel you selected, the sender *encodes* the message. This means that the sender is describing and formatting the message in a way that *makes sense to the sender*. The sender needs to realize that they are trying to pass on the message in their language. This language might include business, technical, or industry jargon, figures of speech, a certain perspective on the subject, or a language barrier in general. Before sending a message to your intended audience, make sure to remove as much jargon as possible. Try to format your message in a simple way. Make it easy for people to understand. And perhaps ask a couple of your team members or stakeholders to review your message before sharing it.

The way you encode your message, and the ability to decode the message by the receiver, greatly impacts the effectiveness of your communication. So, once the message is sent to or shared with the audience, the receiver(s) need to *decode* the message. That is, the receiver needs to interpret what the message means, determine its intent, and try to identify how it will impact them. If you want to make this easier, you can include such aspects in your message: describe or explain what you would like people to do with the information, what you're hoping to achieve, and how it will impact them.

The channel always introduces some form of noise, and just as in any communication system, the signal-to-noise ratio matters. A great example of noise exceeding the signal is when you're reading a document or a book and at some point have to scroll back, thinking, *Hang on, let me read that again*. Composing documents requires a great deal of thought to minimize that effect.

And that's just the tip of the iceberg. This part of communication relates only to the first layer of communication, the message. There are three additional layers to consider. Why would the receiver spend so much time on you? What drives the urge for a quick reply, a free slot in the agenda, not canceling the appointment at last-minute notice? The answer is the relationship you have with the person.

## FOUR LAYERS OF COMMUNICATION

Apart from the message, there is also the process of communicating, the relationship you have with the other person, and your (or their) emotional state. The message is the most visible and tangible part of communication, but the other three layers might be the biggest influencers of successful communication. Figure 31.2 illustrates the four layers of communication. In order to get the right message across, you need to get the other three layers in place.

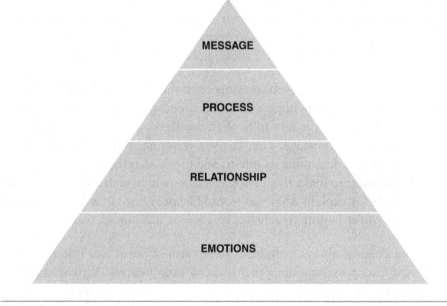

**Figure 31.2** Four layers of communication

How you deliver your message is very important. It has to do with tone, intonation, nonverbal communication, and your connection with the other party. If you communicate in a very rigid, short, and direct way, it will surely affect the other person. They may experience you as domineering and curt, which may lead to irritation or even aggression in an extreme case. So, consider your nonverbal communication and tone of voice.

How do you feel? Are you calm, excited, frustrated? Understand what **emotions** you are experiencing before you communicate. If you are all heated up and frustrated, then you are probably not going to communicate effectively. If you're okay on an emotional level, move forward.

Ask yourself if you have been demonstrating empathy for the other person. Did you spend time building a **relationship** with them? Are you actively listening to the other person, and are you hearing what they say?

What about the **process** of the conversation? Are you heading into exchanging arguments right from the start of the interaction? Or are you having a structured conversation, both being able to talk and listen?

Finally, consider the actual **message** you want to deliver. Is the content of your message interesting for the other party? Are you using a lot of jargon? Or do you have a common vocabulary?

When people struggle with effective communication, the first thing they often consider is whether the contents of their messages should be improved. But in many cases, ineffective communication is caused by the other, underlying layers. Do some personal reflection on those, and inspect your investment in the relationship layer. We often don't spend enough time building high-quality relationships with our stakeholders.

## BUILDING RELATIONSHIPS WITH STAKEHOLDERS

Many people, including Product Owners, have a complicated view of building good relationships. Want to create friendships outside of work? Sure, you can do that. Do you want to build a professional network? That might already be a bit more complicated for you, as networking often feels like a shallow, perhaps even seedy, thing to do, right? Building connections with other people at work? That's just unfair!

But these different types of relationships are still, well, relationships. Especially in your early career as a Product Owner or product manager, you might believe that everyone should be treated equally. You are partly correct in that sense. Everybody should be treated with the same respect, just as we explained in Chapter 28, "Stakeholder Management in Complex Environments." However, we also discussed that you should treat different stakeholders differently. And they are likely to do the same to you. People don't have enough time, energy, and trust to treat everyone the same way. Although they won't likely be treating strangers poorly, chances are that they will treat better relationships in a better way. So, it's worthwhile to invest time in building good relationships, friends, networks, and connections at work.

> *Good work relationships make everything easier. Teammates who trust you won't make you spend as much time justifying your decisions. Partners are more willing to assist you or take on risks. Mentors will take the time to share advice with you and hiring managers will bring you onto their teams.*
>
> — Jackie Bavaro and Gayle McDowell[2]

Building relationships at work doesn't have to be hard. The point of building those relationships is not necessarily for you to become best friends with your colleagues. You just need to be able to collaborate effectively. You just need to be friendly and respectful to your colleagues. If you are already collaborating with some people, but you feel like it's a shallow relationship, then just invite them for a cup of coffee to get to know them better. If you want to expand your connections and network, consider joining a group of people with shared hobbies, passions, expertise, or working groups. If you want to connect with more like-minded product people outside of your organization, then join a Product Owner community or Meetup group. If you want to build

---

2. Jackie Bavaro and Gayle McDowell, *Cracking the PM Career: The Skills, Frameworks, and Practices to Become a Great Product Manager,* CareerCup, 2021.

better relationships at work, including management and executives, then here are some things for you to work on:

## WORK ON YOUR CREDIBILITY

Earning credibility from managerial stakeholders and customers is key for Product Owners and product managers. People tend to be more open to your ideas, opinion, decisions, and influence if they trust your judgment. Stakeholders need to build up confidence in your abilities. They need to know that if you ask them for something, it's for a good reason. They need to know that you know what you're talking about. They need to know that you act in their best interest.

By building credibility, you also increase your autonomy. Doing a good job is important, and working on great products and launching them successfully help to build your reputation. However, doing a good job is not all that matters. You need to gain people's trust, for example, by doing what you said you would do (and making sure they know about it), by being confident (but not overconfident), by communicating your reasoning behind decisions, and by taking ownership of failures, and sharing successes.

## DRIVE DECISIONS FOR YOUR PRODUCT AND TEAM

A frequently heard complaint from managers about Product Owners is that they don't drive decisions well enough. Many product people ask for permission way too often, and they don't steer conversations well enough to reach a good quality decision quickly and effectively.

A better strategy is to take responsibility for making decisions. Great Product Owners are proactive, and they identify decisions that need to be made. They don't procrastinate in making decisions, nor do they hope that someone else will take the lead. In your role as a Product Owner, you should take an active role in decision making and form and communicate your point of view.

## LEARN ABOUT OTHER PERSPECTIVES AND DRIVE PROGRESS TOWARD A SHARED GOAL

Listen to the experts, your customers, and your stakeholders. Capture arguments, options, and research. Do your research if needed. But then drive a discussion to make progress. It's important to learn what other people know and think. If they know more about a topic than you do, it won't make much sense for them to trust you with the decision. So, make sure that people feel like you're all on the same team and are working toward the same shared goals and objectives.

## KEEP MOVING FORWARD

When making a decision, wasting a lot of time on reaching consensus among all stakeholders is often worse than making the wrong decision and moving forward. This common trap is called *analysis paralysis,* and it springs shut if you get stuck overthinking and overanalyzing to the point that you can't make a decision. As we discussed in Part V, "The Decision Maker," product management is a game of incomplete information. Many decisions need to be made using incomplete information. Great Product Owners display good judgment by moving fast on decisions that are easily reversed. Great Product Owners understand that unresolved and pending decisions take a toll on the team.

## ESCALATE DECISIONS AFTER DOING YOUR HOMEWORK

Inevitably, you will need to escalate something to ensure that a problem or decision is resolved quickly. However, before you escalate a problem or decision to your boss, make sure that you have done your homework by

- Clarifying the decision that needs to be made.
- Determining the trade-offs, pros and cons, and potentially conflicting goals.
- Driving agreement among the stakeholders on the most important goals.
- Having done everything you can yourself before escalating in the first place.

If you need to escalate a decision, focus on asking for a decision about which goal is most important to achieve. Don't ask company leaders, executives, or customers about which solution to choose. People you'll be escalating to tend to know how the goals should be prioritized, but they are usually not experts in, and more disconnected from, the details. Stakeholders can provide you with more context, and perhaps you'll be able to make a good decision with that additional context.

## SHARE YOUR IDEAS AT THE RIGHT TIME

Product people are always full of ideas: great ideas to resolve customer problems, great ideas for new product features, and great ideas for making the product generate more value. When shared at the right time, a good idea can have a huge positive impact on people. However, it can also be seen as an annoyance if it's shared at the wrong time.

So, make sure to pay attention to the planning cycles within the company. Presenting new ideas is better done before new quarterly or yearly goals, objectives, and targets are set. Take the product life cycle into account to present the right ideas at the right time. Coming up with great, new, shiny, big initiatives after the goals have just been identified is likely to cause more annoyance than enthusiasm.

## GET BUY-IN BY INCLUDING PEOPLE AND COLLABORATING EARLY ON

You may have heard of the *not invented here (NIH) syndrome*. NIH syndrome describes how people are more attached to things they create themselves than to things bought elsewhere. We've witnessed this syndrome in many organizations where they're developing software, tools, and processes themselves despite standard solutions being available on the market. Sure, those standard tools don't exactly match the company's way of working, but is that a problem? Can't the way of working be adapted slightly to match the industry standard? Wouldn't that be easier, cheaper, and perhaps more effective?

If you want to start something new or move in a different direction, use this concept to your advantage. Build stronger relationships with your stakeholders by including them in the discovery, creation, ideation, design, and development of new products, services, processes, and plans. Do an early kick-off meeting, for example, because people love being included early on and taking part in shaping new directions. Structure meetings in a way that you get the kind of input you want. Host brainstorming sessions so that people can share ideas without your being obligated to use them. And, of course, allow other people to receive credit for their contributions. You'll often increase your influence on people if you allow them to feel like they came up with the ideas themselves. We're all human beings, and at our core, we all want to feel important and impactful. Use this knowledge to your advantage by giving people an opportunity to feel important and valued.

## BUILD TRUST ACROSS TEAMS AND DEPARTMENTS

Large organizations are typically split into groups, departments, and teams. In many cases, these groups are built around silos, like product, sales, marketing, support, operations, IT, and engineering. Those who staff the different silos often feel that they know and understand best how the business is run and how it should be run. When product teams get elitist and dismissive of other departments, distrust starts to grow. As a Product Owner, if you focus solely on doing what's best for your product and team, you will only increase that distrust. You must consider the whole silo.

Understanding that there are other goals, objectives, initiatives, and interests beyond your product and team becomes increasingly important as you advance your career. You need to learn about, understand, and be able to evaluate different interests on a company level. You need to earn trust from the executive team and department managers or directors. Building trust among department leaders (who report to the executives) is a good way to build long-term relationships with some very important people in the company. It takes time to build trust, but it is time well spent. It helps to learn about their interests, goals, and concerns. If you do, they will start to consider you as an ally, and they will become less skeptical of your ideas. Ask them what their most important goals are. Learn about any concerns they have going forward based on their past experiences with other Product Owners. Share the goals and objectives your team is trying to achieve.

## SPEND THE TIME

Make a list of the people in your organization who give you energy when you meet with them, and seek out opportunities to work with them, whether it's officially on an interdepartmental committee or more informally, such as asking them for advice. When you do, be conscious of what it is about them that makes you want to work together, and share this observation with them. Set up coffee with one person per day for a month. Spend the time understanding what they love about their work.

Although it's tempting to eat lunch at your desk and avoid all interaction with the outside world, it's much more beneficial to take a break and eat in the lunchroom. This allows you to get to know your colleagues on a more personal level. Lunchroom chat usually involves any topic (other than work) and is the perfect opportunity to bond with the people you work with. Over time, lunch-break friendships usually blossom into trusting relationships.

Avoid office politics and gossip. Office gossip has the powerful ability to foster disengagement and negative feelings toward your job, management, and your company, resulting in dissatisfaction in the workplace. Rather, try to be a positive force that seeks opportunities.

Most organizations with a good company culture arrange at-work activities and out-of-work gatherings. They provide you with the opportunities to meet people you don't directly work with every day and get to know them beyond the office walls. If it's during working hours, then these activities are mostly compulsory. On the other hand, out-of-work gatherings aren't obligatory, but they are essential if you want to make work friends. Although you don't have to go to every meeting, it's ideal to show your face now and again.

Dedicate some time to the people around you. It takes only five minutes to walk over to a colleague and ask them how they're doing. Have a casual conversation about work or something else. Those five minutes a day will help you build a connection and gain their trust.

## ADAPTING YOUR TUNE TO YOUR AUDIENCE

We cannot always tell people *what* they want to hear. We cannot always give people what they're asking for, but we can communicate our message to stakeholders in the way they want to hear it. We can communicate *how* they like to hear something.

Various models, tests, assessments, and theories exist that seek to capture and explain people's personalities, preferred communication styles, and preferred styles of working. Models such as Dominance, Influence, Steadiness, and Conscientiousness (DISC), Myers-Briggs Type Indicator (MBTI), the Big Five, Management Drives, Insights Discovery, and Leary's Rose are all models that help us to better understand ourselves and others. Some research finds that these models and tests are flawed and ineffective, while other research finds that they are useful. Hence, the famous quote, "All models are wrong, but some are useful," by George E. P. Box applies. Whether you are a fan of these models or hate them, whether you see value in them or discard them completely, just bear with us for a moment.

We have seen often that people do have a preferred style of communication. It may change over time and may be different in different situations. In other words, you can't put people in a certain box. However, if you observe people over a longer time, at their work, in certain settings (e.g., meetings), you will likely spot some patterns. Knowing these patterns, and thus the preferred style of communicating, can be useful to you in building better relationships and improving your communication and stakeholder management skills.

Although we don't necessarily prefer one model over another, we decided to explain the concept based on the DISC model. Why? Mainly because it's rather simple to understand, as it describes only four styles. Guess what the downside is. It describes only four styles and is thus less accurate than some other models.

So, how can we use a model like DISC in practice? First, each of the preferred communication styles—dominant, influential, steady, and conscientious—has certain characteristics or traits, which are displayed by a person's behaviors, things they say, and things they like to hear. These characteristics give you insight into their personalities.

Second, by observing your stakeholders in practice, and by comparing their behaviors, things they say, and things they respond to well, you'll likely be able to classify them in one of the DISC types. But remember that you'll need to observe these behaviors rather consistently over time while taking their work context into account.

Once you know more about your stakeholders' personalities and preferred styles of communicating, you can use that knowledge to tune your communication to your audience.

## DOMINANT: THE EAGLE

Some people prefer a dominant style of communication. They don't want to dive into all the details but prefer the big picture. They quickly find the challenges to be solved, and they prefer to get straight to the point.

This type of stakeholder is typically focused on getting the job done and delivering results. Because they are so focused on getting the job done, they can be quite blunt. They like to hear concrete actions to take, pros and cons, and solutions, and they want to know what decisions they are being called on to make.

This style is often favored by stakeholders who are higher up in the org chart. Product Owners often struggle with this communication style because they are inherently aware of the uncertainty and complexity of product development. Often, there are no easy paths or simple decisions.

Do your homework when you engage with a stakeholder who prefers this communication style. Present a decision to be made. Presenting various options, pros and cons, and solutions for them to decide typically works well for dominant stakeholders.

## INFLUENTIAL: THE PEACOCK

Others want to be part of the exploration process. They are still driving the result but love to cooperate on it and dislike being ignored. These stakeholders can be compared to peacocks. They like to be on stage, in the spotlight, part of the exploration process, and to show off their beautiful feathers. Include these types of stakeholders in workshops, brainstorms, envisioning sessions, and product presentations to leverage their energy to create fans.

Getting into the details works to some extent, but these stakeholders might check out or get bored if they're not doing something new and exciting. Where the eagle-type stakeholders prefer to be presented with clear options to make decisions, the peacock type prefer to be more involved.

Once you realize that peacocks like to show off their feathers, you may want to allow them to take the stage and present the results of your workshops or perhaps the results of the Sprint during the Sprint Review. Take a step back sometimes to offer these stakeholders a place to shine; in that way, you can be more of a servant leader to the success of your product.

> *A leader is best when people barely know he exists. When his work is done, his aim fulfilled, they will say: we did it ourselves.*
>
> — Lao Tzu

## STEADY: THE PENGUIN

Penguins are fascinating animals because you'll always find them huddling together. They also chase their prey together. They prefer to get the biggest bang for their buck by seeking out the best and most nutritious food for the least amount of effort.

You may encounter some stakeholders in your organization who prefer the steadiness style of communication. These stakeholders love to hear about the details or surface those details themselves, especially when making complex decisions. As they are aware that complex decisions require buy-in on many levels, and that the commonly accepted opinion of the group may influence many decisions and outcomes, the steadiness stakeholders dislike being rushed into a decision.

Pressure and deadlines often harm these stakeholders, as they are more focused on people than on results. They care about reaching a consensus in the group, and they value individuals, opinions, and togetherness. Taking a calm approach and acknowledging that you do not know everything and that you need their help might be a useful approach to take. You'll want to ensure that the penguins are on board with your approach and that they don't feel they are being rushed into decisions. Avoiding major changes in favor of several small steps can help to improve the product.

## CONSCIENTIOUS: THE OWL

The fourth type of stakeholder is less focused on reaching consensus in the group. These stakeholders just want to make the right decision, in the right way, using the right process. The conscientious stakeholders often follow a pattern of logic and are somewhat less concerned with people's emotions.[3]

The details, options, facts and figures, data, and proven solutions matter a lot to this type of stakeholder, though. Much like the penguins care about the details and taking small steps, the owls also cannot decide without the details of the matter at hand. They do not necessarily need to be part of the decision-making process or to make the decisions themselves, but they do require you to follow the rules, or they will interfere.

You must be well prepared when you interact with stakeholders who prefer this communication style. Not only must facts and figures be correct, but the way they were gathered should allow for objective reasoning. It's helpful to do your research the right way because chances are that these stakeholders will also do some research themselves. They are usually well prepared for meetings, as they enjoy being independent and objective.

---

3. If you are a *Star Trek* fan, think Vulcans.

## A BRIEF CLOSING NOTE ON THESE FOUR ANIMAL-LIKE STAKEHOLDERS

Great communicators adapt their tune to their audience. When facing an eagle-like stakeholder with little time and the need to make progress, it is not wise to propose organizing an all-hands meeting. The worst thing you can do to an owl is come up with something new and shiny, with little to no data or proof of being successful. Ignoring emotions and people when talking to a penguin is not the brightest of ideas. Being aware of the preferred communication style of your stakeholder allows you to adapt to *how* they best receive what you are trying to communicate, allowing you to keep control over *what* you are trying to communicate.

Our intentions while using these animals are not to offend anyone. These animals are merely metaphors but may not resonate with all readers. In western countries, the owl, for example, represents a wise bird of prey, a reference going back to the representation of the Greek goddess of wisdom Athena. In other mythologies, the owl is sometimes considered a symbol of foolishness or refers to the wealth acquired by illegitimate means. Use the animals as metaphors, but don't call anyone peacock!

# Mastering the Art of No to Optimize Value Creation for the Product

Managing stakeholders is serious business, right? But we also consider stakeholder management to be a game to be played with a smile. Sometimes you win a round and sometimes you lose one, and that's okay. There are plenty more rounds to play, so don't worry about it. Be careful, though, that stakeholder management doesn't become a political game. It isn't about getting in the way of people, blocking them from making progress, or doing things only to your own advantage. What smart strategies can you use to best work with your opponent and maximize the value of your product while building a relationship with them?

Fulfilling the Product Owner's accountabilities in a great way is inseparable from the ability to say no effectively. It is not always easy to say no to stakeholders, customers, users, or your team. However, it is a priceless skill for any Product Owner. Although it might be a bit scary or difficult at times, saying no offers many positive outcomes and benefits for yourself and the people around you. Some positive outcomes of knowing when to say no include the following:

- Colleagues will see that you take responsibility as a Product Owner.
- You will increase clarity and transparency.
- You can maximize the value of the product.

- You create focus (for yourself, the stakeholders, and the Scrum Teams).
- You create the opportunity to have more crucial conversations.
- You increase your authority as a Product Owner.
- You do more things that make you happy.

A well-known quote from Warren Buffett is, "We need to learn the slow yes and the quick no." This is exactly what this chapter helps you with. Despite all the benefits that saying no can bring you, a lot of people struggle to say it. Why is it so difficult to say no? Why do we find it so scary? What drives us to say yes more often than no? How do you say no in an effective manner? We'll figure that out in this chapter, which includes tips to help you become more effective in saying no.

> *People think focus means saying yes to the thing you've got to focus on. But that's not what it means at all. It means saying no to the hundred other good ideas that there are. You have to pick carefully. I'm actually as proud of the things we haven't done as the things I have done. Innovation is saying "no" to 1,000 things.*
>
> — Steve Jobs

## WHAT MAKES SAYING NO SO HARD?

Many people struggle with saying no to stakeholders. The vast majority associate *no* with rejection or a negative result. In addition, many people think that saying no will lead to conflicts. We found that there are five main drivers or patterns that prevent people from saying no:

1. **Fear of conflict:** Fear of conflict is a psychological obstacle that many people suffer from. Many people find conflicts scary, unpredictable, and undesirable. Conflicts can have negative consequences, such as anger, disappointment, and abandonment. Most people try to avoid those negative emotions, even more so in the workplace. Ever since we humans started walking upright and hunting large animals, we discovered that we are more effective in a group. Saying no to other people may cause conflict, and conflict may cause isolation. People naturally want to be part of a group, to belong. Consequently, they avoid conflicts whenever possible. The result? Not saying no often enough.

2. **Fear of disappointing others:** This fear has some similarities to the first one because of people's desire to belong. Many people assume that saying no will disappoint others and result in their being ostracized from the group, so they often refrain from saying no. The disappointment that others might experience when told no is often far greater, however, if the Product Owner has never said no before.

3. **Fear of hierarchy:** In elementary school, you learn to respect authority, listen to the teacher, and perform your assignments. This concept of doing what your bosses tell you to do is ingrained in many businesses, even though company leaders do not always know more about the product, market, and customers than the product people do. However, saying no to the person who decides whether or not you get a salary raise may have some implications on your behavior. Perhaps you don't want to risk that salary raise, bonus, career progression, or other benefits. But will saying no really have such negative repercussions? Keep in mind that it's sometimes better to stand up for something than to just do what you're told.

4. **It's not supported in the culture:** In some teams, organizations, and cultures, it may be viewed as a bad thing to say no. You might consider this pattern to be a combination of the previous patterns (avoidance of conflict, fear of hierarchy, and fear of disappointing others). Being a Product Owner, you need to be aware and respectful of different cultures and their explicit and implicit rules of conduct. You need to understand that you must sometimes be very tactful when saying no. You may even need to put your cultural background aside for a moment to deal effectively with the situation and culture at hand.

5. **Saying no requires you to break your default pattern:** The various fears set aside, saying no is also difficult because it means breaking the pattern of saying yes all the time. Saying yes is, in many situations, much easier than saying no. It leads to a positive feeling in the short term, but it may have some negative long-term effects. Product Owners can consciously break the pattern of saying yes, but they must take care that each no is justified.

## FIVE STEPS TOWARD SAYING NO EFFECTIVELY

There are many ways to say no to your stakeholders. In our Professional Scrum Product Owner training courses, we always joked around with participants that there are at least 50 different shades of saying no. These 50 shades of no are captured in *Master the Art of No*.[1] Before you say no to your stakeholders, though, you need to figure out whom you are dealing with and how to best say it to them. The steps that follow can help you.

## STEP 1: WHO

The first step toward an effective no is to determine whom you are going to say no to. Consider the stakeholder map or stakeholder radar you've created. Consider your communication strategy. Consider how interested and influential this stakeholder is. Remember that not all stakeholders are equal, and this may influence how you respond to a question or request from your stakeholder.

## STEP 2: WHAT

The second step to an effective no is to determine what it is that the stakeholder is asking for. Is it a wish for a new feature? Is it a critical error in the product? Is it an internal issue? Is the issue driven by the customer or perhaps by a request from a legal and compliance perspective? Truly seek to understand what the stakeholder is asking for. Ask clarifying questions until you understand the reasoning behind their request. Learn about their desired outcomes, problems to solve, or the value they hope to gain.

## STEP 3: INTENTION

This step determines, based on the information gathered in the previous two steps, what your intention will be. Are you going to say yes, or no? Consider the potential value, benefits, and outcomes of the request. Consider how valuable the request is in comparison to other items on your product roadmap or Product Backlog. Consider if, and how, it contributes to the product vision and strategy. There are many things to think about, so if you need some time before making a decision, just say so. Make up your mind, though, before you communicate a yes or no. Step 3 is all about making a conscious decision. We need to learn the quick no and the slow yes.

---

1. Robbin Schuurman and Willem Vermaak, Master the Art of No: Effective Stakeholder Management for Product Owners and Product Managers, independently published, 2020.

> *At some point, we had two clients pushing certain feature sets, and we couldn't deliver both in the requested time frame. Upon further investigation, we discovered that one relied on our product for an external deadline that, if met, would lead to great success. The other didn't trust our product could do the job and wanted to test our ability to deliver. We prioritized the first client but had them invite the second client for their launch event. We flew the other client in and made sure they witnessed firsthand the success that others obtained with our product.*
>
> — Chris

## STEP 4: SAY NO

Have you decided to say no? That's great! Identify what way of saying no would be best in this situation. Consider elements such as value, customers, users, timing, impact, or otherwise, in the way you say no.

## STEP 5: HEAR AND BE HEARD

Although we often hope that saying no is the end of a discussion, it typically isn't. When people hear a no, they often experience it as the start or continuation of a discussion. They'll come up with new or additional arguments for you to reconsider. So, in this last step, make sure that the other person understands that you said no and why you said it. You may want to acknowledge the pain of disappointment that your decision may cause for the stakeholder.

An example of how you might frame such a discussion follows: "Look, I understand that you see an opportunity by expanding into that market. However, the Product Vision is to aim for a different market segment. I realize that this will impact your workflow and will not happen overnight. What are some of the things that we can do to ease that transition?"

Product Owners sometimes face fierce resistance when saying no because they only communicate the decision. They only communicate the result: it's a no. Acceptance of your decision will improve if you communicate not only your decision but also the vision, considerations, arguments, and accepted consequences of your decision, preferably from the perspective of the stakeholder. So, check whether the stakeholder has understood (and perhaps accepted) your answer. What is their reaction? Do you want to discuss it now? Or park the discussion for later?

Some discussions seem to go on forever. If you find yourself in such a discussion, you may use the following phrase: "I notice we keep repeating the same arguments. Is there any information that you haven't mentioned yet? Based on the information you have shared with me so far, my decision stands." This opens the door for any new information but allows you to close the discussion if it starts sounding like a broken record.[2]

## THE JEDI MIND TRICK

There is a classic scene in *Star Wars* where Obi-Wan waves his hand and says, "These are not the droids you are looking for," and the stormtroopers just let them pass. As a Product Owner, waving your hand and saying, "These are not the features you are looking for," does not seem to work. But perhaps we can bend the reality of our stakeholders a little bit.

Imagine you are trying to convince your stakeholder of a certain order in which to develop the product, but they have something else in mind. You have been going back and forth a bit. What you can do now is one of the following:

• If your stakeholder leans toward a positive outcome, ask, "What else would improve if we did this?"

• If your stakeholder leans toward a negative outcome, ask, "What kind of problems would we run into if we did this?"

Both approaches put the stakeholder in the driver's seat. Their brains will create neural pathways that support your idea and find issues with their approach.

You can now rephrase and summarize until they reply with a "that's right," firmly fixing the idea. Of course, putting them in the driver's seat means that the conversation could also go sideways.

---

2. That is, for the younger generation, if the argument continues in an endless loop.

# Negotiating with Stakeholders, Customers, and Users

33

It's simple, it's fun, and we all love it: negotiating! Just kidding. The reality is that, while some of us love it, most of us don't. Negotiation is a dialogue between people or parties hoping to reach a beneficial outcome. It typically occurs when dealing with contracts, proposals, quotes, issues, or conflicts, and there is a clear need to resolve those with a positive outcome. Negotiation is an interaction and process between entities who typically make compromises to agree on matters of mutual interest while optimizing their interests at the same time. This beneficial outcome can be for all the parties involved, or just for one or some of them. Negotiators need to understand the negotiation process and other negotiators well to increase their chances to close deals, avoid conflicts, establish relationships with other parties, and gain benefits.

"We've got your son. Give us one million dollars or he dies." Fortunately, it's not a sentence we hear very often unless it's in the movies. However, it is a sentence that Chris Voss, a former FBI hostage negotiator, has heard throughout his career. After working for the FBI for more than 20 years, Voss moved into consulting and training, and he became an author. His book *Never Split the Difference* is a great read for any Product Owner or product manager. In it, Voss shares a ton of negotiation tips, practices, techniques, and examples that worked well for him as an FBI hostage negotiator and in businesses. This chapter summarizes some of the most valuable tips, tools, and techniques for negotiation for Product Owners and product managers.

## BE A MIRROR

Mirroring is a technique you might find familiar, especially when it comes to nonverbal communication. Most people are taught to mirror the nonverbal communication of their counterparts in a conversation. For example, if your partner leans forward, you lean forward. If your partner sits back, you sit back. With remote working becoming normalized, we are learning how difficult it is to mirror your partner in a video call. So, the technique recommended is to mirror the language of your counterpart, for example, by repeating the last one to three words that your counterpart just spoke, followed by a question mark. The intention of doing so is to ask the person, "Please help me understand," but without literally asking that question.

To illustrate, imagine one of your stakeholders comes up to you. It's a stakeholder who has difficulty accepting no for an answer. She asks you, "Hey, can you make sure these two features get delivered?" You might respond, "I'm sorry, deliver two features?" "Yes," the stakeholder says, "these features are really important for our customers." Just by repeating a part of the other person's sentence, typically the last part of it, you'll invite them to elaborate further on their ideas and explain themselves more.

The mirroring technique is used mainly to create a pleasant setting for your counterpart and for you to learn more about their interests. In a negotiating setting, knowledge equals influence, power, and leverage. Here are some key points to keep in mind:

- Prepare yourself well before entering a negotiation by preparing yourself to reveal and adapt to surprises. Surprises will always surface at some point. Great negotiators actively look to surface them.

- Don't commit yourself to any assumptions you made about the other party. Consider the things you (think you) know as hypotheses, which need to be validated.

- Negotiation is not an act of war. Negotiation is a process of discovery. The goal is to learn as much as you can to see if and how collaboration could be valuable for you and the other party.

- Try to silence the voices, doubts, and fears in your head by focusing on the other person. Focus on learning about them. Focus on what they have to say.

- Slow down the negotiation process. The biggest pitfall is to try to hurry. If you are in a hurry, and if you want to close the deal or make agreements fast, the other party can and might use that to their advantage. You'll also risk undermining the trust you've built.

- Put a smile on your face. When people are in a positive mindset, they think more quickly and can solve problems and collaborate more effectively. Being positive helps you and your counterpart to have more mental agility.

## LABEL EMOTIONS

Negotiating might be as scary for your counterpart as it might be for you. In a negotiation setting, we might experience all kinds of emotions, including insecurity, fear, anger, and joy.

Empathy is about understanding the feelings and mindset of someone else. It's exactly like having customer empathy, which is important for us as product people. Tactical empathy is about understanding the feelings and mindset of our counterparts but also about hearing what is behind those feelings. When you closely observe your counterpart's face, gestures, and tone of voice, your brain will start to align with theirs. This concept is called neural resonance and helps you to see what they think and feel more quickly.

When we better understand our counterpart's thoughts and emotions, we can apply a technique called *labeling*. Labeling is a technique for validating someone's emotions by acknowledging them. The first step is obviously to detect your counterpart's emotions. The second step is to label them by sharing them aloud. Labels can be phrased as statements or questions, and typically start with words such as, "It seems like. . ." or "It looks like. . ." or "It sounds like. . . ."

Emotions exist on two levels: visible behaviors (or behaviors) and invisible feelings (or underlying feelings). Behaviors are easier to recognize; they are the things you can see and hear. The underlying feelings, however, are the motivations, thoughts, and feelings you can't see or hear. These are what you read between the lines. Learning about those underlying feelings requires talking, close observation, and labeling those feelings for confirmation. You can address the underlying emotions by the labels, especially negative emotions, which will help defuse them. Labeling positive emotions usually reinforces them. Labeling can help to deescalate a situation because it acknowledges the other party's feelings rather than continuing to act on them.

We are working with other people, with other humans. People want to be heard, appreciated, and understood. Labeling may help you reinforce positive perceptions and dynamics.

## GETTING TO YES!

Much has been said about how you, as a Product Owner, can say no to your stakeholders. But what about when you're the one with the ask? How do you get to a "Yes, we have a deal"? Pushing your counterpart hard for a yes rarely gets you closer to that result. In many cases, it only irks the other party. Although it's not a popular belief, no is the start of a negotiation, not the end of it. So, in a negotiation setting, you'll want to push for a quick and early no from your counterpart. Early noes will help you to identify what they do not want. Once you get clarity on what the other party doesn't want, it opens the way to clarify what they do want. Hearing a no from your counterpart may have different meanings:

- I am not yet ready to agree.
- You make me feel uncomfortable.
- I don't understand.
- I can't afford it.
- I need more information.
- I'd prefer talking to someone else.

Much like there are different types of no, there are also different types of yes:

- **The counterfeit yes:** The counterfeit yes means that the other party wants to say no, but they say yes because it's easier. Saying no isn't common in many companies and cultures, and some people have learned ways to say yes while meaning no.
- **The confirmation yes:** The confirmation yes is rather innocent. It's often a quick response to a black-or-white question based on human reflexes. This type of yes is not a well-considered yes, and although confirmative, it isn't getting you closer to an agreement.
- **The commitment yes:** The commitment yes is the real deal. This type of yes is one that often leads to an agreement, deal, or signed contract. However, because these variants of yes sound similar, you have to learn to recognize which one is being used.

A clear no is far more helpful than a quick yes. For example, if you want to discuss something important with a stakeholder, don't start by asking, "Do you have a few minutes to talk?" Instead, ask, "Is now a bad time to talk?" You'll likely get the response, "Yes, it is a bad time," followed by a good time or a request to go away, or you get "No, it's not," and you'll have total focus.

The word *no* can lead to many positive results, whether you say it yourself to a stakeholder or it is told to you in a negotiation setting. It helps bring the real issues forth; protects you from making poor decisions; slows things down to give you time to analyze decisions and agreements; helps you feel safe, secure, and emotionally comfortable; and moves everyone's efforts forward.

When people get to say no, it makes them feel safe, secure, and in control, so try to trigger an early no. If a stakeholder or client is ignoring you, contact them with a clear and concise no-oriented question, which sounds like you are ready to walk away. Asking, Have you given up on this project? often works very well.

## HOW TO TELL IF A YES IS REAL

You have learned that pushing for a quick yes isn't a good tactic. However, two simple words will transform any negotiation setting: "That's right!" These two words reflect that your counterpart truly believes that whatever was just said is completely correct, and they fully agree. Hearing "that's right" in a negotiation setting means that you've just created a breakthrough.

Alternatives to "that's right," such as "you're right" or "sounds right," are not the breakthrough words you're looking for. "You're right" means that the other person believes you are correct but not that the proposed solution or agreement is right for them. "Sounds right" is similar, but neither is a confirmation that will seal the deal.

To get to a "that's right," it helps if you frequently summarize what was said by your counterpart, connect problems or concerns to solutions, mirror them, paraphrase them, and label their emotions. Combining these techniques in a negotiation setting is the best way to get them to a "that's right" and from there to a real yes.

## BEND THEIR REALITY

The word *fair* is one of the most powerful words during a negotiation. If you want to become a great negotiator, then you'll want to build a reputation for being fair. If you work on tough negotiations, deals, contracts, or agreements, then you'll want to persuade your counterparts that your offer is fair and that they have something to lose if the deal falls through. There are a couple of things you can do to increase your reputation for fairness:

- **Anchor emotions:** You need to start with the basics of (tactical) empathy: observe your counterpart, identify emotions and fears, and label them. You then use the emotions as anchors, which frame their minds for a potential loss. If people feel like they're about to miss out on something great, their human loss-aversion system kicks in, and they'll jump in to avoid that loss. By anchoring their emotions to a potential loss, you're bending their reality.

- **Let the other side go first:** When discussing figures or dates, it's never a good idea to go in first. Let the other side start by anchoring timing or monetary negotiations. When you go in first, you'll either end up with winner's curse or buyer's remorse. However, you need to be prepared to withstand the first offer. If the other party is tough, and they start with an offer that is way below or above what you expected, it might be that they are bending your reality. So be careful to accept that initial offer.

- **Establish a range:** When negotiating figures or dates, establish a ballpark figure with some credible references to support your statement. For example, if a client is asking about timelines, mention that delivering a similar mobile app to that other client took between six and nine months. Or mention that top companies such as XYZ pay people in a Product Owner position between $125,000 and $175,000. By offering ranges and credible references, you can get your point across without making your counterpart defensive.

- **Pivot to nonmonetary terms:** When you are negotiating a new contract, job offer, or salary increase, then it helps to make your offer sound more reasonable by offering things that are not very important to you but might be valuable to them. Alternatively, if your client or potentially new employer's offer is low, you can ask for nonmonetary things that matter to you more than they matter to them. As we lose the nonmonetary element, it might be good to add a clarification, "For example training budget or the time and support for writing and public speaking."

- **When you talk numbers, use odd ones:** Most companies have figured out that offering products at $100 leads to a lower conversion than products offered for $99.95. It seems that figures that end with a zero feel like placeholders. However, any arbitrary number you throw out that sounds less rounded—for example, $8,673—feels like the result of thoughtful calculations.

- **Surprise them with a gift:** You can make your counterpart feel more generous and accepting by setting an extreme figure or date anchor. They will reject your ridiculous number or deadline, but then you offer them a completely unrelated surprise gift.

People generally take more risks to avoid a loss than they will take to realize a gain. Using these techniques may help your counterpart to see that not acting will result in a loss.

## CREATE THE ILLUSION OF CONTROL

Something we've heard many times throughout our careers is that people don't like change. We don't think that this is necessarily the case. People may not like too much change at a time, or big changes frequently following each other. We don't think that people are averse to change per se. However, people don't like to be changed. Just like many people don't like to be told what to do. Keep this in mind during a negotiation setting. Your stakeholders, customers, or users also don't like to get told what to do, nor to get told what their problem is. People prefer to be in control of their own choices and their destiny.

This illusion of being in control can be created in a negotiation setting by using calibrated questions. Calibrated questions are powerful questions that help you to educate your counterpart about their problems. This is preferred over you telling them what their problems are. There are many different types of calibrated questions. Here are some examples you could use:

- What about this is important to you?
- How can I help make this better for us?
- How would you like me to proceed?
- What is it that brought us into this situation?
- How can we solve this problem?
- What are we trying to accomplish here?
- How am I supposed to do that?

The power of calibrated questions is that they make the other party feel like they are in control. However, by asking those questions, it is you who is really driving the conversation.

## GUARANTEE EXECUTION

When you're negotiating, you want to drive decisions. You may want to drive a decision by a client to start working with you, for example. You may want to drive a stakeholder to withdraw their feature request. Or, you may want to drive the decision of changing a deadline.

When you're in a negotiation, you need to design every element of it dynamically and adaptively to get both consent and execution. There are various tactics and tools for verbal and nonverbal communication that may help you to bend the reality of your counterpart. Here are some of these techniques:

- **The 7-38-55 Percent Rule:** This rule, created by Albert Mehrabian, states that only 7 percent of a message is based on the words spoken, 38 percent comes from the tone of voice, and 55 percent comes from the speaker's body language and facial expressions. If you listen to and observe your counterpart closely, you can detect whether the message, tone of voice, and body language align. If they don't align, it is an indicator that your counterpart is bluffing or lying.

- **The Rule of Three:** The Rule of Three is quite simple. It means that you want to get your counterpart to agree to the same thing three times within the same conversation. The first time they agree with you, you have an early confirmation. You can then label or summarize what they said before, allowing them to respond with "that's right," agreeing with you a second time. The third time, you can use a calibrated *how* or *what* question about the implementation or next steps to take, such as, "What do you consider to be the most difficult challenge to get around?"

- **The Pinocchio Effect:** Professor Deepak Malhotra and his colleagues at Harvard Business School found that people who are tempted to bend reality use, on average, more words than people who are telling the truth. They also tend to use more third-person pronouns.

## BARGAIN HARD

When trying to close a deal or settle on your new salary, you may run into some hard bargaining of numbers. If that happens, consider switching to some nonmonetary issues that influence your final number. For example, you could ask your counterpart, "Let's put the numbers to the side for a moment.

What would make this a good deal?" Or you could say something like, "What else would you be able to offer to make that a fair deal for me?"

If negotiations get tough, and you end up bargaining numbers, consider shaking things up a little bit, allowing your counterpart to get out of their rigid mindset. Although you may have some desired and acceptable goals, targets, and numbers in mind, the key is to not be needy. It's also important to remember that the person across the table is not the issue to be solved, the unsolved deal is. A model that may help you when negotiating numbers is the Ackerman model, which describes a six-step process:

1. Set your target price (your goal).

2. Set your first offer at 65 percent of your target price.

3. Calculate three raises of decreasing increments (to 85, 95, and 100 percent).

4. Use lots of empathy and different ways of saying no to get the other side to counter before you increase your offer.

5. When calculating the final amount, use precise, non-round numbers, such as $37,893 rather than $38,000. It gives the number credibility and weight.

6. On your final number, throw in a nonmonetary item that they probably don't want to show you're at your limit.

Before you head into a negotiation about numbers and dates, carefully prepare your Ackerman plan. Having a clear negotiation plan may help you to strike a good deal and should prevent you from being pushed into a lousy deal by your counterpart.

## FIND THE BLACK SWAN

The black swan theory describes our human tendency to find simplistic explanations for unpredictable events. It originates from the book *The Black Swan: The Impact of the Highly Improbable*.[1] The theory is so called because most people in the world were convinced that all swans were white until

---

1. Nassim Nicholas Taleb, *The Black Swan: The Impact of the Highly Improbable,* Random House, 2007.

Australia—and its native black swan—were discovered. The first black swan was an interesting surprise for people, but that is not why this story is important. The story illustrates a limitation to our learning from observations and experience. It shows the fragility of our knowledge because one single observation can invalidate our general beliefs. All you need is a single black bird!

Back to our topic of negotiation. As mentioned previously, people will usually change their behaviors, take action, and/or accept a deal when their fear of losing the deal grows. You could therefore say that it will help to instill an element of fear in your counterpart during negotiations. The fear can offer you leverage in the negotiations. Leverage can be grouped into three types: positive, negative, and normative.

- **Positive leverage:** If you have positive leverage over your counterpart, it means that you can withhold or provide what your counterpart wants. If your counterpart says, "I want . . . ," and you can offer the thing they want, then you have positive leverage.

- **Negative leverage:** If you have negative leverage over your counterpart, it means that you can make the other party suffer. An example of negative leverage is, "If you don't deliver feature X on deadline Y, I will end the contract with your company and destroy your reputation." Negative leverage works because it appeals to our loss aversion. However, be careful with negative leverage—you may need to follow through on it. As with a nuclear deterrent, there will be great pressure and a big mess to clean up. It can break the entire negotiation process, including relationships, collaboration, and trust, which makes these threats hard to recover from. This kind of leverage is not the recommended form to use.

- **Normative leverage:** Using normative leverage means that you're using your counterpart's norms, values, and standards to advance your position. You'll need to analyze the other party's stance and use that as leverage. For example, if you can show them inconsistencies between their norms, values, and beliefs versus their actual behaviors and actions, you have normative leverage. Normative leverage appeals to our feelings of not wanting to be a hypocrite, rather than loss aversion. To gain normative leverage, you'll want to learn from your counterpart about their beliefs, norms, and values, so listen closely and ask many questions. Learn to speak their language.

How do leverage and black swans relate? Well, when people discovered black swans for the first time, it changed their perspectives drastically because swans were believed to be white. This drastic change of perspectives during negotiations often leads to breakthrough results. Black swans can be considered leverage multipliers. Once you discover them, you can use them to your advantage by speaking and mirroring the black swan discoveries back to your counterpart.

To reveal the black swans, let yourself be guided by what you know about the other party, but don't let it blind you. There will always be things you don't know about them. Every negotiation is a new one, so be open, flexible, and adaptable. Remember that negotiation is much more about discovery than it is about winning or arguing. Doing discovery well will help you win. So, learn when to move the discussion away from the actual deal, contract, or proposal. Learn about your counterpart's beliefs and worldviews. Move away from the negotiation table and dig into the emotions and life of the other party. That is where you will usually discover the black swans. People want to be heard and understood. We connect better with people who get us and who are like us. People will more likely concede to someone with whom they share beliefs, values, passions, and a worldview. Try to find common ground with them.

# THE INFLUENCER

# VII

# SUMMARY

## KEY LEARNINGS AND INSIGHTS

This concludes Part VII, in which you explored the Influencer stance. You learned what and who potential stakeholders to your product are. You learned about the tools and practices needed to identify, classify, and group your stakeholders, to create transparency about your stakeholder field and the people you work with in one way or another. You explored how understanding people's goals, interests, motivations, personalities, and other information and insights enables you to be a more effective influencer of and collaborator to your stakeholders. You learned how to translate those stakeholder insights into action by creating a stakeholder management and communication strategy. Understanding how communication works and understanding the different levels of communication well enables you to develop strong relationships with your stakeholders. Ultimately, stakeholder management is all about developing relationships. Adapting your tone, voice, message, communication style, strategy, and tactics contributes to building relationships more effectively.

Winning products are not (just) created by Product Owners or product managers. They are also not (just) created by the winning teams we mentioned in Part VI. They are created in an ecosystem of people who work together to achieve a vision. So, Product Owners and product managers should not be just effective Collaborators in their Product Team. They also need to be strong Influencers to the people outside the team. Great Influencers seek to understand first, before they are to be understood. It's all about understanding your stakeholders, their needs, goals, and desires. This requires continuous effort—collaborating, engaging, and developing relationships with them. In the last chapters of this part, you learned about mastering the art of no, and finally, you explored some of the most successful negotiation strategies and tactics. As a Product Owner or product manager, you need to be an effective Influencer to create a winning product in the marketplace.

## QUICK QUIZ REVIEW

If you took the Quick Quiz at the beginning of Part VII, compare your answers to those in the following table. Now that you have read about the Influencer stance, would you change any of your answers? Do you agree with the following answers?

| Statement | Agree | Disagree |
|---|---|---|
| Stakeholder management is one of the core responsibilities of Product Owners. However, not all stakeholders are equal or need equal attention and influence. | ✓ | |
| Many techniques, such as stakeholder mapping and stakeholder radar, and models such as DISC and MBTI, can help Product Owners to manage stakeholders more effectively. | ✓ | |
| Negotiation is all about achieving consensus. It's often a situation of give and take. | | ✓ |
| In stakeholder management and communication, the most important thing to optimize is the message that you share with stakeholders. | | ✓ |

| Statement | Agree | Disagree |
|---|---|---|
| Negotiation and diplomacy are about getting into the mindset of your partner and aligning their reality with yours. Active listening is key to both. | ☑ | |
| During negotiations with stakeholders—for example, about a feature—you want to get to a yes and agreement from stakeholders as soon as possible. | | ☑ |
| To be an effective value maximizer, a Product Owner should be versatile by applying various stances in various situations to collaborate with various types of stakeholders (e.g., practice situational leadership). | ☑ | |

## WANT TO LEARN MORE?

In this part, you learned about the Influencer stance. Diverse topics, tools, techniques, and concepts will help you to strengthen this stance. If you want to improve your Influencer stance, consider spending more time on building relationships with your stakeholders. Spend time getting to know them. Learn more about their personalities, interests, and goals.

If you struggle to build these relationships, consider taking some time to identify your stakeholder field first. Create a stakeholder map or stakeholder radar, and then create a stakeholder management strategy. Start engaging with your stakeholders based on that strategy, and inspect and adapt it at least every quarter.

In addition, you can learn more about the Influencer stance by catching up with the following materials: *Never Split the Difference: Negotiating as If Your Life Depended on It* by Chris Voss (HarperBusiness, 2016), *Getting to Yes* by Roger Fisher and William Ury (Simon & Schuster, 2011), and *Master the Art of No: Effective Stakeholder Management for Product Owners and Product Managers* by Robbin Schuurman and Willem Vermaak (Independently published, 2020).

# CLOSING SUMMARY: THE STANCES OF THE PRODUCT OWNER

## THE PREFERRED STANCES OF A PRODUCT OWNER

This book has taken you through the six preferred stances of a Product Owner. Becoming a great Product Owner is an amazing, yet never-ending journey. The tools, practices, techniques, and concepts from this book will help you along that journey, but there is much work to be done. You don't become a great product leader by simply attending a two-day course or reading this book. Continuous development of yourself, your product team, your company, and your knowledge and skills is critical to building products that customers will love.

Thank you for taking the time and undergoing the journey through this book and the Product Owner stances. As you continue to learn and grow as a

Product Owner, you'll find that applying the right stance to the right situation becomes second nature to you. To that end, memorizing these six simple sentences can help you to quickly assume the best stance, as needed, in your daily work:

- **Visionary:** It's not about where we are, it's about where we want to be.
- **Customer Representative:** What's the problem to solve for customers and/ or users?
- **Experimenter:** What is the smallest experiment we can run to validate that idea?
- **Decision Maker:** Look at the data and move forward.
- **Collaborator:** Let's get stuff done, together.
- **Influencer:** How can I align people to do what is best for the product?

The purpose of this book was to inspire you with six preferred stances of a Product Owner to adapt ourselves to any given situation. As product people, we need to be versatile in our approach with customers, users, stakeholders, executives, and development teams as well as in our processes, tools, techniques, and communication. We need to master different stances to become a better product leader, and most of all, a better value maximizer.

Thank you.

## OPTIMIZING TRANSPARENCY USING A PRODUCT WALL

Being a Product Owner is not about taking inputs from other people. You're much, much more than a secretary of roadmaps and backlogs. You are the strategic brain behind the product, and it is your job to drive your product forward. The job entails making decisions that support the product and the broader, organization-wide objectives. It includes making decisions based on customer, market, industry, and product insights. It includes continuously communicating product vision and rethinking your strategy. It includes being transparent about what is and isn't known.

Transparency is a powerful asset, which isn't equal to visibility. Being transparent is about making information, processes, and decisions visible, open, accessible, understandable, inspectable, and therefore adaptable.
Transparency is of critical importance in product management and product development. To build great products, information must be transparent to all people involved, such as key (launching) customers, stakeholders, and product developers. There are many ways to improve transparency, and one of them is to use a product wall. Many of the tools, techniques, and practices covered in this book (e.g., product vision, product goals, product roadmaps, and personas) make great additions to your product wall. We therefore encourage you to browse through this book again to identify which concepts might be good additions to your product wall.

A product wall, or obeya room,[1] is a helpful technique to foster transparency within the organization. It's a practice where all product-related information is captured and made transparent in one place. It includes information such as market research, customer insights, technology trends, the product vision, product strategy, goals and objective key results, value measures, product metrics, personas, and much more. Anyone who wants to learn more about your product can go to the product wall to find out.

Combining all product (management) information in one place (either in a physical office or on a virtual product wall) enables better decision making and allows you to collaborate with multiple parties more easily. Stakeholders will gather around the product wall to inspect the information and learn about the product's health and progress, and help you to act. Data, analytics, insights, and evidence can be used to make better decisions, and to improve transparency and communication. There are many advantages to being transparent, and maintaining a transparent product wall. The key, though, is not to try to assemble a perfect product wall all at once. As we do in most of our work, take small steps. Start small. Claim a piece of office or virtual wall, post something there to inspect, and add more elements as you learn. Inspect. And adapt.

---

1. Obeya (from Japanese *obeya*, 大部屋, "large room") originated at Toyota. Comparisons have been drawn between an obeya and the bridge of a ship, a war room, and even a brain.

## EPILOGUE

"What is that, Grandma?" The eyes of the little boy were as large as tea saucers as he stared at the large frame on the wall.

"That, young man, is a reprint of *Relation Aller Fuernemmen und gedenck-kwuerdigen Historien,*" was the reply. The boy looked at the elderly woman with bewilderment and utter confusion. "It is a replica of the first newspaper ever printed, well over 400 years ago," Noa clarified. "It was given to me when I retired from World News. I'm quite fond of it."

The young boy's curiosity wasn't yet satisfied. "So, what would people do with that?" he asked.

"Well, read it, of course," Noa replied. "But fundamentally, they read it to expand their knowledge. By learning more about the world around them, they could make more informed decisions on how to lead their lives."

"But why is it on paper, Grandma?" asked the still-curious boy.

Noa paused for a bit before answering, "In those days, there was no digital news. The world may seem different today, but the problems people faced were not so different."

She pointed out some of the lettering on the ancient titles. "For people to do things that matter, they need to be informed. How we inform people may change over time, but the need for news and knowledge never does."

That explanation seemed to be enough for the boy, as his eyes had traveled down to the small plaque attached to the bottom of the frame. "It says here you were the CEO of World News, Grandma. Has that always been your job?"

Noa smiled as she looked at him and said, "I've certainly always tried to act that way."

# Index